LEGACIES
OF
FAITH
VOLUME II

LEGACIES
OF
FAITH
VOLUME II

by Ed Erny

*Devotional readings for every
day of the year*

*To John. Ina with love,
We recall with joy our stay
in your home.
God Bless,
Ed. Rachel Erny*

Published by OMS International
P.O. Box A, Greenwood, IN 46142

Erny, Ed, 1936
LEGACIES OF FAITH, VOLUME II

1999   98-068725
ISBN 1-880338-26-2   CIP

Printed in the United States of America

FOREWORD

The first volume of LEGACIES OF FAITH was published in 1995. Response has been heartening indeed. Letters come regularly from readers telling of blessings received from the daily selections.

This encouraged me to begin the compilation of this second volume which goes to the printer with a prayer that again the readings that have helped me over the years will prove God's instruments of encouragement.

While many excellent religious books are being published, it has been observed that modern readers tend to prefer shallow writing, popular in style and spiced with lots of illustrations. A quick, easy read. We also tend to be faddists, following current trends in Christian literature and charismatic authors popularized by T.V. and radio exposure whose names are promoted by the large Christian publishing houses. Perhaps this is inevitable in our hyped-up T.V. culture where our tastes are too often shaped by Hollywood, and programs as well as books live and die by the ratings. A sad consequence of this trend is the increasing neglect of many of the older classics of Christian literature. I am dismayed to learn that many of my younger friends have never heard of Fenélon, Madame Guyon, Spurgeon, Hannah Whithall Smith or W.E. Sangster. Such impoverishment is to be truly lamented and it is hoped that this volume may serve to whet someone's appetite for more of the great Christian writers who have left us, in their writings, a priceless legacy.

My heartfelt thanks to Nancy Villareal who patiently, laboriously and always smilingly typed this manuscript. Also to my proofreader wife, Rachel, who proofed every word with the keen eye for detail which I lamentably have always lacked.

As always, in a compilation of this type, the search for owners of copyrights is difficult and time-consuming. With the current trend in mergers, ownership of many works no longer belongs to the original publishers. Where efforts to locate the owner of the copyright have failed, indulgence is begged. When the author is unknown I have used the device employed by Lettie Cowman in STREAMS IN THE DESERT and indicated my ignorance by the word "Selected."

Finally, I confess once more that selections are drawn largely from my favorite authors and I am aware that many worthies are neglected or omitted entirely.

Ed Erny
Manila, Philippines

MAKE US MOUNTAINEERS

Joshua 14:10-12

THE LAST DEFILE

Make us Thy mountaineers;
We would not linger on the lower slope,
Fill us afresh with hope, O God of Hope,
That undefeated we may climb the hill
As seeing Him who is invisible.

Let us die climbing. When this little while
Lies far behind us, and the last defile
Is all alight, and in that light we see
Our Leader and our Lord, what will it be?
Amy Carmichael

He seem to be moved even more deeply by his visit to the tomb of Sir Walter Scott. All of his own eloquence was fired by the memory of this noble Scotchman. Scott's struggle to meet enormous financial losses with his pen had caught the imagination and moved the heart that was later to pour itself out in books of more lasting value than Waverley and Marmion. He quotes: "I will dig in the mind of my imaginations for diamonds, or what may sell for diamonds, to meet all my engagements." What could better portray the closing days of his own life than this tender picture he gives us of the Scott? "But, alas, nature sank in the unequal struggle, and the productions which the world enjoys today are the life-blood of a brave man's heart. His sun was largest at its setting; and though it went down among many clouds, it was a glorious soul, and sank, we trust, to shine in other climes in cloudless light."

THE LIFE OF A.B. SIMPSON
A.E. Thompson

A FAVORABLE MORAL CLIMATE

Psalm 39:3

The Psalm and prophets contain numerous references to the power of right thinking to raise religious feeling and incite to right conduct. "I thought on my ways, and turned my feet unto thy testimonies." "While I was musing the fire burned: then spake I with my tongue." Over and over the Old Testament writers exhort us to get quiet and think about high and holy things as a preliminary to amendment of life or a good deed or a courageous act.

The Old Testament is not alone in its respect for the God-given power of human thought. Christ taught that men defile themselves by evil thinking and even went so far as to equate a thought with an act: "Whosoever looketh on a woman to lust after her hath committed adultery with her already in his heart." Paul recited a list of shining virtues and commanded, "Think on these things."

These quotations are but four out of hundreds that could be cited from the Scriptures. Thinking about God and the holy things creates a moral climate favorable to the growth of faith and love and humility and reverence.

A.W. Tozer

Our achievements of today are but the sum total of our thoughts of yesterday. You are today where the thoughts of yesterday have brought you and you will be tomorrow where the thoughts of today take you.

Pascal

I have often noticed how much depends on stretching ourselves to the limit. Many are spoilt by being satisfied with a mediocrity.

Detrich Bonhoffer

CHARACTER OUT OF DISPOSITION

John 3:3

We make our characters out of the disposition we have, and when we are born again we get a new disposition, the disposition of the Son of God. We cannot imitate the disposition of Jesus Christ; it is either there or it isn't. Our destiny is determined by our disposition; pre-ordination in regard to individual life depends entirely on the disposition of the individual. If the disposition of the Son of God is in me, then heaven and God are my destinations; if the disposition in me is not the disposition of God, my home is as obviously certain with the devil. Our destiny is as eternal and as certain as God's throne; it is an unalterable decree of God; but I am free to choose by what disposition I am to be ruled. I cannot alter my disposition, but I can choose to let God alter it, and redemption means that in my practical experience Jesus Christ can give me a new heredity, a new disposition. Our destiny is something fixed by God, but determined by our disposition. We are all born with a disposition, i.e., the peculiar bent of our personal life, and it is that which determines our destiny. Praying won't alter it, nor science, nor reasoning; if the destiny of a man is going to be altered it must be altered by the Creator. . . .

The Bible does not say that God punished the human race for one man's sin, but that the disposition of sin, i.e., my claim to my right to myself, entered into the human race by one man. The disposition of sin is not immorality or wrongdoing, but my claim to my right to myself.

Oswald Chambers

THE LUST FOR COMFORT

I Timothy 6:8

Declining offers from the best hotels, Gandhi chose instead to stay in an East End slum. He would not even change his uniform or diet for meetings in the palace. Some reporters were scandalized that he would dare meet with a king in a "half-naked" state. Gandhi quietly pondered their objections and replied with a smile, "The king was wearing enough clothes for both of us."

In India, as the issues of independence and partition began reaching the critical mass just before explosion, Gandhi took off on his celebrated barefoot pilgrimage through the riot-torn Noakhali district. Some Congress leaders questioned his decision to waste time in jerkwater villages while the party was negotiating the future of the subcontinent. "A leader," said Gandhi, "is only a reflection of the people he leads. If the small villages do not live in peace, how will the entire nation?"

Gandhi never insisted that political leaders follow his path of rigid discipline; his was a moral and religious crusade and not just a political one. But he did ask that each government minister live in a simple home with no servants and no car, practice one hour of manual labor daily, and clean his or her own toilet box. For more than a decade after his death, Congress leaders wore the homespun cotton uniform he espoused and often conducted party meetings while spinning cotton threads. Despite this cosmetic gesture, Congress soon slipped into wealth, corruption, and venality; nothing pained Gandhi more during the last few years of his life.

Gandhi's adopted style of humility permeates his autobiography. In it, he treats rivals who caused him intense pain and strife with respect and courtesy. Look at your own errors with a convex lens, said Gandhi, and at others' with the reverse.

Philip Yancey

Verily the lust for comfort murders the passion of the soul, and then walks grinning in the funeral.
Kahlil Gibran

USE THE WORD

Psalms 1:2

The Word, the Word, use the Word! That is the whole art and secret regarding the origin, nourishing, growth and maintenance of the spiritual life. It is not true, as some foolish people say, that because such and such a Christian now stands so firmly and steadily in grace, he can therefore believe and live as he does. No, if he has a faith and a life which are the work of the Spirit and not merely of nature, then it is not due to his steadfastness and strength that he can believe and live so, but it is only the result of the fact that he nourishes his soul more diligently with the divine Word. If he neglects it, then the old nature will start to grow again and the truly spiritual life will die away. Yes, pay a visit to him one day when he has neglected the Word for rather a long time. And you will find very little that is spiritual in him. If his faith and peace are still maintained without the Word, then they are not the work of the Spirit. In brief, it is only through the Word of God that the Spirit of God dwells and works in the human being. And note further, not all that read the Word of God get Spirit and life from it. Thousands use the Word and still they do not get the Spirit. The thousands of scribes and Pharisees among us prove that. What is then required? It is required that, in addition to the use of the Word, we bear clearly this in mind, that it is still in the hand of God whether we shall receive its power. It is required that we use the Word with a mind governed by this thought, that we may with humility, fear, obedience and faith appropriate the face of the holy God.

C.O. Rosenius

We can choke God's word with a yawn; we can hinder the time that should be spent with God by remembering we have other things to do. "I haven't time!" Of course you have time! Take time, strangle some other interests and make time to realize that the centre of power in your life is the Lord Jesus and His Atonement.

Oswald Chambers

"THEY RECEIVED MY WORDS"

John 17:8

The secret springs of Abraham's faith then lay away back in his earlier days. He had received ineradicably the words and promises of Jehovah. They had sunk deeply into his soul. They were a rock immoveable, a light that could not be put out, his meat night and day, they were "exceeding great and precious."

The Lord Jesus in His high priestly prayer, as recorded in the seventeenth chapter of St. John, had only one thing to say to His Father in praise of His disciples, *"They have received My words."* There was no mention of their having forsaken all to follow Him, no eulogy of their consecration, their zeal, their love, or their devotion. The only thing that commended them to God's infinite grace was that they had "received the words" of the Savior. Tens of thousands had heard these same words: thousands had wondered and admired them; thousands more had understood them; hundreds had profited by their healing power; but it was only a little flock, a small company that had *"received* them," deeply into their soul. This was the Savior's joy, "They have received My words." Oh! the power of His promises! Oh! the folly of men, with whom the word of man has such weight, causing them to fear or smile, to come or go, fly or follow, to rejoice or despair, and yet who pay no heed to the Word of the living God and trample under foot the exceeding great and precious promises of His Divine Son.

God still talks to men. This is the main theme of the Hebrew Epistle. He talks to men today in clearer fashion than He did in the Old Testament, because He "speaks to us by His Son."

Faith can only come by "hearing" this His Word, the Eternal Word, Jesus the Son of God, in Whom all the promises of God are Yea and Amen.

A. Paget Wilkes

FOUR TEXTS

John 6:63

Dr. A.T. Pierson said four Scripture texts had greatly influenced his life.

1. Psalm 1:1-2 "Blessed is the man that walketh not in the counsel of the ungodly, nor standeth in the way of sinners, nor sitteth in the seat of the scornful; but his delight is in the law of the Lord and in His law doth he meditate day and night." This is the sole secret of prosperity and peace: Meditate in the Word of God and take delight in it. In more than 50 years of study I have only begun to understand it.

2. Proverbs 3:6 "In all thy ways acknowledge Him and He shall direct thy paths." Since the time when my father first gave me that text when I was a boy leaving home, it has been a principle in my life never to make a plan without first seeking God's guidance and never to achieve a success without giving Him the praise.

3. Matthew 6:33 "Seek ye first the kingdom of God and His righteousness and all these things shall be added unto you." This promise has been wonderfully fulfilled in my experience. Whenever I have taken a step of faith, and have sought to devote myself primarily to the advancement of God's interests, He has seen to it that I and my family have lacked nothing. I have made it a practice never to put a price on my services, and yet, even during the last 20 years, when I have received no stated salary, there has never been any lack. On the contrary I have been able to give away more money than ever before.

4. John 7:17 "If any man will do His will, he shall know of the doctrine, whether it be of God or whether I speak of myself." There is no need of skepticism or unbelief or doubt. Any man who is willing to do God's will can *know* and the only way to *know* is to will to do. After more than 50 years of closest study, observation and experience, I can testify that *it pays to be a follower of God.*

D.L. Pierson

NO ONE ELSE TO PREACH

John 12:32

There is no one else to preach but Jesus Christ, and it is the mark of every deviant liberal theology to make him ever smaller and to reduce him to less daunting size. That is why it causes me sometimes to wonder how, with a Christ so immense, so many can say so much in the pulpit about themselves. John the Baptist's remark reads well in the third chapter of his name-sake's Gospel. The text uses a pair of present infinitives, and that tense in Greek contains the notion of a process, a continuity. He said, "He must go on increasing, and I must go on decreasing." Let it be added that there is no implied overwhelming and blotting out of the subject in this blessed process. In becoming more and more like Christ, a Christian discovers the only way to become more and more his true self, the person God had from the beginning in mind and purpose. Yes indeed, that must be every preacher's theme. Mounting the steps of the barrel-like pulpit in the fine old church in Portland Place, my eyes confronted a text pinned under the desk: "Sir, we would see Jesus." We must forget about "bright services." The subject is enthralling enough and Christianity, life itself, is a deadly serious business. The proclamation, like the Lord's Prayer which means increasingly more to me, rakes the soul. Worship calls for adoration, but it is in the stillness of the soul, as Elijah was taught, that God speaks.

And as Christ has grown in my experience, so too has the Word. It speaks with ever greater clarity. I have, as I said, in a small red leather volume, passages of poetry which have moved me and I find lines spring to my mind. Newly-born Saul Kane in Masefield, for example: "Jesus drive the coulter deep, and plow my living man from sleep." Or in life's storms Housman watching the Severn gale toss the Wrekin: "The wind it plies the saplings double, it blows so hard 'twill soon be done." Or Browning: "I was ever a fighter—so one fight more."

E.M. Blaiklock

STORE IT UP

Psalm 119:11

Memorization of key passages is another method of scriptural intake. Without doubt the classic verse for Scripture memorization is Psalm 119:11: "I have hidden your word in my heart that I might not sin against you." The word that is translated in verse 11 as "hidden" is elsewhere translated as "stored up," a phrase which is more descriptive of the actual meaning. In Proverbs 7:1, for example, Solomon says, "My son . . . *store up* my commands within you," and in Proverbs 10:14 he says, "Wise men *store up* knowledge." In Psalm 31:19 David speaks of the goodness which God has *stored up* for those who fear him. From these passages it is clear that the central idea of the psalmist in Psalm 119:11 was that of storing up God's word in his heart against a time of future need—a time when he would encounter temptation and would be kept from that temptation by the word of God.

But the word of God stored in the heart does more than keep us from sin. It enables us to grow in every area of the Christian life. Specifically for our practice of godliness, it enables us to grow in our devotion to God and in the Godlike character that makes our lives pleasing to him.

Yet another method for taking in God's word is *meditation.* The word *meditate* as used in the Old Testament literally means to murmur or to mutter and, by implication, to talk to oneself. When we meditate on the Scriptures we talk to ourselves about them, turning over in our minds the meanings, the implications, and the applications to our own lives.

Jerry Bridges

THE GREATEST OF TREASURES

Psalms 19:10

We are living in a time where Bible ignorance is widespread. Except for a small proportion of those who faithfully and daily study the Word of God, Americans are a Biblically illiterate people. But the Bible is the greatest of treasures. It is the indestructible Word of God, the unconquerable Word of God.

Dr. A.Z. Conrad said:

Century follows century—*There it stands.*
Empires rise and fall—*There it stands.*
Dynasty succeeds dynasty—*There it stands.*
Kings are crowned and uncrowned—*There it stands.*
Emperors decree its extermination—*There it stands.*
Despised and torn to pieces—*There it stands.*
Storms of hate swirl about it—*There it stands.*
Atheists rail against it—*There it stands.*
Agnostics smile cynically—*There it stands.*
Profane, prayerless punsters caricature it—*There it stands.*
Unbelief abandons it—*There it stands.*
Higher critics deny its inspiration—*There it stands.*
Thunderbolts of wrath smite it—*There it stands.*
An anvil that has broken a million hammers—
There it stands.

It is vitally important because not only is the Word of God indestructible, but also its importance extends to every phase of our lives.

William Lyon Phelps observed:
Our civilization is founded upon the Bible.
More of our ideas, our wisdom, our philosophy, our literature, our art, our ideals come from the Bible than from all other books combined.

D. James Kennedy

FORMING THE CHARACTER

II Timothy 2:15

McCheyne's own words will best show his estimate of study and at the same time the prayerful manner in which he felt it should be carried on. "Do get on with your studies," he wrote to a young student in 1840. "Remember you are now forming the character of your future ministry in great measure, if God spare you. If you acquire slovenly or sleepy habits of study now, you will never get the better of it. Do everything in its own time. Do everything in earnest; if it is worth doing, then do it with all your might. Above all, keep much in the presence of God. Never see the face of man until you have seen His face who is our light, our all. Pray for others; pray for your teachers and fellow students." To another he wrote: "Beware of the atmosphere of the classics. It is pernicious indeed; and you need much of the south wind breathing over the Scriptures to counteract it. True, we ought to know them, but only as chemists handle poisons—to discover their qualities, not to infect their blood with them." And again: "Pray that the Holy Spirit would not only make you a believing and holy lad, but make you wise in your studies also. A ray of divine light in the soul sometimes clears up a mathematical problem wonderfully. The smile of God calms the spirit, and the left hand of Jesus holds up the fainting head, and His Holy Spirit quickens the affections, so that even natural studies go on a million times more easily and comfortably."

Andrew A. Bonar

IT CANNOT BE DESTROYED

Matthew 7:24-27

Gold cannot be destroyed; love cannot be destroyed; faith cannot be destroyed; Christian character cannot be destroyed. And we hear the Master saying, "When through fiery trials thy pathway shall lie, My grace all sufficient shall be thy supply. The flame shall not hurt thee; I only design thy dross to consume and thy gold to refine." The flame shall not hurt thee. A man is never more completely man than when he is God's man. A man is never more in possession of his own personality than when he is possessed with God. And the flame of God will only burn those things of which we would be ashamed in eternity. The flame of God will only take those things away which would hinder us from being completely ourselves. The bush burned, but was not consumed; and true lovers of Christ will welcome this flame. God's lovers welcome it, welcome a flame which will be to them what Manoa's fire was for the angel who, as the flame went up toward heaven, ascended in the flame on the altar. The old saints could pray, "I only want to live to be consumed before Thee as a lamp burneth ceaselessly before thine altars."

Archbishop Fenelon wrote, "Where are they who love Thee for Thyself? Where are they, those who love Thee because they were created only to love Thee? Where are they? Are there any on the face of the earth? If there are none, make some, for what use is the whole world if no one loves Thee, or if no one loves Thee enough to lose themselves in Thee? Oh, my God, oh love, love Thyself in me." Or in those burning words of St. Francis Xavier,

> Jesus, I love thee not because
> I hope for heaven thereby;
> Nor yet because if I love not
> I must forever die.
> I love Thee, Saviour dear, and still
> I ever must love Thee.

David McKee

A ROYAL PRIESTHOOD

I Peter 2:9

I knew a young, unmarried man who fell out of work during the long trade depression between the wars. He was a skilled workman and a fine Christian, but how he lived during those lean years I hardly know. His joy when, at last, he got a job in a wireless factory it would be difficult to describe.

There was, however, a fly in the ointment. He soon found that the men with whom he was working regularly used the most filthy language, and it was impossible all the time to close his ears to their obscenities. He was a gentle soul . . . and yet bold with the boldness of those who belong to our "royal priesthood." He could not feel that it was right to make no protest. . . . At the beginning of his second week he told a few of them gently, affectionately, but plainly, how he felt. A word, he hoped, would be enough. It was a vain hope. They laughed till they cried and blasphemed the more. So he got a . . . collecting box from the local infirmary and put a penny in whenever they swore. . . . When they first realized what he was doing, they swore the harder. . . . They said that it was their first opportunity to curse for the cure of the sick. After being out of work for years, that poor, brave, obscure disciple put, by his own act, nearly all his first week's wages in that box.

But he broke them. When they saw what he had done, something happened. The Spirit of God used the simple artifice of it. They saw how much it hurt him and the blasphemy died down. . . . In the passing of time, when it happened, it happened only by accident, and it was followed immediately by an apology, and the offender himself paid the "fine." He was a plain working man, speaking with a provincial accent, but he belonged to the royal priesthood.

W.E. Sangster

"A TEST OF CHARACTER"

Hebrews 12:6

You many not agree with me, but the truth is that the present war is a blessing in disguise to our people and that the burden it imposes and the hardships it has brought upon us are a test of our character to determine the sincerity of our convictions and the integrity of our souls. In other words, this war has placed us in the crucible to assay the metal in our being. For as a people, we have been living during the last 40 years under a regime of justice and liberty regulated only by universally accepted principles of constitutional government. We have come to enjoy personal privileges and civil liberties without much struggle, without undergoing any pain to attain them. They were practically a gift from a generous and magnanimous people—the people of the United States of America.

Now that Japan is attempting to destroy those liberties, should we not exert any effort to defend them? Should we not be willing to suffer for their defense? If our people are undergoing hardships now, we are doing it gladly; it is because we are willing to pay the price for those constitutional liberties and privileges. You cannot become wealthy by honest means without sweating heavily. You very well know that the principles of democracy and democratic institutions were brought to life through bloodshed and fire. If we sincerely believe in those principles and institutions, as we who are resisting Japan do, we should contribute to the utmost of our capacity to the cost of its maintenance, to save them from destruction and annihilation, and such contribution should be in terms of painful sacrifice, the same currency that other peoples paid for these principles. . . .

Douglas MacArthur

THE WINDOW GETS MISTED

I Corinthians 9:27

For myself, personally, I have found that I can only concentrate my thoughts and activities on Christianity and everything connected with it, which is the one subject I care about in life now—if I don't indulge my senses. This applies even to overeating, which is quite a harmless thing. . . .

Actually, I am a vegetarian nowadays and eat rather little. If I eat a lot, still more if I drink a lot or smoke a lot or indulge in sexual activities a lot, this means to me personally with my sort of make-up, that I am shut off from the sight of God. The image which I use to myself is taken from driving. If it's too hot inside the car, if the temperatures outside and inside are all ill-adjusted, then the windscreen mists over and you can't see. In the same sort of way, if I allow myself to become preoccupied with my bodily appetites, my soul's window gets misted over and I can't see out. I do not in any way criticize people who don't feel similarly. I do not think that abstinence is essential to the pursuit of truth through Christianity, though I notice that the figures in the past whom I most admire and whose writings and thoughts most appeal to me usually did take that way. So there must be some connection. Even so, I would never preach abstinence to people as such; I would point out to them that my experience of life, such as it is, suggests that an integral part of looking at the spiritual reality of life is divorcing yourself as far as possible from involvement in the sensual or physical part.

Malcolm Muggeridge

I Would Be True

I would be true, for there are those who trust me
    I would be pure, for there are those who care;
I would be strong, for there is much to suffer;
    I would be brave, for there is much to dare.
I would be friend of all—the foe, the friendless;
    I would be giving and forget the gift.
I would be humble, for I know my weakness;
    I would look up—and laugh—and love—and lift.
Howard Arnold Walter

NOT MEASURED BY THE CLOCK

Romans 8:26

I found that successful prayer cannot be measured by the clock—it must rather be measured in terms of *unhurriedness*. That is to say, we must have a daily spot where we have a sense of release from every other care—where there is nothing else to do but to speak and listen to God. So many of our prayers consist of hugely comprehensive sentences lumped together. How often one hears the prayer, "Lord, bless all the missionaries." That way of praying is not characteristic of praying in the unhurried quiet time, where one can allow himself to be led out into detailed petitions. And one needs time sufficient to be able to stop and listen to God. When we are in a hurry we tend to do all the talking. This is an impertinence. Some are afraid to stop saying something before God for fear of wandering thoughts. But where is there a better place to do our serious thinking than in the presence of God?

"We know not what to pray for as we ought." This serious infirmity can only be corrected by taking enough time before God to let the Spirit teach us. A missionary friend of mine told me that he had used a prayer list until it became as mechanical as a rosary. It is not a discrediting of the obvious value of a prayer list to insist that in our unhurried quiet time we must get to the place where we transcend all mechanics and where on any given day the Spirit may lift something out of the list or inject something not yet written, with a gentle pressure which brings that item into the center of focus, making it the burden of the day, sometimes along with, and sometimes to the exclusion of, the other items on the list.

Everett Cattell

THINGS THAT HINDER

I John 5:15

Amy Carmichael could be severely practical in reminding colleagues of the things that hinder united prayer. Once she noted down "three facts that if remembered save time and energy in a prayer meeting":

1. We don't need to explain to our Father things that are known to Him.

2. We don't need to press Him, as if we had to deal with an unwilling God.

3. We don't need to suggest to Him what to do, for He Himself knows what to do.

"Lord, all my desires are before Thee." "Do Thou for me, O God the Lord."

Concerning the same need which called forth the "three facts" she wrote:

This early morning I looked up about our special prayer for X, a light fell on the words, "We know *that we have* the petitions that we desired of Him." We pray from the ground of that certainty; not towards certainty but from it. (Is that why we have the words, "In everything by prayer and supplication *with thanksgiving*"? We give thanks before we see).

Then the thought came, "What is it that we *have* in this sense already received? Surely just this: that the glory of the Lord will be manifested (for is not this what we desired of Him?), and that the very best will be done from His eternal point of view, for the work committed to us."

Once in the Forest in October, 1933, a prayer meeting was held in her room.

Yesterday [she wrote to Godfrey] we had the prayer meeting in my room, and the one thing we prayed about was Prayer. I know we have all, for some time back, felt the need of something more in our prayer life. I have, personally, and I know others have, and there are many in our Family who come to prayer meetings because it is the custom to do so, but who are not urged by a great desire. It is the lack of prayer-hunger that often makes a big united meeting difficult. The one thing we seem to need most is a revived prayer life in our own souls—then the wave will flow out to the others.

Elizabeth Elliot

"GOD DOES NOT LOVE PEOPLE"

Psalm 139:17-18

The moment we say "The Lord is my shepherd" we feel faintly selfish or even decidedly stupid. "How," we ask, "can God give full time to me as well as every other person in the world?"

Recently, veteran missionary Ann Smith told of a woman in Japan who became a Christian. She knew that she needed to pray, but she felt self-conscious about bothering the Almighty. So, in order to avoid overburdening God, she would stay awake until one o'clock in the morning to pray because she felt that he wouldn't be so busy at that time.

We smile at her simplicity, knowing that one o'clock in Tokyo is noon somewhere else in the world. But still we need to be reminded that not being a prisoner in time, God can take time for each of us.

One day in a lecture, I said, "One thing we know: God loves people."

Albert Donaldson, creative and perceptive friend, met me later. "You made a mistake, Berquist. God does not love people."

I couldn't believe he was serious. But he was. "God does not love people. He loves persons, individuals."

I have to agree. And Al's distinction is important. It is also scriptural.

In another of his psalms, David says:

How precious are thy thoughts unto me, O God.
    how great is the sum of them!
If I should count them,
      they are more in number than the sand;
      when I awake, I am still with thee.
Psalm 139:17-18

God is thinking about you right now. Not only is God aware of the person you know that you are, but God is also aware of the person he knows you can become.

Maurist Berquist

A WATCHMAN FOR THE LORD

Isaiah 62:6-12

An individual who became known worldwide for his involvement in prayer was John Hyde, a missionary to India who has often been referred to as "Praying Hyde." His first twelve years in India saw very little fruit from his labor. All that time he was actively engaged in missionary work, but his prayer life was lacking.

In reflecting on those years, he became convinced that earnest prayer would have made a difference. He determined in his heart that he would become a watchman for the Lord and that he would give himself no rest in his prayer life. Then in 1904, he met with fellow missionaries and together they formed the Punjab Prayer Union, based on five principles that each member was required to affirm.

1. Are you praying for quickening in your own life, in the life of your fellow workers, and in the Church?

2. Are you longing for greater power of the Holy Spirit in your own life and work, and are you convinced that you cannot go on without this power?

3. Will you pray that you may not be ashamed of Jesus?

4. Do you believe that prayer is the great means for securing this spiritual awakening?

5. Will you set apart one half-hour each day as soon after noon as possible to pray for this awakening, and are you willing to pray *till the awakening comes*?

An awakening did accompany Hyde's ministry, but it was not one that was a result of prayer alone. It depended also on his faithful proclamation of the gospel. "He received assurance in prayer that at least one soul would come to the Savior each day during 1908. There were more than 400 converts added that year. The following year the Lord laid two souls a day upon his heart, and prayer was fully answered; the following year his faith was enlarged to claim four a day."

Ruth Tucker

THEY EMBRACED MY GRIEF

Isaiah 59:1

A pastor in the Midwest wrote me about an experience he had several years ago, a "nervous breakdown" the doctors called it.

The most painful part of it was the seeming silence of God. I prayed, I thought, to a silent darkness. I have thought a lot about this. He only seemed silent. The problem was partly my depression and partly the Christian community. For most Christians I was an embarrassment. Nothing they said dealt with what I endured. One pastor prayed for me in generalities and pieties that were utterly unrelated to the situation. They would not feel my pain.

Other people just avoided me. Ironically, Job's friends were probably a help to him, psychologically. At least they forced out feelings, even if angry ones. Their pronouncements were useless, but they did deal with the questions and gave Job the impression that maybe God was around somewhere. No one in the Christian community, except my wife, helped me even to that degree.

Years later the same pastor, with renewed mental health, was reading Psalm 145 from the pulpit. He tried to concentrate, but something was plaguing him: his week-old grandson had just died, grieving the whole family. He couldn't continue reading the words about God's goodness and fairness. His voice choked, he stopped reading, and he told the tense congregation what had happened.

"As people left the church," he remembers, "they said two important and helpful things:

1. 'Thank you for sharing your pain with us.'

2. 'I grieve with you.' This simple statement was the most helpful thing said. I did not feel alone. Unlike during the time of depression before, I was not abandoned by God and His people. They embraced my grief."

Philip Yancey

AN AGE THAT OPPOSES MEDITATION

Psalm 19:14

Most of us would agree with these words of Jacques Ellul even when applied to ourselves:

> The man of our time does not know how to pray; but much more than that, he has neither the desire nor the need to do so. He does not find the deep source of prayer within himself. I am acquainted with this man. I know him well. It is I myself *(Prayer and Modern Man)*.

We live in an age that opposes meditation, contemplation, and prayer. The cultural values of our society have unduly permeated the worship, life, and service of the church. To a great extent, all of us are faced with a mindset characterized by the success syndrome, pragmatic functionalism (if it works, it's good), the myth of self-fulfillment, materialism, a fragmentation and impersonality of life, a frenetic pursuit of pleasure, and tyranny of timepieces— schedules, computers, jet flights, and telephones.

Coupled with this spirit of the times is a marked confusion among many Christians concerning the great framework of God's grace in our spirituality and prayer life. A major problem we have is our failure to recognize that our God and heavenly Father is waiting, ready, and able to help us in our prayers to Him. All too often we fail to trust God and fail to realize the enabling power of His Spirit in and among us.

The life and writing of Teresa of Avila can help us greatly in this vital dimension of *prayer in life*. Her thoughts and example are significant indeed for the church of Jesus Christ these four centuries later. . . .

Prayer for Teresa is much more than just "saying our prayers." It is God giving Himself and we receiving Him. Thus, when we are really in earnest, steadily pursuing God's will, in an attitude of faith and an act of trust and commitment, it will not be long before we are blessed by His life-giving touch. This is the vital reality which permeates her life and writing.

Clayton Berg Jr.
PREFACE TO A LIFE OF PRAYER,
St. Teresa of Avila

MORE THAN THE DEVIL HIMSELF

Mark 11:24

Rugged Martin Luther was intensely human, yet a man of prayer. He wrote, "I judge that my prayer is more than the devil himself; if it were otherwise Luther would have fared differently long before this. Yet men will not see and acknowledge the great wonders of miracles God works in my behalf. If I should neglect prayer but a single day, I should lose a great deal of the fire of faith."

People spoke of Luther as "the man who can have whatever he wishes of God." When they brought a demon-possessed girl to Luther, he put his hand on her head, prayed, and she was completely delivered. Luther's powerful prayers for healing brought people back from the brink of death.

Melanchthon's eyes were set, his speech and hearing seemingly gone. He recognized no one, and he had ceased to take any nourishment. When Luther saw his condition, Luther began to plead mightily with God, took Melanchthon by the hand and said, "Be of good courage, Philip, thou shalt not die. . . . Trust in the Lord who is able to kill and to make alive." While he spoke Philip began to move, breathe again, and was raised to health and strength.

In the last stages of tuberculosis, the beloved leader Myconius lay dying when Luther prayed for him. "May God not let me hear so long as I live that you are dead," Luther wrote him, "but cause you to survive me. I pray this earnestly and will have it granted, and my will will be granted herein, Amen." Myconius said it was as if he heard Christ saying, "Lazarus, come forth." Myconius was healed and outlived Luther.

All of God's saints were human like you and me but became mighty in prayer. You will never be any greater than your prayer. But you can be great in prayer in spite of all else if you will walk with God. Probably most of God's greatest intercessors are almost unknown to all but Him.

Wesley Duewel

PRAYER OF THE HEART

Romans 8:27

There were in this noviciate many novices. The eldest of them grew so very uneasy under his vocation, that he knew not what to do. So great was his trouble that he could neither read, study, pray, nor do scarcely any of his duties. His companion brought him to me. We spoke awhile together, and the Lord discovered to me both the cause of his disorder and its remedy. I told it to him; and he began to practice prayer, even that of the heart. He was on a sudden wonderfully changed, and the Lord highly favored him. As I spoke to him grace wrought in his heart, and his soul drank it in, as the parched ground does the gentle rain. He felt himself relieved of his pain before he left the room. He then readily, joyfully, and perfectly performed all his exercises, which before were done with reluctance and disgust. He now both studied and prayed easily, and discharged all his duties, in such a manner, that he was scarce known to himself or others. What astonished him most was a remarkable gift of prayer. He saw that there was readily given him what he could never have before, whatever pains he took for it. This enlivening gift was the principle which made him act, gave him grace for his employments, and an inward fruition of the grace of God, which brought all good with it. He gradually brought me all the novices, all of whom partook of the effects of grace, though differently, according to their different temperaments. Never was there a more flourishing noviciate.

Madame Guyon

PRAYER MADE EASY

Mark 8:34

Tersteegen said: "Self-denial makes prayer easy and prayer again lightens self-denial. The more the flesh is under restraint, the more liberty and delight is experienced by the Spirit, in living with God in its true element. . . ." The great gain to the questing soul from this fruit of the Spirit is that it offers to God an ordered and obedient personality, not cloyed by comfort nor sluggish from indulgence, but sensitive to guidance and ready for all His perfect will.

What perplexes beginners in the holy life, concerning the discipline of the saints, is that it covers so many good things. They expected the sword of the Spirit to flash out against evil, but it surprises them that those advanced in sanctity are so severe *with themselves* about many things which are either innocuous or unmistakably wholesome. They do not see, with John Wesley, that a thing can be innocent in itself and yet increase the authority of the body over the mind. They do not realize that one can hardly leave the kindergarten of the School of Sanctity until one has seen that the battle is not only against evil but also against the lesser good. Nobody, so far as I know, has claimed sanctity for Jenny Lind, but she was a devout and aspiring soul, and her great renunciation illustrates her clear recognition that the good can be the enemy of the best. Asked by a friend why—still young and at the height of her fame—she had withdrawn from the operatic stage, she answered, as she picked up her Bible: "Because I found it left me so little time for this and"—pointing to the sunset—"none for that." The saints want God. God above all things. All things in God. Nothing is really a sacrifice that gives them more of God. They put down the penny to pick up the pound.

W.E. Sangster

REDOUBLED CONCENTRATION

Mark 9:29

"Why could not we cast him out?" The answer lies in a personal relationship to Jesus Christ. This kind can come forth by nothing but by concentration and redoubled concentration on Him. We can ever remain powerless, as were the disciples, by trying to do God's work not in concentration on His power, but by ideas drawn from our own temperament. We slander God by our very eagerness to work for Him without knowing Him.

You are brought face to face with a difficult case and nothing happens externally, and yet you know that emancipation will be given because *you* are concentrated on Jesus Christ. This is your line of service—to see that there is nothing between Jesus and yourself. Is there? If there is, you must get through it, not by ignoring it in irritation or by mounting up, but by facing it and getting through it into the presence of Jesus Christ. Then that very thing, and all you have been through in connection with it, will glorify Jesus Christ in a way you will never know till you see Him face to face.

We must be able to mount up with wings as eagles; but we must also know how to come down. The power of the saint lies in the coming down and living down. "I can do all things through Christ which strengtheneth me," said Paul, and the things he referred to were mostly humiliating things. It is in our power to refuse to be humiliated and to say, "No, thank you, I much prefer to be on the mountain top with God." Can I face things as they actually are in the light of the reality of Jesus Christ, or do things as they are efface altogether my faith in Him and put me into a panic?

Oswald Chambers

A DIFFERENT AUDIENCE

Matthew 6:3-4

When the excitement of the game mounted and the crowd grew frantic (the other team often becoming rattled), these boys worked like parts of a well-oiled machine. One day as I watched a game, I understood how this could be. Although the crowd might not know if each boy executed his specific assignment well, the coach would know. Their cool operation would be seen on Monday even if the press had missed it. I thought, *these boys are unconsciously playing the game to a different audience, and it has freed them from the franticness of the crowd!*

I had my answer. Whether or not it was true for the football team, it was true for me! All of my life I had been influenced too much by the moods of my associates. When they were excited and panicked, I reflected their anxiety. Now, in my new experiment, although I was still performing in the same circles and in the same social and business "games," I was occasionally finding a calmness and an ability to live with more honesty and integrity than before. I was starting to play my life to a different audience—to the Living Christ.

I wasn't thinking in terms of His "judging" my actions but rather of His living *awareness* of my struggles to be His boy. I began to get up in the morning being conscious of God's awareness of me and my waking movements. I began being able to tell Him that *He* was the one for whom I wanted to perform the day's actions. Just the conscious act of deciding *that* was a new kind of commitment which, by itself, changed all kinds of things.

Keith Miller

NO RESERVE! NO RETREAT! NO REGRETS!

Proverbs 3:7-12

William Borden grew up with abundance and luxury. He was a heir to a vast fortune, acquired through the giant Borden dairy business. As a youth he was primed for the leadership he would one day assume over this financial empire. He enrolled at Yale for his university education and graduated in 1909.

But during his years at Yale, his vision for the future had dramatically changed. During his freshman year he was deeply challenged by a Reformed Church missionary who had committed his life to reaching Muslims with the gospel. "He was a man with a map. Charged with facts and with enthusiasm, grim with earnestness, filled with a passion of love for Christ and the perishing, Samuel Zwemer made the great map live, voicing the silent appeal of . . . two hundred million of our fellow-creatures in the lands colored green on the map—two hundred million under the sway of Islam."

He was a powerful speaker and his message penetrated the heart of this wealthy young man. "Who is there tonight who can always see the shadow of the Cross falling upon his banking account? Who is there who has the mark of the nails and the print of His spear in his plans and life, his love and devotion and daily program of intercession? Who is there who has heard the word of Jesus and is quietly, obediently, every day, as He has told you and me, taking up his cross to follow Him?"

Borden's commitment grew stronger in the succeeding years, and upon his graduation he announced that he was donating his inheritance to the cause of world missions and that he was committed to serving overseas. He was determined to serve with the China Inland Mission in order to reach Muslims living in China. He first went to Egypt for Arabic language study, but only four weeks after his arrival he contracted spinal meningitis and two weeks later he was dead. Later a message was found scribbled on a sheet of paper stuffed under his pillow: "No Reserve! No Retreat! No Regrets!"

Ruth Tucker

"GETTING TOO CLOSE"

II Timothy 2:22

During the Civil War, an attractive young man in his thirties, was a close friend of my father, and had called to pay his respects. As the two old friends were chatting, the orderly, in some perturbation, broke in to say that two Southern ladies were insisting upon speaking personally with the general. . . .

The two women were ushered in and were impressive, indeed. The eldest was a "grande dame" of the Southern aristocracy, and the younger was the loveliest woman my father had ever seen—but one. (My mother was present when he told me the story, and my father was no fool.)

The general seemed fascinated. He could not take his eyes from that beautiful face.

The stillness of the dingy office was broken by the voice of the older woman. "I will at once come to the point. We must have the temporary use of transport facilities to move our cotton. Your country has no wish to antagonize the British to the point of joining the South in the war and, consequently, allows blockade running. It would accordingly not regard with dissatisfaction the use of your wagons. In return, here is two hundred and fifty thousand dollars in gold certificates. And, if you need other inducements," she added with a smile, "this young lady will supply them." And with a bow they walked out, leaving the young lady's address on the desk.

My father said his knees were knocking together as they had never done in battle. But the general's voice was crisp and clear as he turned to him and dictated the following dispatch:

To the President of the United States:

I have just been offered two hundred and fifty thousand dollars and the most beautiful woman I have ever seen to betray my trust. I am depositing the money with the Treasury of the United States and request immediate relief from this command. They are getting close to my price.

Douglas MacArthur

THIS KIND OF CHALLENGE

John 12:25

While Whittaker Chambers was giving evidence in the case of Alger Hiss, a juror leaned forward and asked him, "Mr. Chambers, what does it mean to be a Communist?" Chambers thought a moment and then exposed the spring of his forsaken loyalty. He explained that when he was a Communist, he had three heroes: a Russian, a Pole, and a German Jew.

The Pole was Felix Djerjinsky, later to be head of the Tcheka and organizer of the Red Terror. As a young man, he had been a political prisoner in the Paviak Prison in Warsaw. In the Paviak Prison in Warsaw, Djerjinsky *insisted* on cleaning the latrines of the other prisoners. The most developed member of any community, he held, must take upon himself the lowliest task.

That was one thing, Whittaker Chambers explained, that it meant to be a Communist.

The German Jew was Eugene Leviné. He organized the Workers' and Soldiers' Soviets in the Bavarian Soviet Republic of 1919. When the Republic was suppressed, Leviné was captured and court-martialled. The court came to its inevitable conclusion. "You are under sentence of death," they told him. Leviné answered, "We Communists are always under sentence of death."

That was another thing, Whittaker Chambers explained, that it meant to be a Communist.

The Russian was a pre-Communist named Sazonov. Arrested for a part in the plot to assassinate the Csarist Prime Minister, von Plehve, he was sent to one of the worst prison camps in Siberia where the political prisoners were flogged unmercifully. Sazonov wondered how he could bring this wickedness to the notice of the world. At last he found a way. Choosing his time, he drenched himself in kerosene, set himself alight, and burned himself to death.

And that also, Whittaker Chambers explained, is what is meant to be a Communist.

No one can answer this kind of challenge but the saints. Conventional religion is powerless.

W.E. Sangster

"MAKE THIS BED AN ALTAR"

Romans 12:1-2

Keep your life on the altar. Taylor Smith was a great power for God. He once revealed to a friend a prayer he often prayed. He said that before he even got out of bed in the morning he would say, "Oh God, make this bed on which I rest an altar and my body reclining on it a sacrifice. In the teaching of Romans 12:1, I present it to you again this morning, a living sacrifice." This is a practical prayer. Christian, keep your life on the altar for Christ.

A missionary party outward bound for the Pacific Islands was ridiculed by the ship's captain. The scoffer said, "You will only die out there." A missionary answered, "We died before we started." This death to self-will is the royal road of obedience. Those who walk that road will know and do the will of God. "We must trust and obey God."

Norman Lewis

A few penciled notes in Charles Cowman's diary tell of some of the dealings he had with the Lord on July 15, 1924. "It looks as if the Lord has forbidden my return to the Orient. He was peculiarly present with me this morning about daybreak. Just what He meant to tell me, I am not certain. It may have been my healing, or it may be that He was trying to tell me that the time of my departure is at hand. I would rather remain upon earth a while longer if it be His will, but if He wants me in His presence, I can but say, 'Thy will be done.' I am perfectly willing to leave the work I love so well in His Hands, perfectly willing to leave with Him my unanswered prayers, perfectly willing to let my body return to the dust—dust that He will watch over till the resurrection morning."

Lettie Cowman

"THY HUMBLE SLAVES"

Luke 9:62

The words of the preacher rekindled the fires of love half-smothered in the heart of Raymund Lull. He now made up his mind once and forever. He sold all his property, which was considerable, gave the money to the poor, and reserved only a scanty allowance for his wife and children. This was the vow of his consecration in his own words:

"To Thee, Lord God, do I now offer myself and my wife and my children and all that I possess; and since I approach Thee humbly with this gift and sacrifice, may it please Thee to condescend to accept all that I give and offer now for Thee, that I and my wife and my children may be Thy humble slaves." It was a covenant of complete surrender, and the repeated reference to his wife and children shows that Raymund Lull's wandering passions had found rest at last. It was a *family* covenant, and by this token we know that Lull had forever said farewell to his former companions and his life of sin.

Samuel Zwemer

Are you willing to give the living God a blank sheet of paper, so to speak, and say to Him, "Write upon it what You will. I'm committed to it, not knowing what it is." Are you so committed?

Selected

First, new life can start when a person begins a relationship with Jesus Christ in which, for him, there are no conscious reservations. Our job is not to anticipate no conscious reservations. Our job is not to anticipate the things in someone's life which many need to be dealt with, but to suggest that he give Christ all he sees at the moment.

Bruce Larson

AN AWFUL TOLL

Mark 8:34-35

The earliest to go forth were five young men who sailed for the Congo, Africa, in November, 1884, three years before the Christian and Missionary Alliance was regularly organized. Within a few months of their arrival on the field their leader, John Condit, died of fever. Indeed, the opening of both the Congo and Sudan field proved a painfully costly undertaking. Those deadly climates exacted such an awful toll of lives that for years the missionary graves in both fields outnumbered the living missionaries.

The pioneer Alliance missionary to China, Rev. William Cassidy, was never permitted to reach that land, but died of smallpox contracted on the Pacific voyage and was buried in Japan. Those who followed after him faced a China that was then seething with bitter anti-foreign feeling; and especially in the totally unevangelized provinces of Kuangsi and Hunan, where they were among the early pioneer forces, were they called upon to endure no little hardship and danger. Others pressed on westward to the remote borders of Tibet and knocked at the doors of that hostile and devil-possessed land, to enter which had been one of the main objectives in mind when the Alliance was organized. A little later a band of 45 workers from Sweden penetrated the far north, and amid many vicissitudes planted stations beyond China's Great Wall on the borders of Mongolia. The Boxer uprising of 1900 brought this mission to a tragic end. Twenty-one of its foreign workers and fourteen of their previous children were brutally murdered, and the rest made a hazardous escape across the desert into Siberia and after harrowing experiences reached their European homes.

THE LIFE OF A.B. SIMPSON
A.E. Thompson

FACING THE LION

Mark 8:36-37

"Missiology Faces the Lion" is the title of this article, but what lion are we talking about? What lion stands before missiologists ready to devour them? The lion very clearly is the conviction that mission is primarily helpful activities to other people regardless of what they believe. The lion is the idea that mission (missiology) is primarily helping those great groupings of humankind who are less fortunate than we are. . . . As Christians look out on these multitudes, should they minister to the physical and mental needs regardless of the spiritual need? The lion says they must.

Before us lies a village in which all the inhabitants offer sacrifices to and worship the god represented in the stone image of a bull, or of a woman, or a man. The average income of those who reside here is very low. Half the people in the village are illiterates. The people in this village are divided into several distinct castes or tribes. One of these is, by the religion professed, held to be most superior, another is held to be most inferior. What does this village need? Does it need better systems of agriculture? Does it need to become entirely literate? Does it need a system for the disposal of refuse? Does it need better houses in which to live? Yes, of course, it needs all these things.

However, its crucial need is none of these. Its crucial need is to cease worshiping the stone idols, to cease believing that all sickness is caused by acts of these gods. The crucial need is to believe on God the Father Almighty, who is made known to us in Jesus Christ, his Son. The great need is to move off the animal and human platform and to mount the platform of the divine life. Then and then only will these other advances be made quickly and permanently.

The lion that stands before missiology today must be recognized as the great enemy. Missiology needs to state clearly that no amount of physical or mental advance outranks or equals spiritual rebirth.

MISSIOLOGY-INTERNATIONAL REVIEW

FAITHFULNESS IN A LITTLE THING

Luke 16:10

Alone in his attic room James Fraser was assailed by some real temptations. One was a depressing sense of loneliness in his isolated position. There was virtually no one to talk to, since Embury was more than busy in the work almost single-handed, and James could not converse in Chinese. Another was the boredom of his daily study routine, partly done with his language teacher, partly alone with his books. Overall there was temptation to slacken in his daily communion with God. . . .

James was only 22, and fast learning to school himself against the subtle inroads of apathy and lethargy. He tried hard to be faithful in the seemingly trivial tasks at hand.

"A little thing," said Hudson Taylor, "is a little thing. But faithfulness in a little thing is a great thing."

James wrote at this time:

It has come home to me very forcibly of late that it matters little what the work is in which we are engaged: so long as God has put it into our hands, the faithful doing of it is of no greater importance in one case than in another. . . . The temptation I have often had to contend with is persistent under many forms: "If only I were in such and such a position" for example, "shouldn't I be able to do a great work! Yes, I am only studying engineering at present, but when I am in training for missionary work things will be different and more helpful." Or "I am only just in preparation at present, taking Bible courses and so on, but when I get out to China my work will begin." "Yes, I have left home now, but I am only on the voyage, you know; when I am really in China, I shall have a splendid chance of service." Or, "Well, here in the Training Home, all my time must be given to language study— how can I do missionary work? But when I am settled down in my station and able to speak freely, opportunities will be unlimited!" etc., etc.

It is all IF and WHEN. I believe the devil is fond of those conjunctions.

MOUNTAIN RAIN
Eileen Crossman

WASTED IN INDIA

Mark 14:4

I have known cases of young ministers dissuaded from facing the missionary call by those who posed as friends of foreign missions, and yet presumed to argue: "Your spiritual power and intellectual attainments are needed by the Church at home; they would be wasted in the foreign field." Spiritual power wasted in a land like India! Where is it so sorely needed as in a continent where Satan has constructed his strongest fortresses and displayed the choicest masterpieces of his skill? Intellectual ability wasted among a people whose scholars smile inwardly at the ignorance of the average Westerner! Brothers, *if God is calling you,* be not deterred by flimsy subterfuges such as these. You will need the power of God and the Holy Ghost to make you an efficient missionary. You will find your reputation for scholarship put to the severest test in India. Here is ample scope alike for men of approved spiritual power and for intellectual giants. And so I repeat, *if God is calling you,* buckle on your sword, come to the fight, and win your spurs among the cultured sons of India.

Rev. T. Walker, India

But how often our zeal comes from mixed motives. Horatius Bonar (1808-1889), Scottish preacher and hymn writer, had a dream. He dreamt that the angels took his zeal and weighed it and told him it was excellent. It weighed up to 100 pounds, all that could be asked. He—in his dream—was very pleased at the result. But then the angels wished to analyze it in various ways, with this result:

> *14 parts were from selfishness*
> *15 parts were due to sectarianism*
> *22 parts from ambition*
> *23 parts because of love for humanity, and*
> *26 parts from love for God*

Bonar woke up humbled at the thought, and dedicated himself anew.

FAITHFUL IN CHRIST, URBANA '84

"THESE LOW-BORN MECHANICS"

I Corinthians 1:27-28

Carey and his son have been in Bengal 14 years, the others only nine. They have all had a difficult language to acquire, before they could speak to the people; to preach and argue therein required a thorough and familiar knowledge. The wonder is not that they have done so little, but so much. The anti-missionaries cull from their journals and letters all that is ridiculous, sectarian, and trifling; call them fools, madmen, tinkers, Calvinists, and schismatics; and keep out of sight their love of man and zeal for God, their self-devotement, their indefatigable industry and unequalled learning. These "low-born and low-bred mechanics" have translated the whole Bible into Bengali, and by this time have printed it. They are printing the New Testament in the Sanskrit, Oriyam Marathi, Hindi, and Gujarati; and are translating it into Persian, Telugu, Kanarese, Chinese, and the tongues of the Sikhs and of the Burmans; and in four of these languages they are going on with the whole Bible. Extraordinary as this is, it will appear more so when it is remembered that of these men one was originally a shoemaker, another a printer, and the third the master of a charity school. Only 14 years have elapsed since Thomas and Carey set foot in India, and in that time these missionaries have acquired this gift of tongues; in fourteen years these "low-born, low-bred mechanics" have done more towards spreading the knowledge of the Scriptures among the heathen than has been accomplished, or even attempted, by all the world's princes and potentates, and all its universities and establishments into the bargain.

SOUTHEY'S DEFENSE OF WILLIAM CAREY

HEAVEN EMPTY IN FIVE MINUTES

Acts 26:16

When the angel visited Cornelius he was able to tell him that his alms and prayers were accepted of God, but added, in effect: "I cannot tell you the way of salvation, I cannot communicate to you the gift of eternal life. If you want to know that, you must send to a saved sinner, named Simon Peter."

The angels have no experience of pardoning and regenerating grace. They have never felt rebellion in their hearts; they have never known the mystery of reconciliation; never been plucked from the burning; never been lifted from the slough of sin; never felt the Spirit within crying, "Abba, Father." How, then, shall they speak of these things to men? How shall they be able to communicate eternal life to dead souls?

But to us it is given to be ministers of the grace of God. A friend of mine once observed, "If God gave the command to angels to evangelize the world, heaven would be empty in five minutes."

No man feels the value of the soul of another who has not been made sensible of the worth of his own soul. No man discerns the malignity of sin in the world who has not yet felt its bitterness and terror in his own heart. No man is awake to the peril of the ungodly who has not trembled under the sense of personal danger. No man forms a correct estimate of the value of the atonement who has not had the blood of Christ sprinkled on his own conscience.

Here is a deep secret, and one that is absolutely indispensable for the work of soul-winning. To put it briefly, we may say that the one task that we are called upon to accomplish is to convict men of sin and then to convince them of the love of God in Christ.

The Lord Jesus appeared to Paul that He might make him a *witness*. Unless our divine Lord has in some form appeared to us, humbling us in the dust before Him, our ministry will be no ministry at all, but the telling of what to the hearer will sound as *"idle tales,"* "sounding brass" and "tinkling cymbals."

That it is sadly possible to be ordained to the ministry, and yet to be in utter darkness of soul, unable to be a witness, we are constantly seeing to our sorrow.

A. Paget Wilkes

UPCHUCKING ON SELFISHNESS

I Peter 2:9

In the 1880s and 90s there were only 1/37th as many college students as there are today, but the Student Volunteer Movement netted 100,000 volunteers who gave their lives to missions. Twenty thousand actually went overseas. As we see it now, the other 80,000 had to stay home to rebuild the foundations of the missions endeavor. They began the Layman's Missionary Movement and strengthened existing women's missionary societies.

John E. Kyle

There is a growing number of Christian young people who are upchucking on selfishness. They want something more out of life, more out of themselves and more out of their Christianity.

One of my most earnest prayers for the young is that they will have a purpose in life that is big enough and worthy enough to demand every ounce of their ability, love and creativity. We in the church have been guilty of robbing youth of a world vision large enough to sink their teeth into for the rest of their lives. We should extend the same missionary challenge to today's youth that Francis Xavier, the great missionary to India and Japan, issued to the youth of his day. He urged students to "give up their small ambitions and come eastward to preach the gospel of Christ."

The torch is being passed on. Think of it! For almost two thousand years Christians have dreamed of finally fulfilling the Great Commission. And God has ordained that the young generation—this present generation—run the last lap. "But you are a chosen generation, a royal priesthood, a holy nation, His own special people, that you may proclaim the praises of Him who called you out of darkness into His marvelous light" (I Pet. 2:9).

David Shibley

NOT A DEBATING SOCIETY

John 12:30-32

The Church is not a debating society where we are to contend over the fine points of ecclesiastical life and procedure. I dare to say that it is not merely, or chiefly, a place for worship where we may regale ourselves in the presence of the revealed. Let me say that the church exists for this, and for this only: to give Jesus Christ to the whole world. That is the supreme business of the Church. And I am wondering what He thinks of the loyalty that marks the movement of our days. When I remember that there are a thousand million men and women in the world who have never so much as heard of Christ; when I remember that forty million of them are passing out of the earth into eternity with each revolving year; when I know that a hundred thousand of these men and women are dying every day; when I remember that four of them pass out every time we draw a breath, and that my beloved Church is giving only a few cents per year, per member, in order that Jesus Christ may become their Savior too, I am asking myself, Is my church a real Church of the living God?

From this Conference, we ought to sound a forward march for our beloved Methodism. From this conference we ought to send forth a cry that would pierce, as a flame of fire, every Church in this land, and there ought to be such a calling forth and laying down of lives and dollars during this next year as our Methodism heretofore has never known.

THE MISSIONARY IMPERATIVE
Elmer T. Clark

BROKEN ON THE ROCKS

I Peter 1:7

From our human viewpoint there are many things that must be described as sorrowful. Your child was taken; your dearest hopes were disappointed; your desires and ambitions, which were high and worthy, were frustrated. Often it is with men's plans and hopes as it was with those ships that Jehoshaphat sent for the gold of Ophir: "The ships went not, for they were broken on the rocks."

Then there are those things which have happened to you through the faithlessness or malice or wickedness of others. What shall we say of these things? It is indeed true that you can see how some of these things have taught you patience and sympathy, have softened your life, annealed your heart, and brought a tenderness and earnestness into your life which otherwise would have been lacking. Even death, we can see, has a great ministry for the soul. The legend of Jubal, one of the descendants of Methuselah, tells how when death was only a black spot in the memory of *one* man, Cain, men lived a life of pleasure and idleness, a life that had no greatness or nobility in it. But when the second death came, then a new meaning came into life.

Clarence E. Macartney

Faith was tested in that period through the prolonged illnesses of some members of the family, and the death of others. But the collapse of faith, which would have given free entrance to the devil, never took place. To this time belongs the story of a mud wall which "fell in solemn crashes," all through a night of heavy rain. When the children saw the ruins next morning, one of them said, "Amma will be sorry," but another corrected her. "No," she said, "Amma will say it is the trial of our faith." The phrase became proverbial, and was applied to circumstances which scarcely deserved it, but it did describe Amma's attitude to the whole of life, including events far more painful than the incident which gave rise to it.

AMY CARMICHAEL OF DOHNAVUR
F. Houghton

FALL INTO THE PURE DIVINE

Luke 9:24

When I had lost all created supports, and even divine ones, I then found myself happily compelled to fall into the pure divine, and to fall into it through all those very things which seemed to remove me further from it. In losing all the gifts, with all their supports, I found the Giver. In losing the sense and perception of thee in myself—I found thee, O my God, to lose thee no more in thyself in thy own immutability. Oh, poor creatures, who pass all your time in feeding upon the gifts of God, and think therein to be the most favored and happy, how I pity you if you stop here, short of the true rest, and cease to go forward to God himself, through the loss of those cherished gifts which you now delight in. How many pass all their lives in this way, and think highly of themselves therein! There are others who being called of God to die to themselves, yet pass all their time in a dying life, and in inward agonies, without ever entering into God, through death and a total loss of self, because they are always willing to retain something under plausible pretexts, and so never lose themselves to the whole extent of the designs of God. Wherefore, they never enjoy God in all his fullness; which is a loss that cannot be perfectly known in this life.

Madame Guyon

GOD'S TOOL IN YOUR LIFE

Hebrews 12:15

One of the greatest barriers that prevents us from experiencing God's unsurpassed peace is a root of bitterness. Planted as a seed of anger, rejection, or resentment, bitterness grows into a poisonous emotion that chokes out the peace of God in our lives and defiles the lives of family members and friends.

If you are or have been embittered against someone because of an unjust circumstance, you know the emotional price you pay. It affects you physically and spiritually, releasing its hostile toxins at the slightest upset. You cannot hide a bitter spirit. It spills over into all that you do.

But the good news of the gospel is freedom from every form of bondage, including a bitter spirit. You do not have to be its slave or allow it to fester a day longer. In honest prayer before God, admit your bitterness. Be specific. Acknowledge it as sin and repent, changing your mind and heart about its corrosive influence. This attacks the problem at its root—sin against God—and creates the right climate for healing and restoration.

Next comes one of the most difficult steps toward dislodging the stronghold of bitterness. You must choose to view the offending party or circumstance as God's tool in your life. That is fundamental to long-term freedom. Everything that comes into your life is filtered through the will of God. God has allowed this person or event, as painful as it may be, to touch your life for your personal spiritual growth. This is the extraordinary biblical view that will excavate the root of bitterness from your spirit.

Charles Stanley

BROKEN-WORLD EXPERIENCES

Genesis 50:20

We searched out the biblical biographies of every man and woman whose world had broken for one reason or another. As I've noted elsewhere, we discovered that almost everyone in the Bible was conversant with some kind of broken-world experience. And we came to understand that in almost every case the broken-world moments were the turning points to great spiritual insight, development, and godly performance. That was both a comfort and a marvelous promise.

We also turned to the spiritual classics. Here, our friends became women and men such as Amy Carmichael whose personal world broke through no fault of her own when she suffered a series of accidents and spent the last 20 years of life bedridden; Oswald Chambers whose life was probably shortened through his enormous intensity and physical exertion in serving the Lord during the World War I period; William and Catherine Booth who plowed through powerful ridicule and discouragement to establish the work of the Salvation Army. . . .

Mrs. Charles Cowman's *Streams in the Desert* and Chamber's *My Utmost for His Highest* became a daily spiritual feeding, never failing to provide a word from God to nourish our hearts. The prayers of Quoist, Baillie, and Francois Fenélon, the words of Tozer, and the liturgical worship of the Book of Common Prayer became our spiritual lines to the deep. And out of them all, words came from heaven itself each day to help in the rebuilding process.

Because we had more time here at Peace Ledge, we read more. And both of us came to a similar conclusion as we discussed the books we were reading. Books written by people who had sustained some sort of a broken-world experience—debilitating illness, humiliating failure, intense persecution, conflict with evil, numbing disappointment—were powerful in their ability to reach into our inner spirits.

Gordon MacDonald

ALL SUFFERING EXCLUDED

Philippians 1:29

Suppose, contrary to fact, that this world were a paradise from which all possibility of pain and suffering were excluded. The consequences would be very far-reaching. For example, no one could ever injure anyone else: the murderer's knife would turn to paper or his bullets to thin air; the bank safe, robbed of a million dollars, would miraculously become filled with another million dollars (without this device, on however large a scale, proving inflationary); fraud, deceit, conspiracy, and treason would somehow always leave the fabric of society undamaged. Again, no one would ever be injured by accident: the mountain-climber, steeplejack, or playing child falling from a height would float unharmed to the ground; the reckless driver would never meet with disaster. There would be no need to work; there would be no call to be concerned for others in time of need or danger, for in such a world there could be no real needs or dangers.

To make possible this continual series of individual adjustments, nature would have to work "special providences" instead of running according to general laws which men must learn to respect on penalty of pain or death. The laws of nature would have to be extremely flexible. . . .

One can at least begin to imagine such a world. It is evident that our present ethical concepts would have no meaning in it. If, for example, the notion of harming someone is an essential element in the concept of wrong action, in our hedonistic paradise there could be no wrong actions—nor any right actions in distinction from wrong. Courage and fortitude would have no point in an environment in which there is, by definition, no danger of difficulty. Generosity, kindness, the agape aspect of love, prudence, unselfishness, and all other ethical notions which presuppose life in a stable environment, could not even be formed. Consequently, such a world, however well it might promote pleasure, would be very ill adapted for the development of the moral qualities of human personality. In relation to this purpose it would be the worst of all possible worlds.

John Hick

AN EMOTION THAT HEALS

I John 4:10

Love is an emotion that heals. It is the antidote for fear. The Apostle John writes: "God is love; and he that dwelleth in love dwelleth in God, and God in him. Herein is our love made perfect, that there is no fear in love: but perfect love casteth out fear" (I John 4:16).

Mr. Brown tells of a mother whose daughter had a tumor on the brain that was causing blindness. The mother was frightened as to the future. He and the mother filled their hearts with the love of God and then prayed. The tumor disappeared.

The person who would pray for the healing of others must be filled with love. But we must learn love. As we love one another God's love begins to be perfected in us.

In her book *Love, Hate, Fear, Anger and the Other Lively Emotions*, the Canadian author June Callwood writes:

Love takes 30 years to learn. Love is the only emotion that isn't natural, the only one that has to be learned and the only one that matters. In recent years psychologists and psychiatrists have been making discoveries about love which tend to disprove three thousand years of poetry: real love is a skill rarely learned before the age of 35. No love, not even maternal love, is instinctive or innate. Most people can love only in shabby, suspicious amounts; when they speak of love, they mean getting it, not giving it.

Perhaps not all of us would agree that it always takes 30 years to love. But we certainly agree that love must be learned by being practiced and that the practice of love must begin early in life. How important it is that love be the climate of the home.

Frank Bateman Stanger

DRAW EACH OTHER TO GOD

Matthew 6:21

Our Lord gives the answer to a difficulty continually perplexing honest Christians—"How am I to learn to *love* God? I want to do my duty, but I do not feel as if I loved God." Our Lord gives the answer, "Where your treasure is, there will your heart be also." Act for God, do and say the things that He wills; direct your thoughts and intentions God-ward; and, depend upon it, in the slow process of nature, all that belongs to you—your instincts, your intelligence, your affections, your feelings—will gradually follow along the line of your action. Act for God; you are already *showing* love to Him and you will learn to *feel* it.

Charles Gore

They who, continuing faithful to divine grace, however partially communicated, serve God with their whole lives, will never fail of that one reward, the greatest which even He has to bestow, the being made able to love Him with their whole hearts.

Dora Greenwell

He said he received such a manifestation of the full meaning of those words "God is Love" as he could never be able to express. "It fills my heart" he said every moment. Presently addressing his wife by the pet name for her he said, "O Polly, my dear Polly, God is love! Shout! Shout aloud, God is love." Then because he was getting so weak he could scarcely talk he proposed that they should agree upon a sign between themselves. Tapping her hand twice with his finger, he said, "I mean, God is love—by this we will draw each other into God."

THE LIFE OF JOHN FLETCHER

SOMEONE HELPING SOMEONE ELSE

I Corinthians 13:4-6

Love delivers from self-attention, gives you other attention; and therefore love, not faith, is the method of getting rid of fear. For love produces faith as a by-product of that love.

"Lila of Greece" lives on absolute faith that love is invincible. She is the word of love become flesh in concrete situations. While I write she is at joyous work massaging the sores of lepers with her bare hands. Isn't she afraid of infection? No, perfect love casts out fear. And my conviction is that her love will make her immune.

A servant was sent to the railway station to meet Sir Bartle Creer. The servant had never seen him and didn't know how to recognize him, but the one directing him said, "Look for someone who is helping someone else." The servant saw a man helping an old lady, went up to him and said, "Are you Sir Bartle Creer?" And he was. If you want to recognize a mature person look for someone who is helping someone else. . . .

Without expressed love we are sick. In a sanatorium I announced that the patients would have an opportunity to sew for China relief during the Sino Japanese war. We provide the garments and the patients had only to sew them up. I thought there would be a rush to get the garments at the close of the chapel service. Not a person took a garment. Their love had become ingrown and self-centered and hence they were sick personalities.

E. Stanley Jones

A young man was sent to our neighborhood to recuperate from a nervous breakdown. Visiting him was a gloomy business. "This is a gray world" etc., he would say.

Then one day something happened. He fell in love. He fell hard! He came to see me the day his engagement was announced. "This is a lovely world," he said. "Come out into the garden and listen to that little bird singing fit to burst its heart. Isn't it a glorious morning? How good to be alive."

W.E. Sangster

"NOBODY EVER LOVED ME"
I Corinthians 13:8

I found in the outskirts of the city one of our neglected poor so ignorant of human love that she could not comprehend at first what I meant when I told her of the love of God. She had been neglected, abused, and wronged so long that her hand was against her. When I tried to lead her to the knowledge of Jesus, she looked up into my face and said, "I do not understand you; nobody ever loved me, and I do not even know what love means." I went home that night to my proud and wealthy church, and I told them I wanted them to make a poor sister understand the meaning of love. And so they began one by one to visit her, to give her little tokens of their interest and regard; until at last one day, months later, as I sat in her humble room, she looked up in my face and said with much feeling, "Now I think I understand what love means, and can accept the love of God."

A.B. Simpson

St. Tikhon Zadonsky, the great Russian saint, said: "Christ has loved me for nothing, and I must love Him for nothing too."

St. Therese of Lisieux: "And If I should come into purgatory, well and good: I shall wander at pleasure through the flames like the three young men and in the fiery furnace sing the song of love."

Love for souls:

Catherine Booth: "O, the value of souls. They are worth all the trouble and sacrifice involved—yea a thousand times over. . . . O, how I yearned over them! I felt as if it would be a small thing to die there and then if that would have brought them to Jesus."

Said of Gerald Majella: "He loved all men except Gerard Majella."

- Selected

"WHICH DO YOU SERVE?"

Matthew 22:37

Every Christian would agree that a man's spiritual health is exactly proportional to his love for God. But a man's love for God, from the very nature of the case, must always be very largely, and often must be entirely a "Need-love."

The question whether we are loving God or the earthly Beloved "more" is not, so far as concerns our Christian duty, a question about the comparative intensity of two feelings. The real question is, which (when the alternative comes) do you serve, or choose to put first? To which claim does your will in the last resort yield?

C.S. Lewis

Wherever you get out of love is where you must get back in love. If you have violated the spirit and law of love in dealing with your own wife, you'll have to repent to her as well as to God. You could not be sweet enough with all other women in the world to get back. . . .

How to increase union and in love:

1. Open wide to receive Jesus and His love. "Election is this way; Jesus is all the time voting for us and the Devil is all the time voting against us and the way we vote carries the election."

2. Choose to give Him and his love to all.

3. Pray for perfect love.

4. Do your part in removing the hindrances of love.

5. In every new situation pray and seek to choose the most loving thing. Remember what Jesus did.

Rufus Mosely

"FIRE! FIRE!"

Matthew 3:11

There is a Scottish paraphrase which declares that when the Holy Spirit comes He does two things, not one:

Your minds shall fill with sacred truth,
Your hearts with sacred fire.

Sometimes the Church has been so keen about the first, the quest of sacred truth, that it has rather tended to play down the second, the sacred fire of love. And when that happens, you are bound to get a Church inhibited and crippled, lacking verve and glow and warmth and spontaneity. "I baptize you with water," declared John the Baptist, "but He shall baptize you with fire." "Let your religion," cried G. K. Chesterton impatiently, "be less of a theory and more of a love affair!" There was a day when Father Stanton, in his pulpit of St. Alban's, Holborn, suddenly cried "Fire! Fire!"—and then when the congregation was beginning to panic, he went on. "Everywhere, everywhere—except in the Church!" Do let us remember that what the gospel gives is not a problem but a Person; not an -ism or an -ology, but the Word made flesh: not a metaphysic but a master-passion, a living Lord to love and to be loved by for ever. "Simon, son of Jonas, lovest thou Me?"

It was a simple question. But it was also a *searching question*, a terribly probing question. What short work this question makes of all our shams and sophistries and insincerities!

There was once a Russian artist who painted a picture of the Last Supper. When it was finished, being rather pleased with it, he took it to Tolstoy and said, "I want your opinion of my picture: what do you think of my Christ?" And Tolstoy, having looked carefully at the picture, turned round with blazing eyes on the artist, and in a voice trembling with emotion exclaimed, "You don't love Him! For if you did, you would have painted Him better. And if you don't love Him, what right have you to touch Him at all?"

James S. Stewart

THE POLYPHONY OF LIFE

Song of Songs 1:1-4

There is always a danger of intense love destroying what I might call the "polyphony" of life. What I mean is that God requires that we should love him eternally with our whole hearts, yet not so as to compromise or diminish our earthly affections but as a kind of cantus firmus to which the other melodies of life provide the counterpoint. Every affection is one of these contrapuntal themes, a theme which enjoys an autonomy of its own. Even the Bible can find room for the Song of Songs, and one could hardly have a more passionate sensual love than is there portrayed. It is a good thing that that book is included in the Bible as a protest against those who believe that Christianity stands for the restraint of passion (is there any example of restraint anywhere in the Old Testament?). Where the ground bass is firm and clear there is nothing to stop the counterpoint from being developed to the utmost of its limits. Both ground bass and counterpoint are "without confusion and yet distinct," in the words of the Chalcedonian formula, like Christ in his divine and human natures. Perhaps the importance of polyphony in music lies in the fact that it is a musical reflection of this Christological truth, and that it is therefore an essential element in the Christian life. All this occurred to me after you were here. Can you see what I'm driving at? I wanted to tell you that we must have a good, clear cantus firmus. Without it there can be no full or perfect sound, but with it the counterpoint has a firm support and cannot get out of tune or fade out, yet is always a perfect whole in its own right. Only a polyphony of this kind can give life a wholeness, and at the same time assure us that nothing can go wrong so long as the cantus firmus is kept going. Perhaps your leave and the separation which lies ahead will be easier for you to bear. Please do not fear or hate separation if it should come, with all its attendant perils, but pin your faith on the cantus firmus.

LETTERS FROM PRISON
Detrich Bonhoeffer

BURNING READINESS

Luke 12:49

The coming of the Spirit is to have the effect of fire. Christ desired that all the fiery ministry of the Spirit be active in the life of His own. He kindled the holy flame of God in the hearts of His followers as He began His earthly ministry. Only on the day of Pentecost, as visibly symbolized by the descent of the holy flame of the Spirit, did Christ so empower by His fiery baptism that the 120 began to spread God's holy fire across the world.

Jesus had said, "I have come to bring fire on the earth" (Luke 12:49). While not all commentators are agreed as to the meaning of this fire which Christ so longed to have arrive, yet over the centuries a host of noted scholar-leaders of the church have seen it as referring to or including reference to the mighty ministry of the Spirit.

Zeal for accomplishing God the Father's purpose was burning in Jesus like an unquenchable fire. He had a "burning readiness to do all the Father's will, even though it cost Him His blood." Our flaming-hearted Savior should have disciples with hearts similarly aflame.

Bishop William Quayle, speaking of a leader, said he "stands at the center of a circle whose entire rim is fire. Glory envelops him. He is a prisoner of majesty." He says that even the speechless should become ablaze on such themes as the gospel compels us to grapple with. "We must not be insipid. There is not a dull page in all this age-long story of the redeeming of the race."

Quayle pleads with us not to be apathetic but to be vigilant. We "are burdened with a ministry which must be uttered lest we die, and, what is more consequence, which must be uttered lest this wide world die". . . .

Benjamin Franklin confessed that he often went to hear George Whitfield because he could watch him burn before his very eyes.

Wesley Duewel

MORE THAN A CASUAL ENCOUNTER

Acts 1:8

One lovely morning, during spring break at Asbury College, I went to my place of prayer with such love for Jesus in my heart. For months I had been seeking the Holy Spirit in my life. I was seeking more than just a casual encounter; I wanted the Holy Spirit in my life taking total control.

Over the years I tried to tell about that glorious morning, but words truly fail. He came that morning as he always comes to those who yearn for him with all their heart. He came with a baptism of holy love, with the fire of the Holy Spirit which burned for four days. The burning was so powerful that first day I had to lie down most of the day. The Holy Spirit came revealing Jesus, and I saw him in my heart as I had never seen him before. I was speechless for I did not want to speak and I couldn't. He taught me and loved me during the duration of the burning. His control during this time was overwhelming, for the Holy Spirit absolutely loved me into total surrender.

This experience continued all day, yet it seemed only a few moments. In the late afternoon I called my mother, who has been my spiritual guide, and sought her counsel. As a wise guide she encouraged me, "Continue to be totally submissive and quiet before him, yielding everything to him."

When my husband stepped through the back door, he sensed God's presence and called out to me, "Are you all right?"

"Oh, John, God has come to me today. It has been incredible! The Holy Spirit has revealed Jesus to me."

The vivid reality of Jesus continued with burning for four days, gently diminishing in its intensity each day. Quietly I stayed in his presence and waited on him while doing little else.

THE LOVE EXCHANGE
Margaret Therkelsen

"MY ROOM WAS FULL UP"

John 14:17

This power of the Holy Spirit is of tremendous value to us. The Bible says: "Be filled with the Spirit!" In Haarlem lived a woman who started a prayer meeting in her room. Her brother had not much faith about it and said: "You will never succeed!" But the day after, she told him: "My room was full up!" "All right, but just wait and see what happens next week." But the next time she said: "My room was even fuller." And the third time: "Now it was fuller still!" Her brother said: "That is impossible; when your room is full, it cannot be fuller." "Oh yes," she said. "Every week we took some more furniture out of the room."

When we are filled with the Holy Spirit, then another step may be necessary. It is possible that some furniture must be removed from the heart: television, or some books, friendships, personal hobbies; everything that can hinder us from following Jesus Christ. We can clear out still more for Jesus, so that we can give more room to the Holy Spirit. My glove cannot do anything by itself, but when my hand is in the glove, it can do a great deal. It can even cook, write and do many things! I know that it is not the glove, but the hand. When I put only one finger in the glove, then it cannot do anything! So it is with us. We are gloves; the Holy Spirit is the hand which can do everything, but we must give Him room right into the outer corners of our lives. Then we can expect that He can do a lot in and through us. In John 14:17 it is written: "He is with you now and will be in your hearts!"

Corrie Ten Boom

OTHER THINGS THEY WANT MORE

John 1:29-31

There is another matter that must be settled: You must be sure that you need to be filled with the Spirit.

Why are you interested in this subject? You have received Jesus, you are converted and your sins have been forgiven. You have taken a course in New Testament somewhere. You know that you have eternal life and no man can pluck you out of God's hand. In the meantime, you are having a wonderful time going to heaven.

Are you sure that you can't get along all right the way you are? Do you feel that you just cannot go on resisting discouragement? Do you feel that you cannot obey the Scriptures and understand truth and bring forth fruit and live in victory without a greater measure of the Holy Spirit than you know now?

If you haven't reached that place, then I don't know that there is much I can do. I wish I could. I wish I could take off the top of your head and pour the holy oil of God down into you—but I can't. I can only do what John the Baptist did when he pointed to Jesus and said, "Behold the Lamb of God that taketh away the sin of the world." Then John faded out of the picture. After that, everyone was on his own. Each one had to go to the Lord Jesus Christ and receive help from Christ on his own.

No man can fill me and no man can fill you. We can pray for each other, but I can't fill you and you can't fill me. This desire to be filled must become all-absorbing in your life. If there is anything in your life more demanding than your longing after God, then you will never be a Spirit-filled Christian.

I have met Christians who have been wanting to be filled, in a vague sort of way, for many years. The reason they have not been filled with the Spirit is because they have other things they want more. God does not come rushing into a human heart unless He knows that He is the answer and fulfillment to the greatest, most overpowering desire of that life.

A.W. Tozer

THE ROD IN GOD'S HAND

Acts 2:1-4

Although this, the first meeting of the long campaign, was not especially well received by the congregation, it gave Mr. Moody an opportunity to announce his noonday prayer-meetings and Bible meetings, which were to follow. The noonday prayer-meetings were held in a small upper room (reached through a dark passageway), where the Y.M.C.A. held their meetings. Only six persons attended the first of these meetings. But these meetings were the beginning of days with us—the rising of the cloud of blessing, not larger than a man's hand, but which was soon to overshadow us with plenteous showers, and often with floods upon the dry ground.

It was at one of these noonday meetings that a young minister, pastor of the leading Baptist church of the city, his face lighted up with a light which I had not often witnessed before, rose and said: "Brethren, what Mr. Moody said the other day about the Holy Spirit for service is true. I have been preaching for years without any special blessing, simply beating the air, and have been toiling hard, but without the power of God upon me. For two days I have been away from the meetings, closeted with my Master. I think he has had the victory over my arrogance and pride, and I believe I have made a full surrender of all to him, and today I have come here to join you in worship, and to ask you to pray for me."

This confession and testimony was the rod in God's hand that smote the rock in the desert of doubt and unbelief at York. From that day the work took a new start, and soon there were hundreds of souls crowding the inquiry rooms. We were invited to hold services in this young pastor's chapel, and a large number were taken into his church. From that day on marvelous success has attended his preaching, and his name has become almost a household word in the Church at large. . . . This young preacher, the Rev. F.B. Meyer, B.A., will ever be held in grateful remembrance by tens of thousands in this and other lands.

Ira Sankey

CONSTANT RECOGNIZABLE PATTERNS

Galatians 5:22-24

The history of the Spirit's life in people is light and shadow, illumination and darkness. He is proof of the kingdom of God in our midst—the first installment of our redemption. But he too remains invisible. He is hidden from the world and sometimes from us. Wherever we look for the life of the Spirit, we will find this mixture of light and darkness. We never find the fruit of the Spirit without finding, at the same time some of the fruit of the spirit of this age.

How do I know? After all, some people speak about the Holy Spirit as though they have no sense of darkness. They tell us that they converse with God just as they talk with a friend, that in prayer they are regularly overwhelmed by a physical sense of God's presence. They speak of verbal promises God has made to them: "God spoke to me and told me that the house belonged to me."

I can't see inside people to know what really goes on between them and God. I can, however, look for secondary effects or signs of that relationship on their lives. There are consistent, recognizable patterns in the way the Holy Spirit works.

First of all, the Holy Spirit always works in conjunction with the truth—God's Word. The Reformation recognized this formally as the principle of "Spirit and Word." If people say, "We have the Spirit," but do not exhibit reverent and accurate proclamation of God's Word, they are wrong. If they say, "We preach the Word," but do not evidence such fruit of the Spirit as love and self-control, they are wrong . . . .

Second, the Holy Spirit always produces the fruit of the Spirit, such as love. Where love is lacking, the Spirit must surely be darkened.

And third, the Holy Spirit always produces power. This power is not aimless, for show, like a fireworks display. It is power to do work, to spread the name of Jesus. The Spirit moves, as he moved in Acts, toward the furthest, most remote people, and so will the Spirit's people. They will always be missionary-minded. His mighty power works miracles and breaks down barriers to spread God's kingdom.

Tim Stafford

AN EXPERIENCE AS WELL AS AN ATTITUDE

I Corinthians 6:19

According to the Book of Acts only those full of the Holy Spirit should be considered for top church leadership. This is an interesting qualification because it clearly implies that not all Christians are, in fact, full of the Holy Spirit. This, obviously, is not a statement dealing with the *presence* of the Holy Spirit in the believer, because He is present in all. Paul says, "Do you not know that your body is the temple of the Holy Spirit who is in you?" (I Cor. 6:19).

C. Peter Wagner

I.   The word most often used to describe God's Spirit is this word "Holy."

His word is to glorify Christ and sanctify the saints, making holy the Body of Christ which is His church.

II.   What is holiness?

1. Unfortunately it has accumulated many bad connotations.
2. The concept of holiness is not to be found in pagan literature. The Bible is unique at this point.
3. This quality in God demanded a like quality in His people and to His covenanted people He said, "Be ye holy for I am holy."
4. Holiness is an experience as well as an attitude, a life as well as a separation. Their separation unto God was to be manifested in their likeness to Him. The supreme revelation and standard are in Jesus Christ.

III.   Misapprehensions about holiness

1. The concept that holiness is optional. It is regarded as desirable for certain people in special circumstances but its claims are by no means universal. It is not an alternative way to heaven.

Some regard holiness as an emotional luxury, if not as a spiritual fad. Its claims are deemed to be emotional rather than ethical, operational rather than imperative.

2. Another mistake made by many earnest Christians about holiness is that it comes by gradual growth in grace and a steady progress of spiritual discipline. They are always growing toward it, but they never get into it, always struggling and striving to attain, but never entering into possession. The positive expectation is always seen to be afar off, and they die without having possessed. The hopeful future never becomes the positive now . . . but holiness does not come by growth: neither is it identified with growth. Growth is a process of life; holiness is the gift of abundant life. Growth is the result of health. Holiness is health.

Holiness implies a crisis, a new experience, a transformed life. It is not an achievement or an attainment, but a gift of grace in the Holy Ghost. It comes not by works, but of faith.

Holiness is not in forms and ordinances. It is a spirit, a life, a principle, a dynamic. The spirit of God indwells the spirit of man. He clothes himself with man.

He is no longer a model but a living Presence. Christian faith does not copy Him; it lives Him. Christ is not imitated but reproduced.

The Spirit of Holiness makes the heart clean, the mind true, the face fit, and the life fruitful, by making His holiness ours.

THE SPIRIT OF HOLINESS
Samuel Chadwick

ESSENTIALLY CHRISTOCENTRIC

John 16:5-7

The ministry of the Spirit is essentially Christocentric. His primary concern is to glorify Christ and to secure the acknowledgment and practical manifestation of His lordship in our lives. Although He cannot add anything to the glories of the exalted Christ, He can make Him real and glorify Him in the experience of His followers. It is one of His functions to reveal and explain Him.

"What light is to the earth, the Holy Spirit is to Christ," said Joseph Parker. One cannot see a person in a dark room. But let someone switch on the light and the person stands revealed. The Spirit delights to illumine the face of Jesus Christ as He is revealed in the Scriptures He has inspired. . . .

How does the Holy Spirit show us the things of Christ and make Him real to us? It is preeminently in the Scriptures that He reveals the things of Christ. To the Spirit-anointed eye of the diligent student of the Word, the Old Testament is seen to be full of Christ, every page revealing some new facet of His person and work. In the prophets, His greatness and achievements, as well as His sufferings and glory, were anticipated. Through meditating on the Word, a Spirit-taught believer can again experience the burning heart kindled in the hearts of the Emmaus disciples, when Jesus, "beginning with Moses and with all the prophets . . . explained to them the things concerning Himself in all the Scriptures" (Luke 24:27). Under the illumination of the inspiring Spirit, the words become spirit and life. . . .

The great business of the Holy Spirit is to stand behind the scenes and make Jesus real. Just as the telescope reveals not itself, but the stars beyond, so Christ is revealed by the Holy Spirit, as the medium of our spiritual vision. . . . Through the telephone of prayer, we may catch the very voice of our absent Master and be conscious of the heart-throbs of His love. . . .

The presence of the Comforter but makes Him nearer and dearer, and enables us to realize and know that we are in Him and He in us.

J. Oswald Sanders

A SENSE OF PERSONAL FAILURE

John 15:5

Scorn from cynical foreigners could be tolerated. Opposition from fellow missionaries was a greater test of resilience. But a sense of personal failure and sinfulness when he was sincerely trying to serve and please God he found to be supremely distressing. He wrote to his mother from Ninghai on March 13, 1869, "Oftentimes I am tempted to think that one so full of sin cannot be a child of God at all."

Readers unfamiliar with the pietistic movement of this period may be interested to follow the process of thought which had such far-reaching results. Not surprisingly, he had confessed to "irritability of temper" as his besetting sin, his "daily hourly failure." It was hard to suffer fools gladly. And long separations from Maria subjected him to added tension. During 1869 *The Revival* magazine in Britain carried a series of articles by R. Pearsall Smith, whose influential addresses at Oxford largely gave rise to the Keswick Movement which still draws thousands together annually in several countries around the world. As John McCarthy recalled, his expositions "had led many of us to think of a much higher (plane) of life and service than we had before thought possible." Copies of *The Revival*, reaching every CIM station, were creating a desire in many of the Mission to attain to this spiritual goal which was being called "holiness" or the "victorious life." In the CIM "the exchanged life" and "union with Christ" or just "union" came to sum up their thinking. . . . Many responded with the same longing as Hudson Taylor himself. Only Maria was unmoved, wondering "what we were all groping after . . . (an) experience she had long been living in the enjoyment of. . . . I have rarely met as Christlike a Christian as Mrs. Taylor." In Judd's words "(It) gave her that beautiful calmness and confidence in God (in which) up to that time she so surpassed her husband."

HUDSON TAYLOR AND
CHINA'S OPEN CENTURY
A.J. Broomhall

ALL COME THE SAME WAY

John 3:3

Francis Schaeffer said in a lecture, "True Christianity is a balanced whole. [It is] not only intellectual, it is not only our cultural responsibility. Christianity is being born again on the basis of the finished work of Christ, his substitutionary death in space-time history." As he put it in *True Spirituality*, the book that he later felt should have come first, the only way to be converted is by "accepting Christ as Savior. No matter how complicated, educated, or sophisticated we may be, or how simple, we must all come the same way . . . the most intellectual person must become a Christian in exactly the same way as the simplest person."

There is, he wrote, "no way to begin the Christian life except through the door of spiritual life." Further, Christian life is no mechanical, intellectual exercise. It is, as he had seen again in the hayloft, above all a personal relationship in obedience to God, a "moment by moment communion, personal communion, with God himself . . . letting Christ's truth flow through me through the agency of the Holy Spirit." The classical Christian teachers pointed to two essential differences between Christianity and other religions—the differences in their source and in their effect. Christianity's *source* is God making himself known personally and for all the time—to be sure, within a process of historical development, but not explainable primarily as a natural or predictable result of that historical development. Secondly, Christianity's *effect* is true salvation from sin, deliverance from guilt, despair, and death, based upon God's own coming in Christ. Christianity differs from the religions of the world in that its understanding of God comes, not from human striving, intellect, and will, but from God's own self-disclosure in human history, through the people of Israel, which culminates and clarifies itself finally only in Jesus Christ. After Jesus, religion can never be the same.

Christopher Catherwood

A CHRISTIAN PRINCE

Psalm 2:6

Erasmus wrote this advice in his work The Education of a Christian Prince which he dedicated in 1516 to the sixteen-year-old Charles of Burgundy, the future Emperor Charles V.

Whenever you think of yourself as a prince, remember you are a *Christian* prince! You should be as different from even the noble pagan princes as a Christian is from a pagan.

Do not think that the profession of a Christian is a matter to be lightly passed over, entailing no responsibilities unless, of course, you think the sacrament which you accepted along with everything else at baptism is nothing. . . . You share the Christian sacrament alike with all others—why not its teaching too? You have allied yourself with Christ—and yet will you slide back into the ways of Julius and Alexander the Great? You seek the same rewards as the others, yet you will have no concern with His mandates.

But on the other hand, do not think that Christ is found in ceremonies, in doctrines kept after a fashion, and in constitutions of the church. Who is truly a Christian? Not he who is baptized or anointed or who attends church. It is rather the man who has embraced Christ in the innermost feelings of his heart, and who emulates Him by his pious deeds. . . . You compel your subjects to know and obey your laws. With far more energy you should exact of yourself knowledge and obedience to the laws of Christ, your king! You judge it an infamous crime, for which there can be no punishment terrible enough, for one who has sworn allegiance to his king to revolt from him. On what grounds, then, do you grant yourself pardon and consider as a matter of sport and jest the countless times you have broken the laws of Christ, to whom you swore allegiance in your baptism, to whose cause you pledged yourself, by whose sacraments you are bound and pledged?

Erasmus

MANY A HAMMER

Matthew 16:18

Predictions about the decay and early dissolution of the Church are of course no new thing in history. But long ago they were answered in the memorable words of Theodore Beza to King Henry Navarre. "Sire," said Beza, "it belongs in truth to the Church of God, in the name of Whom I speak, to receive blows, and not to give them, but it will please Your Majesty to remember that the Church is an anvil which has worn out many a hammer."

St. Matthew's gospel, in Chapter 16, throbs with a similar conviction of the indestructible nature of the Church. At Caesarea Philippi on the way to the Cross, Jesus, with a passionate intensity which we feel when we read the words, said, "Simon . . . thou art Peter, and upon this rock I will build my church; and the gates of hell shall not prevail against it."

This is the Church's secret weapon. She may unerringly diagnose the modern malaise, master the problem of communication and assimilate contemporary philosophies, but unless, in the name of Christ, she can say to men enslaved by habit and broken by life, "Simon, thou art Peter," the message she proclaims is as useless as a high explosive shell without a fuse.

Arnold Toynbee, in his Gifford Lectures, pays generous tribute to the character of the early Christians. He writes: "The Christian Church won the heart of the masses because it did more for the masses than was done for them by any one of the higher rival religions, or by either the imperial or the municipal authorities, and the Christians were the only people in the Roman Empire, except the professional soldiers, who were prepared to lay down their lives for the sake of an ideal."

Murdo Macdonald

"YOU IMPS OF SATAN"

II Corinthians 2:14-17

Harriet Winslow was a pioneer in the American Sunday school movement—the movement that was very controversial in the early days. "Hearing of what was then new in America, the Sunday-school, she gathered a little Sunday-school in the galleries of her home church. The church authorities deemed this a desecration of the house and day, and they drove her and her charges out from the church. Then she gathered the little ones in a neighboring schoolhouse. But public sentiment would not tolerate this there, and again she and her charges were expelled. Nothing daunted, she taught the little ones on the church steps in the open air, until public sentiment was changed and the gallery was again opened to her."

In her efforts she was, as the apostle Paul affirms, "to the one . . . the smell of death; to the other, the fragrance of life." In one instance, when an "old pastor, in his knee breeches and cocked hat, passed the schoolhouse where this young and devoted teacher had her Sunday-school class for a season, he shook his ivory-headed cane towards the building, and said in honest indignation, `You imps of Satan doing the Devil's work!'"

She was the first one in her family to make a profession of faith in Christ. "But her father and mother followed her into the church, and so did every other member of the . . . family. When she became a foreign missionary three of her sisters followed her in that step. One of her brothers died just before he entered the ministry. Another brother . . . went West as a home missionary. A daughter of hers labored as a missionary's wife in India." She indeed was "the fragrance of life."

Ruth Tucker

LOSING THE VISION

Matthew 13:22

A first generation gathers by conviction around highly motivating issues and devotes its resources to a narrowly defined set of goals. In the second generation, resources and attention are diverted to the education and nurture of children in the ways of the movement. This generation fails, however, to grasp the original vision with the same intensity and finds subtle ways to twist the movement's institutions to its own concerns. This process continues through several generations until in many cases the very opposite of what was originally intended is finally produced. This dynamic may be seen in the successive history of the movements. . . .

Discipline and a reordered life-style enable converts to rise in social class and economic level, a process culminating in a middle-class church like those against which the movement originally protested. This new church is subtly transformed into a bastion against those who would threaten its life, especially the lower classes that were once a source of vitality.

Sensitive leaders of such movements, often intuitively aware of this dynamic, have warned against the "dangers of riches" that undercut the original force of revival movements. John Wesley often commented on this problem. "Christianity, true scriptural Christianity, has a tendency, in the process of time, to undermine and destroy itself. For wherever true Christianity spreads, it must cause diligence and frugality, which, in the natural course of things, must beget riches! And riches naturally beget pride, love of the world, and every temper that is destructive of Christianity. . . . Wherever it generally prevails, it saps its own foundation."

Donald Dayton

A CONVENTIONAL PARISH

Luke 4:18

A. B. Simpson, who came to New York's 13th Street Presbyterian Church in 1879, struggled for two years to turn this church outside itself to the poor of New York City and described the increasing polarization in these words: "What they wanted was a conventional parish for respectable Christians. What this young pastor wanted was a multitude of publicans and sinners."

Finally Simpson resigned, announcing his decision in an address based on the text "the Spirit of the Lord is upon me because he hath anointed me to preach the gospel to the poor." He then began a series of moves around the city that climaxed in founding the "Gospel Tabernacle" for immigrants located in the Times Square area. Out of Simpson's work grew the Christian and Missionary Alliance, a movement that originally understood itself to have a special call to serve the "neglected classes both at home and abroad."

The Church of the Nazarene was an inter-denominational movement which brought together a number of people who shared the belief that it was the Christian's responsibility to minister to the poor. After years of service in some of the most beautiful churches and well-paid pulpits of California Methodism, Phineas F. Bresee felt called in the 1890s into ministry to the poor of inner-city Los Angeles. Bresee originally hoped to maintain his ministerial relationship in the Methodist conference while engaging in this work, but the bishop and his cabinet refused this request, forcing him to sever his lifelong relationship to found in 1895 the Church of the Nazarene.

The original "Articles of Faith and General Rules" described the "field of labor" of the new church as "the neglected quarters of the cities." The name Church of the Nazarene was chosen to symbolize "toiling, lowly mission of Christ" by taking a "name which was used in derision of Him by His enemies."

Donald Dayton

THE SICKENING UNDERSIDE

II Corinthians 6:10

The Salvation Army originated in England as the Christian Mission founded in the 1860s by William and Catherine Booth. This mission was a protest against "respectable churches" whose life cut them off from the masses. . . .

The Salvation Army came to America about 1880 and by the end of the century had thousands of officers engaged in relief and evangelism throughout the cities of the world. A living critique of the bourgeois churches and a disturber of the peace by revealing the sickening underside of a supposedly respectable society, the army generated intense opposition from both mobs and church people. In one twelve-month period about 1880, 669 Salvationists were reported "knocked down, kicked, or brutally assaulted," 56 army buildings were stormed, and 86 Salvationists imprisoned.

Though primarily concerned with salvation and preaching the gospel to the poor, the Salvation Army, like other slum workers soon found itself providing other services. Most immediate were the needs for food, clothing and shelter. A "poor man's bank" was established. Day-care centers were provided to permit mothers to get out to earn a living for their families. The army discovered that the legal system was biased toward those who could afford to hire counsel, and it therefore provided free legal aid. Special attention was given to work among prisoners. The Army sought to become the custodian of first offenders to prevent their being sent to prisons that would turn them into hardened criminals. (Other work among prisoners yielded some unexpected dividends; one army post in 1896 reported that 47 of its 48 members had prison records!)

Prostitution was a particular concern of the army. The Booths startled many with sympathy for the prostitute, arguing that social conditions more than inherent evil forced young women into the "world's oldest profession."

Donald Dayton

A TREMENDOUS ORGANIZATION

Ephesians 4:14-15

During World War II a story was going around about a German soldier who was wounded at the front. He was ordered to go to the military hospital for treatment. When he arrived at the large and imposing building, he saw two main doors, one marked "For those slightly wounded" and the other, "For those seriously wounded." He entered through the first door and found himself going down a long hall at the end of which were two more doors, one marked "For officers" and the other, "For non-officers." He entered through the latter and found himself going down another long hall at the end of which were two more doors, one marked "For Party members" and the other, "For non-Party members." He took the second door, but when he opened it, he found himself out on the street.

When the soldier returned home, his mother asked him, "Son, how did you get along at the hospital?"

"Well, Mother," he replied, "to tell the truth, the people there didn't do anything for me, but you just ought to see the tremendous organization they have!"

Is this a picture of the American church today? A lot of organization—many wheels turning, much busyness. But are we really doing business for the Lord? Are we bringing spiritual health and strength to those who are sick at heart and wounded in spirit?

J.T. Seamands

Many times as a layman and as a businessman I have wanted to shout out in vestry meetings, "Men, we are not doing anything which is relevant to anyone's real needs—even our own. We are just keeping the church machine going because . . . well, because we don't know anything else to do! For God's sake, let's take a new look at what we are doing!"

Keith Miller

THIS VAST UNIMAGINABLE WORK

I Corinthians 6:2-3

Here and now I share God's work in only a handful of lives. As part of his church, I participate in the faltering spread of goods news, the reconciliation of the world. Sometimes supernatural power may be evident in what I do; more often not. Even my secular tasks may be included in his work; I do my daily work with all the love I can muster, even when I cannot see its purpose in the eternal scheme. At the very least I am maintaining the world, keeping it running, until my Master comes. My children are not the only ones who need food and water and clothing while they go through the transformation. But all that I do in God's work and all that I see of his work comes to very little. In the end, even Mother Teresa and Billy Graham transform only corners of the world. I may pray with power, proclaim the gospel with power, do powerfully merciful acts, work powerfully for justice, but my corner is small. Still, it is not at all insignificant. Like an employee at IBM, my individual contribution is swallowed up in a vast movement. My own meaning and my intimacy with God come from my participation in something much bigger than myself: a corporate achievement that I love. I love it because it belongs to God.

God's broader strokes, his great universal movements that are preparing the day when all the universe will be overturned, when earthly powers will vanish and one vast audience will be judged and separated, when a chorus of praise will erupt from the throat of the redeemed—this work I hear of, but I hardly feel I work on it personally. I feel too small for that. Yet Scripture more than hints that even on that day God intends to make me a co-worker. In all Jesus' parables, when the king comes home he appoints his faithful servants to rule the land with him. Paul wrote, "Do you not know that we will judge angels? How much more the things of this life!" Perhaps I will then "see him as he is" partly as I participate in this vast and unimaginable work.

Tim Stafford

THEY ARE GOD'S PEOPLE

Colossians 4:12

Epaphras was . . . ready to notice and to praise the virtues of his people. He wasn't obsessed only with their faults. They had them! . . . The little church at Colossae . . . was like most other churches; it had its imperfections. Nobody was more aware of his people's faults than Epaphras . . . I can imagine him going over them in his mind at the hour of his private devotions. There's Claudius, who prides himself on his modern ideas and is drawn to this gnostic heresy. . . . There's Fulvius, who is so hard to get into . . . regular work for the Master. There's Flavia, who is in danger of thinking more of her beautiful home than of her soul . . . and Mundanus, whose spiritual life is rather shallow; who never seems to get above the spirit of the counting-house. . . . But when he made the journey from Colossae to Paul in Rome, he didn't greet the Apostle with the list of his people's imperfections. He said, `Paul, let me tell you of their love in the Spirit. There's Claudius—he has a big heart. I have only to tell him of somebody's need and he is asking me "What can I do to help?" And there's Fulvius, so free from criticism . . . so willing to believe the best. And there's Flavia; she is given to hospitality. . . . And there's Mundanus, who is so conscientious in the business affairs of the church, so . . . attentive to detail and wise in administration. They have their faults of course, and I do not minimize them, but they are God's people with all their faults and His grace will sanctify them yet.'

And Paul listened gladly, and when he settled down to write to the Colossians he spoke of their dear fellow-servant Epaphras, `your faithful minister of Christ, who declared unto us your love in the Spirit.'

W.E. Sangster

ROTARIAN CHUMMINESS

II Timothy 1:12

The Church can never hope to win the war of conflicting ideologies until she possesses a creed not less positive but infinitely more dynamic. The tide of history will not be turned by idealists who pride themselves on how little they believe, nor will the cynical masses be convinced by those who have shorn Christ of His cosmic stature and reduced the religion of the Cross to the level of a well-meaning Rotarian "chumminess". For society as well as for the individual a creed, far from being a decorative fringe, is a central basic necessity.

Another fallacy is the one which would divorce creed from conduct. Theology, according to this attitude, is useless and irrelevant. Belief is something secondary and unimportant. Morality is not a by-product of religion; it is absolutely autonomous and its sanctions have nothing whatever to do with the mystical experience of the saints or the traditional dogmas of the Church. Behavior is what really matters.

Two eminent Victorians are cited to support this theory—John Morley and Thomas Huxley. Both were professedly agnostic, yet no one could point a finger at their morals. Not only were they good in the conventional sense of that term, they also loved their fellowmen and were prepared to do battle for all good causes. Disciplined in conduct and dedicated to truth, these men are held up as having sabotaged the claim that there is any necessary connection between creed and conduct.

But there is one awkward question. Is this kind of morality self-creating and self-sustaining? Will it continue to operate indefinitely under its own momentum?

Murdo Macdonald

A BARBARIAN IN EACH OF US

Matthew 15:16-20

One could say that a barbarian is in each of us. To some extent the barbarian can be temporarily tamed in the best situations. And one needs only look at the deteriorating moral situation in many parts of the Western world to understand that the barbarian in us is very much alive. That man loves darkness rather than light.

Many of the temptations to sin first come from this source within. Paul had several lists of these, which included "sexual immorality, impurity and debauchery, idolatry and witchcraft; hatred, discord, jealousy, fits of rage, selfish ambition, dissensions, factions and envy; drunkenness" (this one from Gal. 5:19-20). Jesus, of course, noted that the motives and designs for man's worst behavior come from within the heart and often find a receptive climate in the public world.

We are on safe ground when we listen to this carefully, when we conclude that each of us is capable of the worst sort of behavior that will eventually break a personal world to pieces. No environment is more vicious, none more dangerous, than the dark side of the human heart and its capacity to promote evil.

Alexander Whyte quotes John Bunyan:

Sin and corruption would bubble up out of my heart as naturally as water bubbles up out of a fountain. I thought now that everyone had a better heart than I had. I could have changed hearts with anybody. I thought none but the devil himself could equalize me for inward wickedness and pollution of mind. I fell, therefore, at the sight of my own vileness, deeply into despair, for I concluded that this condition in which I was in could not stand with a life of grace. Sure, thought I, I am forsaken of God; sure I am given up to the devil, and to a reprobate mind.

Gordon MacDonald

"OTHERS ARE AS BAD AS WE"

Romans 1:24-25

Before the Great War it had been Paris which had seethed with sinful romance, illicit intrigue. . . . No more; it now was Berlin. "Along the Kurfürstendamm," wrote Stefan Zweig, "powdered and rouged young men sauntered, and in the dimly lit bars one might see men of the world of finance courting drunken sailors;" while at transvestite balls, "hundreds of men costumed as women and hundreds of women as men danced under the benevolent eye of the police."

The role model for thousands of German girls in the Weimar years was Anita Berber, who danced naked, mainlined cocaine and morphine, and made love to men and women sprawled atop bars, bathed in spotlights, while voyeurs stared and fondled one another. Anita was dead at twenty-nine. So, by then, was the Weimar Republic.

William Manchester

Thielicke went on to remind his congregation that the German people had "had some conception of our guilt after the collapse at the end of the last war and many of us had uttered the prayer of the publican, 'God be merciful to me a sinner! Remove not thy grace from our sunken people.' But then came one of the most dreadful moments in the spiritual history of our nation when suddenly we began to say, 'Others are just as bad as we.' Then suddenly our aloneness with God vanished, then repentance and spiritual renewal were gone, then began the fateful measuring of ourselves by looking downward and comparing ourselves with the hypocritical democratic Pharisees among the victors." *(The Waiting Father)*

Gordon MacDonald

"NOTHING BUT EMPTIES"

Ephesians 5:15-17

We look forward at ways of life that are not-the-way. Jude (Moffatt) reads, "They look after none but themselves—rainless clouds." Are those who look after none but themselves "rainless clouds"? Do they inevitably become noncontributive, useless to themselves and others? Down in Texas where they want rain badly someone pointed to a cloud in the sky in hope of rain, but an old Texan shook his head and said, "Nothing but empties." Are people who live for themselves "nothing but empties"?

Again, the same verse describes the self-centered as "trees in autumn without fruit." They come down to the autumn of their lives, the period of ripe fruitfulness when life should be laden with peace and calm and memories of life well spent, and instead what do they show themselves to be? Autumn trees without fruit. The saddest thing in life is to see a person come to the autumn time with nothing to show except a decadent self.

A verse says, "These people are murmurers, grumbling at their lot in life." The self-centered are always complaining of their lot in life. They haven't the key to life, so they try to find the cause of their failure in other persons or in circumstances around them. They blame others for everything, but do not realize that their self-centered attitudes are the cause of their grumpiness and dissatisfaction. Of all the unhappy people on earth the most unhappy are those who have nothing to do but sit on hotel porches and think about themselves, their aches and pains and troubles—most of them produced out of their own self-centered attitudes.

A passage says that "an unclean spirit . . . roams through dry places" (Matt. 12:43, Moffatt). Is it a fact that when you are "unclean" with self-centeredness and other wrong ways of life, life "roams through dry places"? Does life turn insipid, dull, stupid? And do you have to do as one person said of himself, "I have to invent more and more ways to make life tolerable"? The inane stupidity and dullness of evil makes its devotees invent more and more extremes to get the same result. It is under "the law of decreasing returns."

E. Stanley Jones

DISTINCTIONS IN OUR OWN FAVOR

Proverbs 23:7

For this reason, the scholars of the Church, who gain, by profession, great opportunities of knowing human nature, have generally determined that what it is a crime to do it is a crime to think. Since by revolving with pleasure the facility, safety, or advantage of a wicked deed, a man soon begins to find his constancy relax and his detestation soften; the happiness of success, glittering before him, withdraws his attention from the atrociousness of the guilt, and acts are at last confidently perpetrated, of which the first conception only crept into the mind, disguised in pleasing complications, and permitted rather than invited.

No man has ever been drawn to crimes by love or jealousy, envy or hatred, but he can tell how easily he might at first have repelled the temptation; how readily his mind would have obeyed a call to any other object, and how weak his passion has been after some casual avocation, till he has recalled it again to his heart, and revived the viper by too warm a fondness.

Such therefore, is the importance of keeping reason a constant guard over imagination, that we have otherwise no security for our virtue, but may corrupt our hearts in the most recluse solitude, with more pernicious and tyrannical appetites and wishes than the commerce of the world will generally produce: for we are easily shocked by crimes which appear at once in their full magnitude; but the gradual growth of our own wickedness, endeared by interest and palliated by all the artifices of self-deceit, gives us time to form distinctions in our own favor; and reason by degrees submits to absurdity, as the eye is in time accommodated to darkness.

Samuel Johnson

THE ULTIMATE DEGRADATION

Jude 4

Des Pres refers to the Nazi attempt to create the ultimate "Skinner box" of behaviorism, where environment was engineered to reduce inmates to mindless creatures whose behavior could be predicted and controlled. The camps used pain and death as "negative reinforcers" and food and life as "positive reinforcers," applying them consistently and horribly. Yet, the experiment did not succeed. Some prisoners gave in, some withdrew, but many resisted and found their own ways of coping.

Some survivors of such camps emerged, not with the warped, distorted view of cruelty and inhumanity you might expect, but with a resurrected concept of virtue and hope. One such man is George Mangakis, who wrote:

I have experienced the fate of a victim. I have seen the torturer's face at close quarters. It was in a worse condition than my own bleeding, livid face. The torturer's face was distorted by a kind of twitching that had nothing human about it. . . .

In this situation, I turned out to be the lucky one. I was humiliated. I did not humiliate others. I was simply bearing a profoundly unhappy humanity in my aching entrails. Whereas the men who humiliate you must first humiliate the notion of humility within themselves. Never mind if they strut around in their uniforms, swollen with the knowledge that they can control the suffering, sleeplessness, hunger and despair of their fellow human beings, intoxicated with the power in their hands. Their intoxication is nothing other than the degradation of humanity. The ultimate degradation. They have had to pay very dearly for my torments.

Philip Yancey

ALL IN THE WILL

John 7:17

I saw at this time, or rather experienced the ground on which God rejects sinners from his bosom. All the cause of God's rejection is in the will of the sinner. If that will submits, how horrible soever he be, God purifies him in his love and receives him into his grace; but while that will rebels, the rejection continues; though for want of ability seconding his inclination, he should not commit the sin he is inclined to, yet he never can be admitted into grace till the cause ceases, which is this wrong will, rebellious to the divine law. If that once submits, God then totally removes the effects of sin, which stain the soul, by washing away the defilements which he has contracted. If that sinner dies in the time that his will is rebellious and turned towards sin, as death fixes forever the disposition of the soul, and the cause of its impurity is ever subsisting, such soul can never be received into God; its rejection must be eternal, as there is such an absolute opposition between essential purity and essential impurity. And as this soul, from its own nature necessarily tends to its own center, it is continually rejected of the Lord, by reason of its impurity, subsisting not only in the effects, but in their cause. It is the same way in this life. This cause, so long as it subsists, absolutely hinders the grace of God from operating in the soul. But if the sinner comes to die truly penitent, then the cause, which is the wrong will, being taken away, there remains only the effect or impurity caused by it. He is then in a condition to be purified. God of his infinite mercy has provided a laver of love and of justice, a painful laver indeed, to purify this soul. And as the defilement is greater or less, so is the pain; but when the cause is utterly taken away, the pain entirely ceases. Now, I say, it is the very same here. Souls are received into grace, as soon as the cause of sin ceases; but they do not pass into the Lord himself, till all its effects are washed away. If they have not courage to let him, in his own way and will, thoroughly cleanse and purify them, they never enter into the pure divinity in this life.

Madame Guyon

"SECRETLY THEY ALL LOVE IT"

John 3:19

When we are ill we call for a trained physician, whose degree is a guarantee of specific preparation and technical competence—we do not ask for the handsomest physician, or the most eloquent one; well then, when the whole state is ill should we not look for the service and guidance of the wisest and the best? To devise a method of barring incompetence and knavery from public office, and of selecting and preparing the best to rule for the common good—that is the problem of political philosophy.

But behind these political problems lies the nature of man; to understand politics, we must, unfortunately, understand psychology. "Like man, like state" (wrote Plato); "governments vary as the characters of men vary; . . . states are made out of human natures which are in them." The state is what it is because its citizens are what they are. Therefore we need not expect to have better states until we have better men; till then all changes will leave every essential thing unchanged. "How charming people are!—always doctoring, increasing and complicating their disorders, fancying they will be cured by some nostrum which somebody advises them to try, never getting better, but always growing worse. . . . Are they not as good as a play, trying their hand at legislation, and imagining that by reforms they will make an end to the dishonesties and rascalities of mankind—not knowing that in reality they are cutting away at the heads of a hydra?"

Will Durant

Men love crime, they love it always, not at some `moments.' You know, it's as though people have made an agreement to lie about it and have lied about it ever since. They all declare that they hate evil, but secretly they all love it.

F. Dostoyevsky

A PIT THAT IS UNFATHOMABLE

Jeremiah 17:9

I trust that your own studies get on well, dear friend. Learn much of your own heart; and when you have learned all you can, remember you have seen but a few yards into a pit that is unfathomable. "The heart is deceitful above all things, and desperately wicked: who can know it?" Learn much of the Lord Jesus. For every look at yourself, take ten looks at Christ. He is altogether lovely. Such infinite majesty, and yet such meekness and grace, and all for sinners, even the chief! Live much in the smiles of God. Bask in His beams. Feel His all-seeing eye settled on you in love, and repose in His mighty arms. . . .

Do you think you have been *convicted of sin?* This is the Holy Spirit's work, and His first work upon the soul (John 16:8; Acts 2:37). If you did not know your body was dangerously ill, you would never have sent for your physician; and so you will never go to Christ, the heavenly Physician, unless you feel that your soul is sick even unto death. Oh! pray for deep discoveries of your real state by nature and practice. The world will say you are an innocent and harmless girl; do not believe them. The world is a liar. Pray to see yourself exactly as God sees you; pray to know the worth of your soul. Have you seen yourself *vile*, as Job saw himself (Job 42:5-6)? undone, as Isaiah saw himself (Isa. 6:1-5)? Have you experienced anything like Psalm 51? I do not wish you to feign humility before God, nor to use expressions of self-abhorrence which you do not feel; but pray that the Holy Spirit may let you see the very reality of your natural condition before God!

I seldom get more than a glance at the true state of my soul in its naked self. But when I do, then I see that I am wretched, and miserable, and poor, and blind, and naked (Rev. 3:17). I believe every member of our body has been a servant of sin (Rom. 3:13-18)— throat, tongue, lips, mouth, feet, eyes. Every faculty of our mind is polluted (Gen. 6:5). Besides, you have long neglected the great salvation; you have been gain-saying and disobedient. Oh, that you were brought to pass sentence on yourself, *guilty of all!*

Andrew A. Bonar

IN CLEAN CARPETED OFFICES

Ephesians 6:12

Now, Tom Brokaw is not sitting in his New York office either growling—I'll concede that—or plotting the overthrow of Western civilization and expulsion of Christians from the United States. He is an educated, professional newscaster, urbane and fairly dispassionate in his reporting. But the demeanor is precisely the point.

As C.S. Lewis wrote, "The greatest evil is not done in those sordid 'dens of crime' that Dickens loved to paint . . . it is conceived and . . . moved, seconded, carried, and minuted . . . in clean, carpeted, warmed, and well-lighted offices, by quiet men with white collars and cut fingernails and smooth-shaven cheeks who do not need to raise their voices."

Today's barbarians are ladies and gentlemen. Yet behind their pleasant, civilized veneer lurks an unpleasant intolerance that threatens the very processes of pluralism and freedom they claim to defend.

Charles Colson

Who am I, and what manner of man? What evil have not either my deeds been, or if not my deeds, yet my words; or if not my words, yet my will? But thou, O Lord, art good and merciful, and thy right hand had respect unto the profoundness of my death, and drew forth from the bottom of my heart that bottomless gulf of corruption: what was to nil all that thou willedst, and to will all that thou nilledst.

CONFESSIONS
St. Augustine

UTTER HOPELESSNESS

Hebrews 2:14-15

The boast of heraldry, the pomp of power,
And all that beauty, all that wealth e'er gave
Awaits alike the inevitable hour;
The paths of glory lead but to the grave.

"Were all their lifetime subject to bondage!" And the world today is as terrified of death as it has ever been. Much for the excitement concerning the hydrogen bomb has this as its cause. Men of the world have no hope beyond this world, and beyond death and the grave, so they are protesting; and that is the reason for it. They know nothing about the life in the Glory; this life is everything to them, so the most horrible thing conceivable is death. They are confessing that unconsciously. That is quite apart from one's own personal views about the use of hydrogen bombs, which on any showing is sheer madness. But it is interesting to note the type of person who gets most excited about it. Unwittingly these offspring of Adam are just acknowledging that death is reigning over them, and they are horrified and terrified. Again, the modern cult of trying to keep young and to look young instead of ageing gracefully is all part of the same thing. . . . Let me quote another bit of poetry, this time, Walter Savage Landor:

I strove with none, for none was worth my strife;
Nature I loved, and next to Nature, Art.
I warmed both hands before the fire of life'
It sinks; and I am ready to depart.

Let me quote also the words of the President of an Oxford college from his autobiography written during the last war. He said, `But for me the war brought to an end the long summer of my life. Henceforth I have nothing to look forward to except chill autumn, and still chillier winter. Yet I must somehow try not to lose hope!' I know of nothing more hopeless than that.

D. Martyn Lloyd-Jones

"WHAT'S WRONG WITH ME?"

II Corinthians 5:17

How Does Christ Save?

He begins by convincing the people who think they don't need to be saved that they do. Millions of men deny their need of a Savior. `What's wrong with me?' they say. `I don't do anybody any harm. I am always doing good turns.' So they say, and so they sincerely believe.

When these men meet Christ—that is, when they get a clear picture of Him as given in the Bible, and feel themselves in His presence—they know themselves unclean. Nobody need tell them so. They know it themselves, and they know at once that they need saving.

Nobody has the power to do this like Christ. Men are seldom convinced by argument that they are sinners. Most arguments on this point are a waste of breath. Just get them to see what Christ is like and introduce them to Him. They feel dirty at once. And because nobody wants to be saved until he knows he is lost, that is the first thing which must happen.

Then Christ goes to work. To a man who knows he is unclean and wants help, Christ says, `I can change your nature, if you will let me. If a man will take Christ into his life, his soiled past can be forgiven, and he will be given sound judgment and moral power in every day as it comes. He will cease to be the man he was and become another—the same personality but transformed. He is changed as a son, brother, husband, father, friend, workman, citizen . . .; all relationships are affected by that change.

Consequently, his personal change affects society, too. His home is different, his club, workshop . . . even his town and country to some extent, and (as the number of those changed multiply) this influence begins to affect the world.

Christ's power to save is unlimited. He hacks down the barrier of class, race, and color, and He leads also on the war against war. If people who call themselves Christians really followed him, His power would be more obvious that it is.

W.E. Sangster

"THEIR MISERY SPEAKS LOUDER"

Acts 8:23

The spirit that is within Christians will not suffer them to live wickedly, nor to sin as the ungodly do. But with the unconverted it is far otherwise. They are in the gall of bitterness, and in the bond of iniquity, and have yet no part nor fellowship in the pardon of their sins, or the hope of glory. We have, therefore, a work of greater necessity to do for them, even 'to open their eyes, and to turn them from darkness to light, and from the power of Satan to God; that they may receive forgiveness of sins, and an inheritance among them that are sanctified.' He that seeth one man sick of a mortal disease, and another pained only with the toothache, will be moved more to compassionate the former, than the latter; and will surely make more haste to help him, though he were a stranger, and the other a brother or a son. It is so sad to see men in a state of damnation, wherein, if they should die, they are lost forever, that methinks we should not be able to let them alone, either in public or in private, whatever other work we may have to do. I confess, I am frequently forced to neglect that which should further increase of knowledge in the godly, because of the lamentable necessity of the unconverted. Who is able to talk of controversies, or of nice unnecessary points, or even truths of a lower degree of necessity, how excellent soever, while he seeth a company of ignorant, carnal, miserable sinners before his eyes, who must be changed or damned?

Richard Baxter

No man can see his sin by looking at it; he can only see it by looking away from it. Only by the vision of purity can I learn my impurity. I never find that I am in rags until my Father brings forth the best robe. I never know that I am in discord until my Father's house reveals its music. I never realize that I am hungry until my Father says, "Let us eat and drink and be merry!" I never am conscious that I am a prodigal until the voice of my Father cries, "This my son was dead and is alive again, was lost and is found!"

George Matheson

FULL OF CONTRADICTIONS

Genesis 3:17-19

Could a God of Love have Made a World like this?

The world in which we live is full of contradictions. We have mentioned already many of the lovely things it contains, but there are many others which are far from lovely.

Think of the wickedness in men which has expressed itself in wars, persecutions, slavery, torturings, concentration camps, and gas chambers. Civilization often seems only a thin veneer covering something worse in men than the nature of a wild beast.

Yet although these are the causes of our greatest pain and horror, they are not the cause of the greatest perplexity, because they are all traceable to the evil in man. There are other evils which seem built into the very structure of creation, and almost to leap out of the hand of God. Think of the diphtheria germ and other germs of vile disease, which all seem to be a part of creation. Think of earthquakes, epidemics, famines and floods. . . .

Nor is there any easy answer to any of these questions. Nowhere is the Christian more frankly agnostic than when he faces these problems. Light falls on some of them. To others he must frankly say, 'I do not know.'

But the people with alternative explanations are in a worse plight. Those who say that there is no purpose in the world and it all 'just happened' strain our credulity to the breaking point. Could this amazing and intricate world have just happened? They admit 'purpose' in all the parts of nature—in bees and beasts and men, for instance—and none in the whole! The people who say that a devil made the universe have a harder task to explain the good in the world than we have to explain the evil. What a devil, to have made the lovely things which we enjoy!

If for other impressive reasons we believe that there is a good God behind the universe, let us approach the problem honestly and humbly, and see how a God of love could have made a world like this.

W.E. Sangster

TWO POINTS OF VIEW

Galatians 3:13

Scripture teaches us that there are two points of view from which we may regard Christ's death upon the cross.

The one is *the redemption of the cross:* Christ dying for us as our complete deliverance from the curse of sin. The other, *the fellowship of the cross:* Christ taking us up to die with Him, and making us partakers of the fellowship of His death in our own experience.

In our text we have three great unsearchable thoughts. The law of God has pronounced a curse on all sin and on all that is sinful. Christ took our curse upon Him, yea, became a curse, and so destroyed its power, and in that cross we now have the everlasting redemption from sin and all its power. The cross reveals to us man's sin, as under the curse, Christ becoming a curse and so overcoming it, and our full and everlasting deliverance from the curse.

In these thoughts the lost and most hopeless sinner finds a sure ground of confidence and of hope. God had indeed in Paradise pronounced a curse upon this earth and all that belongs to it. On Mount Ebal, in connection with giving the law, half of the people of Israel were twelve times over to pronounce a curse on all sin. And there was to be in their midst a continual reminder of it. "Cursed is every one that hangeth on a tree" (Deut. 21:23, 27:15-20). And yet who could ever have thought that the Son of God Himself would die upon the accursed tree, and become a curse for us? But such is in very deed the Gospel of God's love, and the penitent sinner can now rejoice in the confident assurance that the curse is forever put away from all who believe in Jesus Christ.

The preaching of the redemption of the cross is the foundation and center of the salvation the Gospel brings us. To those who believe its full truth it is a cause of unceasing thanksgiving. It gives us boldness to rejoice in God. There is nothing which will keep the heart more tender towards God, enabling us to live in His love and to make Him known to those who have never yet found Him. God be praised for the redemption of the cross!

Andrew Murray

"HE DIDN'T SEEM TO SAY MUCH"

John 14:9

About twenty years ago Toyohiko Kagawa spoke in the chapel at Princeton University. After the address a student was walking from the chapel with an older friend. Both were quiet for a short time; then the student remarked: "I had heard so much about Kagawa. After hearing him today, I am a bit disappointed. He didn't seem to say much." A moment later the student continued: "I noticed as he read the New Testament, that he held the pages close to his eyes." The older friend then asked: "Do you know why he held the page near his eye? Some years ago, when Kagawa was living in the slums of Kobe, a beggar from the street asked Kagawa to give him shelter for the night. Kagawa let him stay that night in his shack, and caught a disease of the eyes, trachoma, from the vagrant; this disease almost blinded him. That is why he holds the printed word so close to his eyes." After a few quiet moments, the student replied: "Well, I guess a man doesn't need to say a great deal when he's hanging on a cross."

Thomas S. Kepler

To ten men who talk about the character of Jesus there is only one who will talk about His Cross. "I like the story of Jesus Christ's life, I like the things He said. The Sermon on the Mount is beautiful, and I like to read of the things Jesus did; but immediately you begin to talk about the Cross, about forgiveness of sins, about being born from above, it is out of it." . . . When we come to the *Cross* of Jesus Christ, that is outside our domain. If Jesus Christ was only a martyr, the New Testament teaching is stupid.

Oswald Chambers

THE POSSIBILITY OF AFFLICTION

Galatians 2:20

So long as we are not submerged in affliction all we can do is to desire that, if it should come, it may be a participation in the Cross of Christ.

But what is in fact always present, and what it is therefore always permitted to love, is the possibility of affliction. All the three sides of our being are always exposed to it. Our flesh is fragile; it can be pierced or torn or crushed, or one of its internal mechanisms can be permanently deranged, by any piece of matter in motion. Our soul is vulnerable, being subject to fits of depression without cause and pitifully dependent upon all sorts of objects, inanimate and animate, which are themselves fragile and capricious. Our social personality, upon which our sense of existence almost depends, is always and entirely exposed to every hazard. These three parts of us are linked with the very center of our being in such a way that it bleeds for any wound of the slightest consequence which they suffer. Above all, anything which diminishes or destroys our social prestige, our right to consideration, seems to impair or abolish our very essence—so much is our whole substance an affair of illusion.

When everything is going more or less well, we do not think about this almost infinite fragility. But nothing compels us not to think about it. We can contemplate it all the time and thank God for it unceasingly. We can be thankful not only for the fragility itself but also for that more intimate weakness which connects it with the very center of our being. For it is this weakness which makes possible, in certain conditions, the operation by which we are nailed to the very center of the Cross.

Simone Weil

THE VERY SUBSTANCE OF OUR LIFE

Mark 8:34

The Cross of Christ should become the very substance of our life. No doubt this is what Christ meant when he advised his friends to bear their cross each day, and not, as people seem to think nowadays, simply that one should be resigned about one's little daily troubles—which, by an almost sacrilegious abuse of language, people sometimes refer to as crosses. There is only one cross; it is the whole of that necessity by which the infinity of space and time is filled and which, in given circumstances, can be concentrated upon the atom that any one of us is, and totally pulverize it. To bear one's cross is to bear the knowledge that one is entirely subject to this blind necessity in every part of one's being, except for one point in the soul which is so secret that it is inaccessible to consciousness. However cruelly a man suffers, if there is some part of his being still intact and if he is not fully conscious that it has escaped only by chance and remains every moment at the mercy of chance, he has no part in the Cross. This is above all the case when the part of the soul which remains intact, or even relatively intact, is the social part; which is the reason why sickness profits nothing unless there is added to it the spirit of poverty in its perfection. It is possible for a perfectly happy man—if he recognizes, truly, concretely, and all the time, the possibility of affliction—to enjoy happiness completely and at the same time bear his cross.

But it is not enough to be aware of this possibility; one must love it. One must tenderly love the harshness of that necessity which is like a coin with two faces, the one turned towards us being domination, and the one turned towards God, obedience. We must embrace it closely even if it offers its roughest surface and the roughness cuts into us.

Simone Weil

If Jesus Christ were only a martyr, His cross would be of no significance; but if the cross of Jesus Christ is the expression of the secret heart of God, the lever by which God lifts back the human race to what it was designed to be, then there is a new attitude to things.

Oswald Chambers

"I DON'T WANT SACRIFICE"

I Corinthians 1:23

Let me make this quite personal. Someone may say, `Sacrifice? I don't want sacrifice. I am sick of the sound of the word. I am bored with Christianity's reiteration about taking up a cross. It is such a dismal dirge, such an outmoded ethic. Self-realization—that is my goal: to be the arbiter of my own destiny, going ahead and fulfilling even what Christianity would tell me was an unfulfillable desire.'

But I am only asking you to look into your heart and look up at the cross. Does not your own heart tell you that the wisdom of God is there, and that life will work no other way? Canon Streeter once put it memorably: `The primrose path of dalliance is early overrun with briars; and if we must be pierced with thorns, it is more kingly to wear them as a crown.' More kingly, yes, and infinitely more satisfying too. For Christ will be there to help and strengthen you; and, as Principal David Cairns used to say, `What God did with the cross of His first-born Child Jesus, He can do with all the crosses of all his other children.' He can make them shine with glory.

When you reach that point in your thinking— `Christ crucified the wisdom of God'—suddenly it flashes upon you, `I must be in this with Jesus. I must be identified and united with Him in His sacrifice and passion—in that self-offering of which the dear Lord said, "To this end was I born, and for this cause came I into the world."' He is bearing now, this very hour, the shame and suffering of all the earth. And I know He is looking round on me and saying, `Will you stand in and share with Me in this, or is it nothing to you?' For today Christ, the Power and the Wisdom of God, stands at the door and knocks. While the sands of time are running out, and the hurrying hours mold our destiny, He stands at the door and knocks. It is so urgent that we should make our dedication real.

James Stewart

THE MOST SACRED SYMBOL

I Corinthians 1:18

Christians never seem to be able to plumb the depth of meaning in the Cross. It is no wonder that it has become the most sacred symbol of the faith in every branch of the Church. That God should suffer men to nail him on two pieces of wood staggers the minds of Christ's followers whenever they strip away their familiarity with it and look at it afresh. But here are a few of the things which make it unspeakably dear to them:

I. It shows how bad men are. Men don't like to admit their badness. Most of them think they are quite nice fellows and in no need of a Savior. But Christ, the noblest soul who ever walked this earth, was crucified by men—not peculiarly *bad* men, not the `criminal types'; He was done to death by some of the `best' people of His day. Nothing like the Cross reveals the basic evil in men and shows the vile depths to which our nature can sink. . . .

II. It shows how loving God is. Christ came to save. He meant to fight wickedness with love and beat it. By mere power He could have blasted His enemies, but He let them murder Him and prayed for them as they did it.

III. The Cross shows the supreme power of God to transform evil into good. In some senses, the Cross was the worst thing our race ever did. But God made it, at the same time, the best disclosure of His love to men. . . . How can we help but wonder at times what God is like? If we really want to know, we must go to the Cross. The answer is clearest there. He loves like that.

IV. The Cross shows . . . Christians . . . how they must live. Self assertion must be canceled out . . . and all this is but the fringe. However much Christians make of the Cross, they can never make enough of it.

W.E. Sangster

"LET US GO TO THE CROSS"

Philippians 2:8

If all I knew of Jesus Christ was "wonderful servant of men," He could have my heart. I must love Him supremely. But that is not all. "He took upon Him the form of a servant, and was made in the likeness of men; and being found in fashion as a man, He humbled Himself, and became obedient unto death, even the death of a cross."

Let us go to the cross. I want to take the arm of Barabbas and press up through the throng quite close. Listen! Barabbas is telling me something. There were three robbers in jail. The soldiers made three crosses, one for each robber. See the crosses. There are two robbers, each on his own cross. That middle one was made for Barabbas. Why isn't Barabbas hanging on it? Only because Another is dying where Barabbas ought to have died! Barabbas is weeping and I release his arm and gaze and somehow that form on that cross is transfigured before my gaze and I *know* that this cross was not only for Barabbas—it was for me, for all the whole sinful world. Whole libraries have been written to explain the Cross. But all that is necessary is for each of us to see it through the eyes of Barabbas. He died for me. Where I should have died, He died in my stead.

Oh God, what is this? Not merely a Suffering Servant but a man dying in my place! He is identifying Himself with my sin—made sin for me. He is identifying Himself with the punishment of my sin—the sinner shall surely die and He died for me.

Let me take the arm of the Centurion right up close at the foot of the Cross. Listen, Jesus is saying something. "Father forgive them for they know not what they do." As He says it, He looks full into the eyes of the Centurion and He is also looking into mine. How can we bear it? Nothing like this ever happened on earth before. Again transfiguration occurs and we know, we *know*, we KNOW, that "surely this is the Son of God."

Eugene Erny

THAT GHASTLY SYMBOL!

Galatians 6:14

Nobody in his right mind composes hymns extolling the hangman's noose or sports a replica of the guillotine or decorates a church steeple with a model of Sing Sing's electric chair. Why, then, glory in the cross, that ghastly symbol of cruelty, shame and death?

Years ago when Christianity was first propagated in China, a native editor, antagonistic to the gospel, mockingly inquired: "Why should the followers of Jesus reverence the instrument of his punishment and consider it so to represent him as not to venture to tread upon it? Would it be common sense, if the father or ancestor of a house had been killed by a shot from a gun or a wound from a sword, that his sons and grandsons should reverence the gun or sword as if it were their father or ancestor?" That is a question which cries out for a satisfactory answer. Why do Christians glory in the cross?

We do so for one overwhelming reason. To us the cross of Calvary is the time-abiding, heart-assuring, all-sufficient revelation of God's love. In the words of I John 3:16: "Hereby perceive we the love of God, because he laid down his life for us, and we ought to lay down our lives for the brethren." That, in brief, is why we glory in the bloody gibbet on which a young Jew was done to death. For that young Jew was really God incarnate laying down his life for us in a love which eludes the grasp of human thought.

Perhaps we do not realize that apart from Calvary there is simply no convincing evidence to support the New Testament credo, "God is love."

Vernon Grounds

A TRAIL OF CHANGED LIVES

I Corinthians 15:14

Today we stand at that holy season of the year when throughout the world Christians are rejoicing in the central fact of our faith that Jesus Christ is risen.

The French thinker, Auguste Comte, once told Thomas Carlyle that he was going to start a new religion that would replace Christianity. "Very good," replied Carlyle. "All you will have to do is to be crucified, rise again the third day, and get the world to believe you are still alive. Then your new religion will have a chance."

From the very first Easter until now the Christian faith has moved forward based on the fact that Jesus Christ did rise from the dead and the fact that he is alive and changing lives. Whenever people met the historic Jesus, they were changed. And this transforming influence of Jesus Christ did not fade out in the first century. Ever since it has left a trail of changed lives.

I know a vicious gang leader in Harlem who has now become a preacher of the Good News that God is love. I have heard a savage Indian chief in South America who butchered the missionaries who came to tell him about God, but who now is the leader of the church in his tribe. I once met a prize-winning biochemist at the University of Minnesota who had a profound Christian experience when he was fifty years old and deeply influenced his colleague by the way that he calmly faced death by cancer. And I can think of thousands of others. To the Christian these changed lives are evidence that Jesus Christ is indeed alive.

Leighton Ford

WHAT EXPLANATION CAN YOU GIVE?

Acts 26:25-26

Several months ago a very unusual meeting took place at Harvard University. Hundreds of students gathered to hear an address by Professor J. N. D. Anderson, who is dean of the faculty of law at the University of London. His brilliant address surveyed the evidence for the resurrection of Jesus from the eyes of a lawyer. He smashed many of the theories which have tried to explain away the resurrection of Jesus Christ. And then he closed his address by listing a series of historic facts that must be explained in some other way if the resurrection didn't happen.

If there were no resurrection, he asked, how do you explain the Christian church that can be traced back to the first century? The New Testament says it began because its Founder was raised from the dead. Is there any other theory that fits the facts?

How do you explain the success of the early Church? he asked. How did the apostles make thousands of converts in Jerusalem by preaching the resurrection when anyone who wanted to check out the tomb to see if Jesus were still dead and buried could have done so simply by taking a short walk?

What changed the apostles? he asked. What changed Peter from a man who denied Jesus three times before the Cross to someone who defied the chief priests after the resurrection? What happened to James, the brother of Jesus? During Jesus' lifetime he didn't believe in him, but he became a leader of the church in Jerusalem after the resurrection. What changed Paul from persecutor to apostle of Christ?

You see, as Paul said, "this thing was not done in a corner." The documents are there to examine. The evidence is there to consider. And I challenge you today, if you will not and cannot accept the resurrection, what explanation can you give?

Leighton Ford

THAT'S IT! FREEDOM

John 8:32

I shall tell you what Easter means;
To me, that is:
Not so many tulips and daffodils,
Bonnets and bunnies,
Baked hams and lambs.

It is the Creator suddenly bursting
The chrysalis in my heart,
With my consent,
Setting me free, uncongruously.
The words return: "If the
Son therefore shall set you free,
Ye shall be free indeed."

That's it! Freedom.
Freedom to live, to love,
And thus to give,
To take a glorious chance on life,
To be both liberated
And lost—in wonder.

I shall tell you what Easter means;
To me, that is:
The Eternal whispering, "Behold,
I am arisen in you,
Rising higher and higher,
Expanding, enveloping.
Can you bear My being?
Courage, child."

Easter comes so many moons after
This or that,
But also, now and tomorrow.
I pray,
"In me arise, my Lord!
And keep on rising."

That is what Easter means;
To me, that is.
Sallie Chesham

DON'T FEAR THE SUMMONS

John 14:1-2

One hundred and seventy-one years ago in Vermont a man named John Todd was born. In a little while his family moved to the small community of Killingsworth, Connecticut. Before he was six years old, he was made an orphan by the death of both his father and mother. He and his brothers and sisters were sent out among relatives to be brought up. John was assigned to a kind-hearted aunt who lived about ten miles away. She was both his father and his mother and saw him all the way through Yale College and into his chosen profession. Years later she was taken seriously ill and knew that she was close to death. She was afraid to die and uncertain about the experience she had to face. In her anxiety and distress she wrote to John who had been more like a son to her than a nephew. Since he couldn't go to her bedside, he wrote her this letter:

It is now nearly thirty-five years since I, a little boy of six, was left quite alone in the world . . . I have never forgotten the day when I made the long journey to your house in North Killingsworth. I still recall my disappointment when instead of coming for me yourself you sent your hired man Caesar to fetch me. And I can still remember my tears and anxiety, as perched on your horse and clinging tightly to Caesar, I started out for my new home. As we rode along, I became more and more afraid and finally said anxiously to Caesar, "Do you think she will go to bed before we get there?" "Oh no," he answered reassuringly, "she'll sure stay up for you. When we get out of these here woods, you will see her candle shining in the window."

Presently we did ride out into a clearing, and there, sure enough, was your candle. I remember you were waiting at the door, that you put your arms around me, that you lifted me down from the horse. There was a fire on your hearth, a warm supper on your stove.

After supper, you took me up to bed, heard my prayers, and then sat beside me until I dropped asleep.

You undoubtedly realize why I am recalling all these things . . . Some day soon God may send for you, to take you to a new home. Don't fear the summons, the strange journey, the dark messenger of death. At the end of the road you will find love and a welcome; you will be safe, there as here, in God's love and care. Surely he can be trusted to be as kind to you as you were years ago to me.

This is the final word and a fulfillment of the promise of his amazing grace. It is what we recall at the Easter season. It is what Easter is all about.

Gerald Kennedy

THE PLUS SIGN

Job 14:14

A little girl came into the church and saw a cross on the altar. She said, "What is the plus sign doing on the table?" That is it. The cross is the plus between God and man. "The way of the cross leads home," we sing. That is the only way.

He rose again the third day. . . . If Christ had not risen, Paul points out five dreadful consequences: 1. Our preaching is vain, 2. our faith is vain, 3. we are false witnesses, 4. we are yet in our sins, and 5. those who have fallen asleep in Christ are perished.

Take away the empty tomb and you destroy the Christian faith. The fact of his resurrection is the only assurance we have of eternal life. There are reasons why we might live in life after death, but the resurrection of Christ changes mere hope into actual certainty.

Because he lives, we shall live also. We mortals become immortal. Why do we crowd our churches on Easter Sunday? We talk about the "Easter Parade," but it is not to show our new clothes. We go that Sunday especially because we long to have that assurance that we shall never die. "Death is swallowed up in victory," he said.

It is a fact that people attend church on Easter Sunday in much larger numbers than on any other day. Why is this?

Down deep in the heart of every person is a longing to know, to be sure of eternal life. A friend of Maud Royden once said, "Do not bother me now. Don't bother me never; I want to be dead, forever and ever." But that is not the feeling of very many. Most of us want to hear a word of certainty concerning life after death.

And on Easter Sunday we have the surest and most certain word that man possesses. In the long ago, Job asked, "If a man die, shall he live again?" And through the ages that question has been on the lips of humanity.

Charles L. Allen

HE DIES OF BOREDOM!

James 4:14

We who live in the latter half of that twentieth century are the inheritors and victims of that prevailing mood of spiritual emptiness. Much of modern art, with its chaos and confusion, is trying to tell us this. The theater reflects the same loss of meaning. Man is "Waiting for Godot" (which could mean "God") and Godot never comes. . . . The novelist Saul Bellow speaks for many modern writers and playwrights when he says in *Herzog*:

> . . . what is the philosophy of this generation? Not God is dead, that period was passed long ago. Perhaps it should be stated death is God. This generation thinks—and this is its thought of thoughts—that nothing faithful, vulnerable, fragile can be durable or have any true power. Death waits for these things as a cement floor waits for a dropping light bulb.

The psychiatrist Rollo May describes too many of us in *Man's Search for Himself:*

> The clearest picture of the empty life is the suburban man, who gets up at the same hour every weekday morning, takes the same task at the office, lunches at the same place, leaves the same tip for the waitress each day, comes home on the same train each night, and has 2.3 children . . . goes to church every Christmas and Easter, and moves through a routine, mechanical existence year after year until he finally retires at sixty-five and very soon thereafter dies of heart failure.

May adds, "I've always had the secret suspicion, however, that he dies of boredom!" The real tragedy of it all is that, although he "goes to church every Christmas and Easter," the man doesn't realize that the message which he hears on those great days is supposed to transform his very existence!

Donald B. Strobe

THE GREAT ESCAPE

I Peter 1:3-9

Easter took all of Christ's friends by surprise. Christ had warned them that he would rise from the dead, but they missed the meaning of his promise. And who wouldn't? We just don't expect the dead to rise. Nothing seems so permanent to us as death. It is inescapable.

I thought of this when I was in Winnipeg, Canada, speaking at the University of Manitoba and I heard a radio broadcast about Harry Houdini, the great escape artist. Maybe some of you who are older can remember seeing him or reading about his fantastic, incredible feats. Chained, handcuffed, he was locked in trunks and dumped into rivers, but he always managed to escape before drowning. But when appendicitis struck him in 1926, Harry Houdini, the great master of escape, could not struggle free from the chains of death.

Death is inescapable. But Christ rose. That's why we have a New Testament; that's why we have a Christian Church. That first Easter, which took all of Jesus' disciples by storm, became the center of their thinking, their living, their preaching. Christ had escaped death and brought new hope to all men. That was their message.

In the first century deep darkness had settled upon the world. The religions of the world seemed to be dying, or at least irrelevant and ineffective. Military power and might ruled the nations. Cruelty and evil were everywhere, and human life was cheap. But then, on a Judean hillside, there came a message which has reverberated down the corridors of history with hope: "Fear not! For behold, I bring you good tidings of great joy, which shall be to all the people! For unto you is born this day in the city of David a Savior, which is Christ the Lord!" (Luke 2:10-11). With that great message of hope the early Christian movement got its start.

Donald B. Strobe

WE NEGLECT IT TO OUR PERIL

Romans 5:5

Christian hope is a basic part of our faith, and we neglect it to our own peril. For, as Nietzsche said, man can put up with almost anything if he feels that there is meaning and purpose behind it. But if he becomes convinced that life is only "a tale told by an idiot, full of sound and fury, signifying nothing . . ." then there is little hope for his life, and his joy quickly turns to ashes. In one of his books Leslie Weatherhead has written a good parable to describe the uses of hope:

On a long sea journey round the world I once meditated on what would happen if the captain, one day, in the middle of the Pacific Ocean, summoned us all to the saloon and said something like this: "There is plenty of food on board. Life will proceed as before. Meals will be served, games played, dances arranged, concerts provided, but I have decided not to make for a port. We shall just cruise round and round in the ocean until our fuel is exhausted and then I shall sink the ship."

Mark this. The next few days would *appear* just the same as those which preceded them. Only one thing would be different. The captain's speech would have snatched from every mind the concept of purpose, meaning and goal. And, in my opinion, very soon afterwards, on a dark night, first one and then another passenger would jump overboard. The mind hates meaninglessness.

Can it be, then, that the *why* of life is just as important as the *how?* Can it be that most of us have been asking the wrong questions? We want to know how to make a living, when the prior question is more important: how to make a *life.* In all our preoccupation with the question, "Will a man survive?" have we forgotten to ask the more important questions, "What will man do if he does survive?"

Donald Strobe

GLORY! GLORY! GLORY!

Ephesians 5:15-20

Nobody ever doubted the genuineness of Billy Bray's conversion. He was a miner in Cornwall, England, who after a long day of work spent his nights in the beer shops of the mining district. Night after night, his wife had to go out and find him and help her drunken husband home. But he was not without conscience. "I never got drunk without feeling condemned for it," Billy recalled. But, he was convinced that the Devil had a hold on his life.

Then one night in 1823, after he had attended a meeting of the Bible Christians, he came home and cried out to God for mercy and was converted. "In an instant," he testified, "the Lord made me so happy that I cannot express what I felt. I shouted for joy."

A year after his conversion Billy became a lay preacher for the Bible Christian Church, and he was often called upon to preach when no one more qualified was available. His most effective ministry, however, was in the mines. He would pray for his fellow miners before they went to work in the mornings. "Lord," he would say, "if any of us must be killed, or die today, let it be *me*; let not one of these men die, for they are not happy and I am, and if I die today I shall go to heaven."

He was an eccentric character, often dancing and singing in the streets, and professing to be joyful no matter what the circumstances. "I can't help praising God," he said. "As I go along the street I lift up one foot, and it seems to say, `Amen;' and so they keep on like that all the time I am walking." Even at the time of his wife's death, he shouted for joy: "Bless the Lord! My dear Joey is gone up with the bright ones! My dear Joey is gone up with the shining angels! Glory! Glory! Glory!"

Ruth Tucker

NOT SOME LIMP SUBSTITUTE

Psalms 16:11

John, in his epistle (I John), uses the word "joy" only once, but the idea of joy runs through the entire letter. Joy is not something that we manufacture for ourselves; joy is a wonderful by-product of our fellowship with God. David knew the joy which John mentions; he said, "In Thy presence is fullness of joy" (Ps. 16:11).

Basically, sin is the cause of the unhappiness that overwhelms our world today. Sin promises joy but it always produces sorrow. The pleasures of sin are temporary—they are only for a season (Heb. 11:25). God's pleasures last eternally—they are for evermore (Ps. 16:11).

The life that is real produces a joy that is real— not some limp substitute. Jesus said, the night before He was crucified, "Your joy no man taketh from you" (John 16:22). "These things have I spoken unto you, that My joy might remain in you, and that your joy might be full" (15:11).

Karl Marx wrote, "The first requisite for the people's happiness is the abolition of religion." But the Apostle John writes, in effect, "Faith in Jesus Christ gives you a joy that can never be duplicated by the world. I have experienced this joy myself, and I want to share it with you."

Warren Wiersbe

But the misfortune is that people want to direct God, instead of resigning themselves to be directed by him. They want to show him a way, instead of passively following that wherein he leads them. Hence many souls, called to enjoy God himself and not merely his gifts, spend all their lives in running after little consolations, and feeding on them; resting there only and making all their happiness to consist therein.

Madame Guyon

UNUTTERABLE SWEETNESS

I Peter 1:8

I was so strongly absorbed in God, that I could neither open my eyes nor hear anything. I found that thy Word, O my God, made its own impression on my heart, and there had its effect, without the mediation of words or any attention to them. And I have found it so ever since, but after a different manner, according to the different degrees and states I have passed through. So deeply was I settled in the inward spirit of prayer, that I could scarce any more pronounce the vocal prayers. . . .

I was penetrated with so lively a dart of pure love, that I could not resolve to abridge by indulgences the pains due to my sins. "O, my Love," I cried, "I am willing to suffer for thee. I find no other pleasure but in suffering for thee. . . ."

My only pleasure now was to steal some moments to be alone with thee, O thou who art my only Love! All other pleasure was a pain to me. I lost not thy presence, which was given me by a continual infusion, not as I had imagined, by the efforts of the head or by force of thought in meditating on God, but in the will where I tasted with unutterable sweetness the enjoyment of the beloved object; yet not as I came to do afterwards, by an essential union, but by a real union in the will, which brought to me to discern, in a happy experience, that the soul was created to enjoy its God.

Madame Guyon

THE MOST LASTING PLEASURES

Proverbs 3:17

It is a man's proper business to seek happiness and avoid misery.

Happiness consists in what delights and contents the mind; misery in what disturbs, discomposes, or torments it.

I will therefore make it my business to seek satisfaction and delight, and avoid uneasiness and disquiet; to have as much of the one, and as little of the other, as may be.

But here I must have a care I mistake not; for if I prefer a short pleasure to a lasting one, it is plain I cross my own happiness.

Let me then see wherein consists the most lasting pleasures of this life; and that, as far as I can observe, is in these things:

FIRST Health, without which no sensual pleasure can have any relish.

SECOND Reputation, for that I find every body is pleased with, and the want of it is a constant torment.

THIRD Knowledge, for the little knowledge I have, I find I would not sell at any rate, nor part with for any other pleasure.

FOURTH Doing good, for I find the well-cooked meat I eat today does now no more delight me, nay, I am diseased after a full meal. The perfumes I smelt yesterday now no more affect me with any pleasure; but the good turn I did yesterday, a year, seven years since, continues still to please and delight me as often as I reflect on it.

FIFTH The expectation of eternal and incomprehen-sible happiness in another world is that also which carries a constant pleasure with it.

John Locke

"THAT IS HOW I TREAT MY FRIENDS"

Nehemiah 8:10

Teresa constantly urged the nuns to criticize her own faults as they would those of others. She would also submit to humiliating mortifications with all the meekness that she would expect of her daughters. This would be repugnant if we did not recognize the all-important value she attached to the practice of humility. Humility was the chief of all virtues in her eyes.

This was all the more remarkable when we consider a prevailing cultural Spanish characteristic which Clissold discusses.

> In a Spain dominated by the cult of "honor"— pride of lineage, disdain for plebian occupation and manual work, and a touchiness which led to ferocious revenge for every imagined injury— the practice of self-abasement stood in dramatic contrast. Even her pious father and brothers had not been immune from the poisonous obsession with "honor."

Certainly the surest antidote to this terrible obsession was the practice of humility. . . .

A side to Teresa's character which may be related to humility is her incredible sense of humor. She professed to dislike "moody people" and asked to be delivered from "frowning saints." As a matter of fact, at the heart of her life of poverty and penance throbbed a tremendous joy and spontaneity. Furthermore, this profound inner joy seemed to be developed even further by privation.

There is her famous dialogue with the Lord when, fighting with a river crossing in her advanced age, she complained to the Lord that she had a sore throat and high temperature. She added, therefore, that this prevented her from enjoying the incidents of the journey as she might. The Lord was alleged to have said, "But that is how I treat my friends." To which Teresa replied, "Yes, Lord, and that is why you have so few of them!"

PREFACE TO A LIFE OF PRAYER
St. Teresa of Avila

SOMETHING TRANSCENDING BEAUTIFUL

Psalms 43:4

Christianity and Stoicism unite in contempt of self-pity, but in place of the chilly acceptance of life which Stoicism teaches, Christ would make us wise to transmute it into something transcendingly beautiful, and can instruct us how, even, to *use* our woes. Nor is it hard to quote instances of His triumph in this task. One thinks of St. Teresa, in constant and cheerful conflict with ill-health, battling all the time with her terrible headaches, those rushing waterfalls in the head and with bouts of chronic fever, and at least one paralytic stroke. Yet nothing could daunt her courage or quench her gaiety. . . . A smile and a jest were never far away. In 1580 she fell a victim to influenza, and under the awful depression which influenza brings even her conquering cheerfulness seemed to wilt. But not for long. When she shrank from the dreadful cold of a winter journey, the Voice said `Do not mind the cold. I am the true warmth' and she went forth, as ever, with a cheerful courage.

Catherine Booth was never well. . . . Yet she lived to be the glorious mother of the Salvation Army, and to do a work for God almost unparalleled in feminine biography. Two years of terrible pain completed her titanic life, pain which she would never permit to be dulled, despite her husband's pleadings, by the kindly numbness of a drug. . . . She could say on her death-bed that she could not recollect a single day when she had really been free from pain. But . . . thankfulness and courage were with her to the end. The doctor who attended her at the last was an agnostic, and she was full of concern for his conversion. He said himself: "Her courage and anxiety for my welfare were beautiful."

W.E. Sangster

"HAPPY ABOUT WHAT?"

Ecclesiastes 5:10

Tolstoy was not averse to this hum of guests, servants and children. He loved to feel himself surrounded by a noisy, simple life. It was his overcoat, to shield him from cold and death. . . . But did you have right to make merry when a trap-door was about to yawn beneath your feet? He looked at himself in the mirror. A fifty-year-old face: hair cropped short above a high furrowed brow, broad bushy eyebrows overhanging two sharp gray eyes sunk deep in their sockets, a shapeless nose, fleshy ears, a sensuous mouth, and, framing the whole, a forest of stiff, tangled graying hair, thick as wire. He had never been in better condition. . . . Everything he had wanted when he was young he had obtained, and in the prime of life. He had wanted literary fame, and he shared with Dostoyevsky the honor of being universally acclaimed as the greatest living Russian author; he had hoped to spend calm years working in the home of his ancestors, surrounded by a loving wife and many children, and thanks to Sonya, he was savoring this family happiness to the full. He had dreaded being forced to write in order to earn a living, and his financial circumstances allowed him to work in total freedom.

And yet, he was not happy. Or rather, the form of happiness that had become his lot did not content him.

TOLSTOY
Henri Troyat

Another one of the great financiers of our nation was asked awhile ago, "Aren't you exceedingly happy?" And he said, "Happy about what?" "Happy because you have so much wealth." He said, "All I get out of it is my board and clothing, and endless worry. This is all I get out of it."

George W. Truett

ON A MAD QUEST

Ecclesiastes 12:1

A French philosopher said, "The whole world is on a mad quest for security of happiness."

The president of Harvard University said, "The world is searching for a creed to believe and a song to sing."

A Texas millionaire confided, "I thought money could buy happiness. I have been terribly disillusioned."

A famous film star broke down, "I have money, beauty, glamour and popularity. I should be the happiest woman in the world but I am miserable. Why?"

One of Britain's top social leaders said, "I have lost all desire to live, yet I have everything to live for. What is the matter?"

A man went to see a psychiatrist. He said, "Doctor, I am lonely, despondent and miserable. Can you help me?" The Psychiatrist suggested that he go to see a famous circus clown. His patient said, "I am that clown. . . ."

One of the world's great statesmen said to me, "I am an old man. Life has lost all meaning. I am ready to take a fateful leap into the unknown. Young man, can you give me a ray of hope?"

Billy Graham

On that happy Magdalene's day my soul was perfectly delivered from all its pains. I was then indeed only like that of a dead person raised, though not yet unbound from his grave-clothes. But on this day I was, as it were, in perfect life, and set wholly at liberty. I then found myself as much raised above nature, as before I had been depressed under its burden. I was inexpressibly overjoyed to find him, whom I thought I had lost forever, returned to me again with unspeakable magnificence and purity. It was then, O my God, that I found again in thee with new advantages, in an ineffable manner, all I had been deprived of; and the peace I now possessed was all holy, heavenly and inexpressible; all I had enjoyed before was only a peace, a gift of God, but now I received and possessed the God of peace.

Madame Guyon

A GARDEN SONG

Song of Songs 8:13

A garden gay is my garden dear,
In it the trees grow tall;
My shining flowers are seen
The little leaves between,
The joyfullest things of all.

When th' glad sun calleth, "Here I am,"
And the dawn-wind, "And I too."
Then over tree-trunks brown
Joy danceth up and down,
And my heart it danceth too.

The good rain causeth in all my buds
A stir, a laugh, a voice;
Then doth each little spray
Swing merrily and say,
Rejoice, O rejoice, rejoice.

In moonlight nights the angels come,
They step most delicately;
Then is my garden drest
In colours made for rest,
The loveliest that there be.

A garden gay is my garden dear,
Of gentle joys the prime;
Where often He doth talk
Whose wont it is to walk
In gardens at evening time.

Amy Carmichael

"SOMETHING NATIVE TO MY BLOOD"

John 15:11

There are a great many who still stink with Ephraim, of whom God complained: "Were I to write for him my laws, he would but think them foreigner's saws" (Hos. 8:12, Moffatt). Ephraim felt that God's laws were foreign sayings, or saws—something imposed from the outside. God says that His laws are native to us.

"There is something in the autumn that is native to my blood," wrote the poet Bliss Carman. There is something in Christ that is native to my blood. He is the author of my blood. He is at home there. It flows better, is warmer and purer when He is in it. He is native to my nerves. When He controls them, they are calm and creative and contributive. He is native to every organ of my body. When He controls them, they function well, perfectly, in fact, for they are made for His control. When they get under the control of resentments, of fear, of selfishness, they function badly.

Jesus said, "I have told you this, that my joy may be within you and your joy complete" (John 15:11, Moffatt). Note: when His joy is within us, then our joy is complete, for His joy and our joy are the same. He is not imposing a foreign joy, trying to make me happy in something I can't be happy in. He is giving a joy which, when I take it, is my very own. My own joy is complete. Every joy, other than His, leaves me dissatisfied, incomplete. It doesn't hit the spot.

T.S. Eliot says: "We may say that religion implies a life in conformity with nature . . . and that not toward nature implies a wrong attitude toward God, and the consequence is inevitable doom. . . ."

We must have hold of this until it becomes a basic axiom: My will and God's will are not alien. When I find His will, I find my very own. The idea that God's will always lies along the line of the disagreeable is false. The will of God is always our highest interest. It could not be otherwise and God be God. I am fulfilled when I make Him my center. I am frustrated when I make myself the center. I am destined to be a Christian.

E. Stanley Jones

LOVE AND LAUGH

Philippians 4:4

If your morals make you dreary, depend upon it they are wrong.

Robert Louis Stevenson

Learn daily the sublime lesson of trust and calm in the midst of storm. Whatever of sorrow or difficulty the day may bring My tender command to you is still the same—*Love and Laugh.*

Love and laughter, not a sorrowful resignation, mark real acceptances of My will. Leave every soul the braver and happier for having met you. For children or youth, middle or old age, for sorrow, for sin, for all you may encounter in others, this should be your attitude. *Love* and *laugh.*

Do not fear. Remember how I faced the devil in the wilderness, and how I conquered with "the sword of the spirit which is the word of God." You too have your quick answer for every fear that evil may present— an answer of faith and confidence in Me. Where possible say it aloud.

The spoken word has power. Look on every fear, not as a weakness on your part due to illness or worry, but as a real temptation to be attacked and overthrown.

GOD CALLING

"HE NEEDS TO TELL YOU"

I Corinthians 9:16

A friend of mine was a missionary in Burma. One day while he was standing on a street corner preaching the Gospel, a hostile crowd gathered around him. They tried to shout him down and constantly interrupted his message with catcalls. Vainly he struggled to deliver his sermon, but the sentiment of the crowd was too much against him. Just as he was ready to give up a Buddhist monk came by. The monk silenced the crowd with a loud cry and then he said, "Listen to this man. Don't you know *he needs* to tell you about his God?"

What an interesting observation. The Buddhist monk was sensitive to the fact that my friend *needed* to preach his sermon more than the crowd needed to hear it. . . . I do not know how much others need what I have to say but I know that I need to say it.

Anthony Campolo

God never says, "Revive yourselves and convert the world." God's word to His servants is "Preach the gospel to every creature." Their word to Him is "Revive Thy work, O Lord."

In the laws of the spiritual universe faithful evangelism is normally followed by genuine revival. Let the church realize as its first responsibility and the first charge upon its strength the duty of preaching the gospel of Jesus Christ, and there will be added to it revival: that is, a constant renewal of its vital energy and increase of moral force which will be manifest in the spiritual growth of its own members and in the attraction to it of them that are without. But let it be well understood that the church is not directly responsible for revival. It *is* directly and immediately responsible for its duty of evangelism. There is a type of revival which condemns the evangelism which produced it. A superficial scratching of the surface which does not reach down to the roots of moral being is a mockery of the gospel.

Warren Wiersbe

"WHAT KIND OF FELLOW IS THIS?"

Galatians 6:10

When Dr. Gordon Torgerson crossed the Atlantic one summer he noticed a dark-skinned man sitting in a deck chair and reading a Bible. One day he sat beside him and said, "Forgive my curiosity, but I'm a Baptist minister. I see you come here everyday and read your Bible. I assume you're a Christian, and I'm interested to know how it happened."

"Yes," said the man, setting aside his Bible, "I'm very happy to talk about it. I'm a Filipino. I was born in a good Catholic home in the Philippines, and some years ago I came to the United States to one of your fine universities to study law.

"My first night on campus, a student came to see me. He said, 'I've come over to welcome you to the campus and to say that if there is anything I can do to help make your stay more pleasant, I hope you'll call on me.' Then he asked me where I went to church, and I told him I was Catholic. He said, 'Well, I can tell you where the Catholic church is, but it's not easy to find; it's quite a distance away. Let me make a map.' So he made a map to the Catholic church and left.

"When I awakened Sunday morning it was raining. I thought to myself, I'll just forego church this morning. . . .

"Then there was a knock on the door, and when I opened it, there stood that student. His raincoat was dripping wet, and on one arm he had two umbrellas. He said, 'I thought you might have a hard time finding your church, especially in the rain, and I shall walk along with you and show you where it is.' As I got dressed, I thought *What kind of fellow is this?* As we walked along in the rain under the two umbrellas, I said to myself, *if this fellow is so concerned about my religion, I ought to know something about his.* I asked, 'Where do you go to church?'

'Oh,' he said, 'my church is just around the corner.'

"I said, 'Suppose we go to your church today and we'll go to my church next Sunday.' I went to his church, and I've never been back to my own. . . . I am Bishop Valencius, Bishop of the Methodist Church in the Philippines."

Dan Johnson

THE "GO" IN SOUL WINNING

Psalm 126:5-6

"He that goeth forth and weepeth, bearing precious seed, shall doubtless come again with rejoicing, bringing his sheaves with him."

Analyze the verse and you will find these five parts in God's plan of soul winning:

1. "He that goeth forth"—the GO in soul winning.

2. "And weepeth"—the BROKEN HEART in soul winning.

3. "Bearing precious seed"—the WORD OF GOD in soul winning.

4. "Shall doubtless come again . . . bringing his sheaves with him"—the CERTAINTY OF RESULTS with God's method.

5. "Rejoicing . . . bringing his sheaves with him"—the JOY OF THE REAPERS, or a soul-winner's reward.

God's Word puts going as the first requirement in soul winning. How like the Great Commission, when Jesus said, "Go ye into all the world" (Mark 16:15), and again, "Go ye therefore" (Matt. 28:19). The main reason Christians do not win souls is that they simply do not get at it. The one who wins souls is the one who tries to win souls, the one who talks to sinners, the one who makes it his business.

Many have the impression that the best man or woman is the best soul winner—that the Christian who has the highest moral standards, pays his debts, avoids worldliness, attends church, tithes, etc., will automatically be the best soul winner; but that is not true. If it were true, then every Pharisee would have been a wonderful soul winner, but they were not. And many a Christian today prays, reads his Bible, attends church and carefully watches his daily life, yet never wins a soul. That is tragic, but true.

How often in revivals a good sister or brother rises to testify and says, "I want to live such a godly life that sinners will see my daily walk and be saved!" The fact is, their living a godly life does not win sinners to Christ.

John R. Rice

TAKE UP THE CRY

John 4:10

A number of travelers were making their way across the desert. The last drop of water had been exhausted, and they were pushing on with the hope that more might be found. They were growing weaker and weaker. As a last resort they divided their men into companies and sent them on, one in advance of the other, in this way securing a rest they so much needed. If they who were in the advance guard were able to find the springs, they were to shout the good tidings to the men who were the nearest to them, and so they were to send the message along.

The long line reached far across the desert. They were fainting by the way when suddenly, every one was cheered by the good news. The leader of the first company had found the springs of water. He stood at the head of this men shouting until the farthest man had heard his cry: "Water! Water!" The word went from mouth to mouth, until the whole company of men heard the sound, quickened their pace, and soon were drinking to their hearts' content. I have found the Water of Life; it is flowing fully, it is flowing freely; and so I stand and cry: "Water! Water!" Take up the cry, every one, until every thirsty soul shall drink and live. But I have found another blessing, too. It is that of sweet communion with the Lord. It is that of the closest fellowship with Him. It is at the brink of the upper spring.

Wilbur Chapman

YOU CANNOT ACT FOR HIM

James 4:8

It is essential to give people a chance of acting on the truth of God. The responsibility must be left with the individual, you cannot act for him, it must be his own deliberate act, but the evangelical message ought always to lead a man to act. The paralysis of refusing to act leaves a man exactly where he was before; when once he acts, he is never the same. It is the foolishness of it that stands in the way of hundreds who have been convicted by the Spirit of God. Immediately I precipitate myself over into an act, that second I live. All the rest is existence. The moments when I truly live are the moments when I act with my whole will.

Never allow a truth of God that is brought home to your soul to pass without acting on it, not necessarily physically, but in will. Record it, with ink or with blood. The feeblest saint who transacts business with Jesus Christ is emancipated the second he acts; all the almighty power of God is on his behalf. We come up to the truth of God, we confess we are wrong, but go back again; then we come up to it again, and go back; until we learn that we have no business to go back. We have to go clean over on some word of our redeeming Lord and transact business with Him. His word "come" means "transact." "Come unto Me." The last thing we do is to come; but everyone who does come knows that that second the supernatural rush of life of God invades him instantly. The dominating power of the world, the flesh and the devil is paralysed, not by your act, but because your act has linked you to God and His redemptive power.

Oswald Chambers

IT HAS TO BE PROCLAIMED

Romans 1:14

For people who *do* believe in the Christian God, evangelism is a duty and privilege so plain, so incontrovertible, that all talk of 'relevance' is a half-vulgar intrusion of the utilitarian in a realm where it cannot apply. One could as soon enquire of a son concerning the 'relevance' of his love for his mother, or a lover for the beloved, or a great scientist for his devotion to truth. One could as sensibly enquire of people bound together in Christian marriage of the 'relevance' of their mutual vows. . . . [There are] things which soar above utilitarian tests and are right in themselves and not simply because of ends they serve.

The proclamation of the gospel is such a task. It is right in itself. . . . The preaching of the gospel has never seemed relevant to unbelievers. . . . But it has to be proclaimed! Not apologized for, or watered down, or twisted in the interests of immediate relevance, or half-altered to suit the 'time-spirit' or disguised to get it past an unbeliever's guard. It has to be preached—in all its seeming irrelevance; above the cat-calls and sneers of those who hate or despise it; in the face, also, of the amused contempt of those whose vanity leads them to feel superior to it. "I, if I be lifted up from the earth," said Christ, "will draw all men unto me."

Let us lift Him up, therefore!—in the atomic age, as in all others, and leave God to prove His relevance to those who will some day profit by our faith.

W.E. Sangster

EXPECT IT!

II Timothy 4:2

You must also believe in the power of that message to save people. You may have heard the story of one of our first students, who came to me, and said, "I have been preaching now for some months, and I do not think I have had a single conversion." I said to him, "And do you expect that the Lord is going to bless you and save souls every time you open your mouth?" "No sir," he replied. "Well, then," I said, "that is why you do not get souls saved. If you had believed, the Lord would have given the blessing." I had caught him very nicely; but many others would have answered me in just the same way as he did. They tremblingly believe that it is possible, by some strange mysterious method, that once in a hundred sermons God might win a quarter of a soul. They have hardly enough faith to keep them standing upright in their boots; how can they expect God to bless them? I like to go to the pulpit feeling, "This is God's Word that I am going to deliver in His name; it cannot return to Him void; I have asked His blessing upon it, and He is bound to give it, and His purposes will be answered, whether my message is a savior of life unto life, or of death unto death to those who hear it."

Now, if this is how you feel, what will be the result if souls are not saved? Why, you will call special prayer-meetings, to seek to know why the people do not come to Christ; you will have enquirers' meetings for the anxious; you will meet the people with a joyful countenance, so that they may see that you are expecting a blessing, but, at the same time, you will let them know that you will be grievously disappointed unless the Lord gives you conversions.

Charles H. Spurgeon

"THINK NO MORE ABOUT IT"

Jeremiah 6:14

If you can teach a man how to ignore sin, you have him. If you can tell him how to ignore pain successfully and disease and trouble, he will listen to you. If you can tell him how to ignore the possibility of judgment coming on him for wrong-doing, he will listen to you. If you can show a man how he can be delivered from the torture of sin, delivered from a pain-stricken body, loosened from a bad past, then you have him. Mark you, every one of these points is right; the prince of this world delivers on that line, and so does the Lord Jesus Christ. Watch Jesus Christ's life—the people would take all His blessings, but they would not get rightly related to Him; and our difficulty is in presenting men with Jesus Christ apart from what He can do. How does Jesus Christ teach a man to forget sin? By forgiving him. How does a pagan teach a man to forget sin? "Ignore it, think no more about it, realise yourself!" Can it be done? Of course it can be done. If you will just sin long enough, you will forget how sinful you have been, and is it likely that a man who has forgotten how wrong he has been is going to be willing to face Jesus Christ, who, as soon as He sees him, will flash through him his past wrong? The first thing Jesus Christ does is to open a man's eyes wide to the wrong and then delivers him from it.

Oswald Chambers

Fervent lovers of souls do not wait till they are trained; they serve their Lord at once.

C.H. Spurgeon

NON-CONFRONTIVE APPROACH

Acts 8:30-31

The first step in a non-confrontive approach to witnessing is to pray and remind ourselves to be calm and completely natural in manner and tone of voice. The next step varies from person to person. Some prefer to open the conversation by making a simple statement such as, "You know, I'm quite interested in spiritual things." A statement like this is usually casually acknowledged. This opens the way to ask, "May I ask you a question about spiritual things?"

A simple variation is to ask, "Would it be all right if we talk about spiritual things for a few minutes?" When there is an affirmative reply, we immediately ask permission to ask another question so that the non-confrontive questioning can continue.

One of my more enthusiastic pastor friends told me of still another approach. After experimenting, he came up with a very acceptable variation that fits his personality and style. He simply finds something in the conversation that enables him to say, "Oh, are you interested in spiritual things?" He seems to be able to find something spiritual in almost every sentence! Others have suggested lead-in comments such as: "You know, whenever I see you I feel a little guilty. I've known you for many years (months, weeks) and have never taken the time to talk to you about the most important thing we could possibly talk about—spiritual things."

How the transition is made is not important. What is important is that we always ask permission to ask another question.

If the casual acquaintance says no to our original question, our reply should be, "That's fine. I appreciate your honesty." Then we simply change the subject. There is no confrontation. But we shouldn't be surprised if at a later date the same casual acquaintance starts a spiritual discussion. It happens all the time.

Walter S. Bleecker

"GO AND SET ALL ON FIRE"

Acts 8:1-4

In 1739 arrived among us from Ireland the Reverend Mr. Whitfield, who had made himself remarkable there as an itinerant preacher. He was at first permitted to preach in some of our churches; but the clergy, taking a dislike to him, soon refused him their pulpits, and he was obliged to preach in the fields. The multitudes of all sects and denominations that attended his sermons were enormous, and it was a matter of speculation to me, who was one of the number, to observe the extraordinary influence of his oratory on his hearers, and how much they admired and respected him, notwithstanding his common abuse of them, by assuring them they were naturally *half beasts and half devils*. It was wonderful to see the change soon made in the manners of our inhabitants. From being thoughtless or indifferent about religion, it seemed as if the world were growing religious, so that one could not walk through the town in an evening without hearing psalms sung in different homes on the street.

Benjamin Franklin

The next eleven months Francis Xavier was travelling to and fro along the west coast from Cape Comorin, its southernmost point, to Punicale, northern extremity of the kingdom of Comorin. The return to daily life after the first fervour of conversion, the drudgery of organising work which has been begun on the high tide of enthusiasm, these are the things which try men's mettle and prove their perseverance. "Go and set all on fire," had been Father Ignatius's parting words to his son. They had been obeyed. Now the flame had swept through the Fishery Coast.

Margaret Yeo

THE OPPOSITE OF THE FACT

Romans 3:4

The things said most confidently by advanced persons to crowded audiences are generally those quite opposite to the fact: it is actually our truisms that are untrue. Here is a case. There is a phrase of facile liberality uttered again and again at ethical societies and parliaments of religion: "the religions of the earth differ in rites and forms, but they are the same in what they teach." It is false; it is the opposite of the fact. The religions of the earth do *not* greatly differ in rites and forms; they do greatly differ in what they teach. It is as if a man were to say, "Do not be misled by the fact that the *Church Times* and the *Freethinker* look utterly different, that one is painted on vellum and the other carved on marble, that one is triangular and the other hectagonal; read them and you will see that they say the same thing." The truth is, of course, that they are alike in everything except in the fact that they don't say the same thing. An atheist stockbroker in Surbiton looks exactly like a Swedenborgian stockbroker in Wimbledon. You may walk round and round them and subject them to the most personal and offensive study without seeing anything Swedenborgian in the hat or anything particularly godless in the umbrella. It is exactly in their souls that they are divided. So the truth is that the difficulty of all the creeds of the earth is not as alleged in this cheap maxim: that they agree in meaning, but differ in machinery. It is exactly the opposite. They agree in machinery; almost every great religion on earth works with the same external methods, with priests, scriptures, altars, sworn brotherhoods, special feasts. They agree in the mode of teaching; what they differ about is the thing to be taught. Pagan optimists and Eastern pessimists would both have temples, just as Liberals and Tories would both have newspapers. Creeds that exist to destroy each other both have scriptures, just as armies that exist to destroy each other both have guns.

G.K. Chesterton

THE COLLAPSE OF INTEGRITY

Genesis 3:5

Distinctions between right and wrong, justice and injustice have become meaningless. No objective guide is left to choose between "all men are created equal" and "the weak to the wall."

In Year Zero no one could have predicted the consequences that the void at the heart of the nations would produce. But philosopher Blaise Pascal had foreseen, three centuries earlier, the chilling consequences. He argued that in a spiritual vacuum, men can pursue only two options: first, to imagine that they are gods themselves, or second, to seek satisfaction in their senses. Unknowingly, he predicted the routes that would be followed in the East and West in the aftermath of World War II.

Charles Colson

Thomas Huxley's grandson, Aldous, in his book, *Ends and Means*, confesses that a creedless morality leads in the end to disillusionment and the collapse of inner integrity. An atheist may continue for a time to manifest the fruit of Christian love but at best it is only a temporary phenomenon. After all, as Principal John Baillie writes: "a railway engine does not stop as soon as the driver shuts off the steam, nor does a turnip wither and die as soon as it is pulled out of Mother earth."

Europe within recent memory was shocked by the hideous recrudescence of savagery practiced with all the sadistic refinement of modern science. Hitler and his regime liquidated millions of Jews and set up the torture laboratories which went by the name of Buchenwald and Belsen. Civilized men were deeply shocked, but if they had read the signs of the times they should have anticipated such events. Any one who reads *Mein Kampf* can see this barbarous conduct was but the logical consequences of a creed which denied God and, therefore, the sanctity of personality.

Murdo Macdonald

OUT OF JOINT WITH YOURSELF

Jeremiah 17:5-8

When you get out of joint with God, do you get out of joint with yourself? Do you become cynical and bitter—inevitably? When Bertrand Russell said that "life is a bottle of very nasty wine," did his judgment of life have any connection with his lack of faith in God? When God goes, does the meaning drop out of life? And does life actually become "a bottle of very nasty wine"? Do we then live in "generally devaluated world"? Does life turn sour? There is only one answer: Yes! And the whole of life is one long comment on it!

I once saw in New Mexico, on a corrugated-iron-roofed mud hut, with a couple of other mud huts around it, and a mangy dog lying in front, this sign: "Radium Springs—Park Your Pains Here." Those surroundings—that sign! When you "park your pains" in some place other than God—in intoxicants, in money, in sex license, in yourself—do they stay parked, or do they come back to you multiplied? Is evil the great illusion?

E. Stanley Jones

Pontius Pilate, Judea's notorious governor, stood eyeball to eyeball with Jesus of Nazareth. In the judicial process of interrogation, he heard Christ refer to "everyone who is of the truth," to which Pilate replied, "What is the truth?" That question hangs heavily on the thin wire of reason in many a mind this very hour. Pilate never waited for an answer. He whirled away in confused disgust. He should have stopped running and waited for the answer. Jesus could have told him that He alone had satisfying words of life . . . for He alone *is* "the way, the truth, and the life" (John 14:6).

Christianity is not a system of human philosophy nor a religious ritual nor a code of moral ethics—it is the impartation of divine life through Christ. Apart from the Way there is no going . . . apart from the Truth there is no living."

God says . . . Be in Christ, rest yourself.

Charles Swindoll

"I AM NOT MYSELF"

Luke 15:17

All the real argument about religion turns on the question of whether a man who was born upside down can tell when he comes right way up. The primary paradox of Christianity is that the ordinary condition of man is not his sane or sensible condition; that the normal itself is an abnormality. That is the inmost philosophy of the Fall. In Sir Oliver Lodge's interesting new Catechism, the first two questions were: "What are you?" and "What, then, is the meaning of the Fall of Man?" I remember amusing myself by writing my own answers to the questions; but I soon found that they were very broken and agnostic answers. To the question, "What are you?" I could only answer, "God knows." And to the question, "What is meant by the Fall?" I could answer with complete sincerity, "That whatever I am, I am not myself." This is the prime paradox of our religion; something that we have never in any full sense known is not only better than ourselves, but even more natural to us than ourselves. And there is really no test of this except the merely experimental one . . . the test of the padded cell and the open door. It is only since I have known orthodoxy that I have known mental emancipation. But, in conclusion, it has one special application to the ultimate idea of joy.

G.K. Chesterton

THE BEST ARGUMENT

Acts 16:25

That night I wrote in my Journal:

The best argument for Christianity is Christians: their joy, their certainty, their completeness. But the strongest argument *against* Christianity is also Christians—when they are somber and joyless, when they are self-righteous and smug in complacent consecration, when they are narrow and repressive, then Christianity dies a thousand deaths. But, though it is just to condemn some Christians for these things, perhaps, after all, it is not just though very easy to condemn Christianity itself for them.

If minds like St. Augustine's and Newman's and Lewis's could wrestle with Christianity and become fortresses of that faith, it had to be taken seriously. I writhed a bit at the thought of my easy know-nothing contempt of other years. Most of the people who reject Christianity know almost nothing of what they are rejecting: those who condemn what they do not understand are, surely, *little* men. Thank God, if there is a God, we said, that we are at least looking seriously and honestly at this thing. If our Christian friends— nuclear physicists, historians, and able scholars in other fields—can believe in Christ, if C.S. Lewis can believe in Christ, we must, at least, weigh it very seriously . . . .

We did not at all suppose that we *were* Christians, just because we were more or less nice people who vaguely believed there might be some sort of a god and had been inside a church. We were right outside of the fold. Thus we were perfectly aware that the central claim of Christianity was and always had been the same God who made the world had lived in the world and been killed by the world, and that the (claimed) proof of this was His Resurrection from the dead. This, in fact, was precisely what we, so far at least, did not believe. But we knew that it was what *had* to be believed if we were to call ourselves Christian.

Sheldon Vanauken

THE GREATEST QUESTION

Psalms 2:1-3

The greatest question of our time is not communism versus individualism, not Europe versus America, not even the East versus the West; it is whether men can live without God.

Will Durant

For it was death he now had continually on his mind. His atheism—or the fractured geometry of the imagination his atheism was a feature of—began to engender in him a mortal fear. Once, speaking of Alfred's death, I remarked to him that there was one thing I'd drawn from it all. I now was not afraid to die. My father was standing with his back to me but whirled, looked straight into my eyes and asked, "You're not? You're really not?" . . . .

For he was by then the loneliest man I ever knew. Save for these evoked reminiscences, he had shut the door on his past, seemed unable to find solace in his grandchildren, and whatever agency of a free imagination might have provided him structures of existential relief—real or illusory, what difference would it have made?—had been for fifty years forbidden to stir.

We walked on the beach. He had lost the power of easy communication and had to have a topic given him. So I chose a "topic of our walk" each day, each day another philosophy of one school or another. I didn't need to discourse myself, nor could I have. It was enough to prod him.

"Contemporary philosophers," he said, "don't treat the perennial questions. They think my ideas are blurred. They look for sharp, small answers to small questions. I have devoted my life to the wide, unfocused ones."

What does it matter, I thought at the time. Now there was only one question that weighed in the air:

Where do the dead go?

MEMOIRS OF A MODERNIST'S DAUGHTER
Eleanor Munroe

IMPORTANT LOSSES

Psalms 14:1-2

But are there any important losses to set down beside the `gains' the atheist appears to enjoy? There are. We must look at most of them more fully later, but some of them can be mentioned here.

He must give up all hope of finding any deep meaning of life. If he himself loves beauty, truth, and goodness, his own love of them are inexplicable and their origin a complete mystery. (Did matter alone produce beauty, truth, goodness . . . and his own deep care for them?) All noble men, sacrificing themselves for their ideals, are an enigma; Jesus Christ (whom the atheist can classify only as a man) is the greatest enigma of all. When the atheist is grateful, he has no one to thank. He has no hope of re-union with his dear ones beyond the grave. He misses the companionship of God in this life (life's greatest treasure, as Christians think) and may get so firmly fixed on the path which leads to outer darkness that he will miss the best in the next life as well.

W.E. Sangster

His father's suffering increased. There came before long a period of organic disintegration. His mind eroded, the higher faculties he most prized going first. And as these went, ancient forest fears and visions became real to him.

He'd shored himself on his assurance, following Locke and Hume, that gods and demons had no existence since the senses afforded no evidence of them. Now his mind released visions of a kind our ancestors may also have "seen." There were faces in the trees, figures in the window. . . .

Wasn't there some dreadful revenge being exacted here, I asked myself, by the primitive against the hyper-conscious man who all his life denied the existence of the unseen? . . . .

Now he lay open to self-examination, performing an autopsy on himself. Stripped of the repressions of a lifetime, he began exposing buried attitudes that had sucked at his roots and destroyed his peace.

MEMOIRS OF A MODERNIST'S DAUGHTER Eleanor Munroe

"I HAVE NO OTHER RESOURCE"

Isaiah 57:20-21

May 27th. As I said last time, I attempt to work according to my principles without the smallest expectations of reward, and even without using the light of conscience blindly as an infallible guide. . . . It is very difficult for anyone to work aright with no aid from religion, by his own internal guidance merely. I have tried and I may say failed. But the sad thing is that I have no other resource. I have no helpful religion. My doctrines, such as they are, help my daily life no more than a formula in Algebra. But the great inducement to a good life with me is Granny's love and the immense pain I know it gives her when I go wrong. But she must I suppose die some day and where then will be my stay? I have the very greatest fear that my life hereafter be ruined by my having lost the support of religion. I desire of all things that my religion should not spread, for I of all people ought, owing to my education and the care taken of my moral well-being, to be of all people the most moral. So I believe I might be were it not for these unhappy ideas of mine, for how easy it is when one is much tempted to convince oneself that only happiness will be produced by yielding to temptation, when according to my ideas the course one has been taught to abhor immediately becomes virtuous. If ever I shall become an utter wreck of what I hope to be I think I shall bring forward this book as an explanation.

THE AUTOBIOGRAPHY OF
BERTRAND RUSSELL

IN THE NAME OF NOTHING

Psalms 10:4

The essential amorality of all atheist doctrines is often hidden from us by an irrelevant personal argument. We see that many articulate secularists are well-meaning and law-abiding men; we see them go into righteous indignation over injustice and often devote their lives to do good works. So we conclude that "he can't be wrong whose life is in the right"—that their philosophies are just as good guides to action as Christianity. What we don't see is that they are not acting on their philosophies. They are acting, out of habit or sentiment, on an inherited Christian ethic which they still take for granted though they have rejected the creed from which it sprang. Their children will inherit somewhat less of it.

Joy Davidman

"Agnosticism," wrote Thomas Merton, "leads inevitably to moral indifference."

That is why there was something peculiarly strange and funny about the feeble efforts of the bourgeois generations of the late nineteenth and early twentieth centuries to bring up their progeny with a respect for moral and social obligations but with no belief in God. . . . "In the name of whom or what do you ask me to behave? Why should I go to the inconvenience of denying myself the satisfactions I desire in the name of some standard that exists only in your imagination? Why should I worship the fictions you have imposed on me in the name of Nothing?"

At the end of the twentieth century, Merton's words have a haunting, prophetic ring.

Philip Yancey

"THERE ARE TRAPS EVERYWHERE"

Jeremiah 5:12

While in bed, by one of those chances that can influence your whole life, he (C.S. Lewis) picked up and read a book of G.K. Chesterton's essays. You may have read some of his poems. Now, this fearless writer of the first half of this century, was a practicing and believing Christian, a devout Roman Catholic. At the same time his writing was so strong and robust, so full of vitality and often humor that Jack had to confess, `I like him for his goodness.' But he went on to say, `I felt the charm of goodness as a man feels the charm of a woman he has no intention of marrying.' He later made the humorous comment, `A young man who wishes to remain a sound Atheist cannot be too careful of his reading, for,' he added, `there are traps everywhere.'

Anne Arnott

For man has not outgrown, nor ever will, the religious necessity. There is still a God-sized vacuum in the human heart, and the return to worship is the return home. The way back to worship emphasizes the need, the *will* to believe. We almost live as if doubt and uncertainty were signs of superiority. We indicate the big man, the intellectual man, as the man who doubts. The little man is able to believe. But it is Karl Barth who tells us that unbelief in God is faith in self. Unbelief is not the sign of a giant intellect, but of a corrupted will. "He that cometh to God *must* believe that He is, and that He is a rewarder of them that diligently seek Him."

David Mckee

MY FUNDAMENTAL DILEMMA

Romans 1:19-20

My fundamental dilemma is this: I can't believe in Christ unless I have faith, but I can't have faith unless I believe in Christ. This is `the leap.' If to *be* a Christian is to have faith (and clearly it is), I can put it thus: I must accept Christ to become a Christian, but I must *be* a Christian to accept Him. I don't have faith and I don't as yet believe; but everyone seems to say: `You must have faith to believe.' Where do I get it? Or will you tell me something different? Is there a proof? Can Reason carry one over the gulf . . . without faith?

Why does God expect so much of us? Why does he require this effort to believe? If He made it clear that He is—as clear as a sunrise or a rock or a baby's cry—wouldn't we be right joyous to choose Him and His Law? Why should the right exercise of our free will contain this fear of intellectual dishonesty?

Sheldon Vanauken

There is no hope for us unless God in His kindness and grace and love chooses to *reveal Himself.* Now the full position for which we stand is that God *has* definitely done just this. . . . Let me put it in the words of Blaise Pascal: `The supreme achievement of reason is to bring us to see that there is a limit to reason.' There, it seems to me, is the starting point . . .   Now as soon as we, as evangelical Christians, approach this great subject or revelation, we come immediately to the great, the central fact of the Lord Jesus Christ. God has revealed Himself in other ways. He has revealed Himself in nature, and the apostle Paul argues in Romans (1:19ff) that we are without excuse if we do not see Him there. Yet, there we do not see God as He really is because of our sin. The revelation is there, but we do not see it. God has also revealed Himself in history. Further, God has revealed Himself to the Old Testament fathers in various ways. But, as evangelical Christians, we start with the great central fact of the Lord Jesus Christ. The whole Bible is really about *Him.*

D. Martyn Lloyd-Jones

"FAITH MUST PRECEDE"

Hebrews 11:6

Augustine could be caught in contradictions and absurdities, even in morbid cruelties of thought; but he could not be overcome, because in the end his own soul's adventures, and the passion of his nature, not any chain of reasoning, molded his theology. He knew the weakness of the intellect; it was the individual's brief experience sitting in reckless judgment upon the experience of the race; and how could forty years understand forty centuries? "Dispute not by excited argument," he wrote to a friend, "those things which you do not yet comprehend, or those which in the Scriptures appear . . . to be incongruous and contradictory; meekly defer the day of your understanding." Faith must precede understanding. "Seek not to understand that you may believe, but believe that you may understand—*crede ut intelligas*. The authority of the Scriptures is higher than all the efforts of the human intelligence."

Will Durant

I felt that the Christian faith proceeding was more unassuming and honest, in that she required to be believed things not demonstrated (whether it was that they could in themselves be demonstrated but not to certain persons, or could not at all be); whereas among the Manichees our credulity was mocked by a promise of certain knowledge, and then so many most fabulous and absurd things were imposed to be believed, because they could not be demonstrated. Then Thou, O Lord, little by little with most tender and most merciful hand, touching and composing my heart, didst persuade me— considering what innumerable things I believed, which I saw not, nor was present while they were done, as so many things in secular history, so many reports of places and of cities, which I had not seen. . . . unless we should believe, we should do nothing at all in this life; lastly, with how unshaken an assurance I believed of what parents I was born, which I could not know.

*THE CONFESSIONS OF
ST. AUGUSTINE*

A PROVER OF GOD

Psalm 96:8

I promise to fulfill my function as a "prover of God." That is every Christian's function, regardless of his occupation or spiritual gift. A prover of God brings God out of the Bible and makes Him alive today.

God loves to be proved. "Prove me *now*" (Malachi 3:10, KJV, italics added). "Ask a sign for yourself from the LORD" (Isaiah 7:11). He knows that each generation is born skeptical. The Bible must be reborn to every generation. God must break out of print into live action and re-create Bible scenes and activities. Just as God wrote the Bible, so He must repeat the Bible in us. That is why He needs Abrahams, Gideons, Davids, and Pauls today. In short, He needs God-provers.

George Mueller said he began his orphan home in Bristol for one purpose, "To prove God in our day as formerly." Exactly! So with us.

Proving God, however, is not easy. It involves the impossible. You do not prove God when you pray for a healing that will occur naturally. Or when you ask God for $10,000 when you already have $20,000 in the bank. Proving God is asking Him to cure the *incurable*. It is asking Him to give you $10,000 when you have nothing.

But who is sufficient for those heroics? Isn't life fairly humdrum and prosaic? Doesn't God come in the "still small voice" (I Kings 19:12, KJV)?

If so, there is something wrong with our faith. If Satan is still alive, if sin is still man's habit, and if disease, hunger, and death still stalk, then God must find "provers." He needs the ordinary man who has extraordinary faith.

The question is, am I willing to risk embarrassment and failure to be a prover of God? That is the nub of it all—to dare God and risk everything on His simple Word. Provers of God are always winners with God.

W. Glyn Evans

SHOPWORN FAITH

Ephesians 4:11-16

Helen Barrett Montgomery, who was the first woman to translate the New Testament from the Greek and the first woman to serve as the head of a major Protestant denomination (American Baptist), was a well-known missions and ecumenical leader of the early twentieth century. She wrote books and lectured on the subject of foreign missions, pleading for the cause which was very dear to her.

During her youth and early years at Wellesley College, she was a doctrinaire Baptist, and as such refused to join in fellowship with her classmates from other denominations. "Stiff little Baptist that I was," she wrote, "I used to walk to Natick and take communion in the church there." She wrote home lamenting her lonely course of action: "Oh, you don't know how it seems to feel that you are an outsider, that you are regarded as narrow, bigoted."

As time went on, however, Helen slowly began to recognize that there was a better path to follow. She began to see the value of other points of view and the futility of arguing over minor points of doctrine. She expressed her feelings on this after she had been in the company of a dogmatic Baptist who was convinced he was orthodox on every doctrinal point.

In reflecting on him, she was philosophical about her own religion: "I tell you this Christian faith of ours is all shopworn being handled over the counter and mussed and creased and discussed. We want to get it off the counter and cut into coats to over the naked. My own soul is sick with theory—I'm getting so I don't care how or when or where or whether the Pentateuch wrote Moses or Moses, the Pentateuch. There is good news, the gospel, the love of God, the life of Jesus, and here am I, sinful and selfish and blind as a bat—for the secret of the Lord is with them that fear him. I know enough things now to make me a saint if I lived 'em. I'm going to live more and talk less."

Ruth Tucker

THE UNANSWERABLE ARGUMENT

John 9:25

He refused to be intimidated or abashed. `All I know is this: once I was blind, now I can see.' That was as much as to say—You can argue till doomsday that nothing has happened. You can use all the syllogisms of your logic to demonstrate that the alleged power of Jesus is myth and moonshine and delusion. You can prove to your own satisfaction that I am nothing but the pathetic victim of an unintelligent hallucination. Talk of intelligence? It is you who are unintelligent ones! Do you not know the difference between light and darkness? All your fine arguments are wrecked on this: `One thing I know, that whereas I was blind now I see!'

It is of course the unanswerable argument. If the Christian case were simply based on theory, it could doubtless by theory be demolished. If it were just a psychological phenomenon, the psychologists could tear it to shreds. But because it is based on actual events and history, on solid facts—lives redeemed, men made new, blindness turned to seeing—because of that, there is nothing that can shake it: it stands in its own right. *James S. Stewart*

Grace is the overflowing, immeasurable favor of God; God cannot withhold; the only thing that keeps back His grace and favor is our sin and perversity.— *"Noah walked with God."* To walk with God means the perpetual realization of the nature of faith, viz., that it must be tried or it is mere fancy; faith un-tried has no character-value for the individual. There is nothing akin to faith in the natural world; defiant pluck and courage is not faith; it is the *trial* of faith that is "much more precious than gold," and the trial of faith is never without the essentials of temptation. It is to be questioned whether any child of God ever gets through the trial of his faith without at some stage being horror-stricken; what God does comes as a stinging blow, and he feels the suffering is not deserved; yet, like Job, he will neither listen to nor tell lies about God. Spiritual character is only made by standing loyal to God's character no matter what.
Oswald Chambers

THE BANK OF FAITH

John 20:29

Seeing is never believing; we interpret what we see in the light of what we believe. Faith is confidence in God before you see God emerging, therefore the nature of faith is that it must be tried. To say "Oh yes, I believe God will triumph" may be so much credence smeared over with religious phraseology; but when you are up against things it is quite another matter to say, "I believe God will win through." The trial of our faith gives us a good banking account in the heavenly places, and when the next trial comes our wealth there will tide us over. If we have confidence in God beyond the actual earthly horizons, we shall see the lie at the heart of the fear, and our faith will win through in every detail. Jesus said that men ought always to pray and not 'cave in'—"Don't look at the immediate horizon and don't take the facts you see and say they are actuality; the Reality lies behind with God."

Oswald Chambers

The intellect knoweth that it is ignorant of Thee because it knoweth Thou canst not be known, unless the unknowable could be known, and the invisible beheld, and the inaccessible attained. . . .

If anyone should set forth any concept by which Thou canst be conceived, I know that that concept is not a concept of Thee. . . . So too, if any were to tell of the understanding of Thee, wishing to supply a means whereby Thou mightiest be understood, this man is yet far from Thee . . . forasmuch as Thou art absolute above all the concepts which any man can frame.

Nicolas of Cusa

THREE THINGS

Romans 10:9-10

"You will observe," I said, "that according to this Scripture there are *two* things which a man must *believe* to be a Christian, and *one* thing which he must *do*. The first premise that you must accept is that Jesus Christ was and is the Son of God. Do you believe that?"

The professor nodded, and said, "I do. I have never seen any proof against it, and certainly we cannot explain Him any other way. Yes, I can say that I do believe that Jesus was the Son of God."

"Good!" I answered. "Now the second thing you have to believe is that Jesus died for our sins according to the Scripture, and rose again from the dead to be our Savior. Do you believe that?"

"Certainly," he replied. "I am not completely ignorant of the historical facts of the death and resurrection of Jesus—any educated person ought to believe that!"

"All right," I continued. "You believe the two essentials, that Christ, the Son of God, died and rose to save sinners. That's all you have to *believe* to be saved, now here is the one thing you have to *do*. Will you, here and now, accept Christ as your personal Savior and commit your life to Him?"

I held our my hand and the professor quickly grasped it. "I will," he said, "and I do."

Harry Rimmer

IT CAN PROVE ITSELF

Psalm 19:1-4

Earlier we came to the conclusion that God is, that in character He is like Christ, and that this is the highest and noblest—and to me the ultimate— conception of God. If I cannot think of God in these terms, I cannot think of Him in any terms. If He is not like Christ, I'm not interested. It is this—or nothing.

Can I prove this to you? No! But better, it can prove itself to you. As you follow through these pages you will come, I trust, not to a faith which you will hold, but to a faith which will hold you. It will be a faith that will hold not only your mind but also your emotion and your will. It will hold the total *you*. For this is not only an intellectual or an emotional or a volitional quest; it is a life quest. The whole person is involved—you and all your relationships.

The man who wants this proved to him is like a man who stands with his back to the sunset. I describe its breathtaking beauty. He says, "I don't believe it. Prove it to me." I reply, "I can't prove it to you. But turn around and look at it; it will prove itself to you." He replies, "I won't. Prove it to me." Is he fair? I hold a rose in my hand and describe the sweetness of its fragrance to him. He closes his nostrils and says, "I don't believe it. Prove it to me." "I can't," I reply, "but open your nostrils , and it will prove itself to you."

You are going to be fair to God, to life, and to yourself in this quest, aren't you? You are going to let down all your barriers of prejudice, of self-defense, of fear, and make this a life adventure, a life quest. You are going to find God, life, yourself. You are going to put your feet upon the Way. And the moment you do, something within you will whisper, "This is it. You've struck it—at last." And the whisper will be more certain than certainty, more real than reality. For it will not be a bare certainty or reality—it will be warm and tender and satisfying to the depths. It will satisfy the mind, appeal to the emotion, commit the will. It will have *you*.

E. Stanley Jones

THE MIND IS AT REST

John 6:1-9

Comfort came through the story of the feeding of the five thousand. `When Jesus then lifted up His eyes and saw a great multitude come unto Him, He saith unto Philip, Whence shall we buy bread that these may eat?'

`We' was the first word of reassurance here. *We,* not *you.* Then the one hundred pennyworth of bread, something between six and seven pounds, was just about the sum I had had to send for that child. The remote became near as I thought of it. What are years to the King of Eternity?

But between verses 6 and 7 occurs, Westcott tells us, a break filled by the day's work. Can I in this new work go on all day sure that in the evening help will come?

Then as never again for fifteen years I was allowed to taste of the cup which would be poured out for me if it did not come. Allan Gardiner for some hidden, good purpose was allowed to starve to death. Therefore such an issue could not be regarded as impossible. The children . . . I need not track in writing the end of that thought. But I did that day tread every foot of it in imagination and came to this: Suppose the children die, and we all (of course) die with them, and the Christian world cries shame on the one responsible, what will it matter after all? The children will be in heaven and is that not better than the temple?

But it did seem more likely to be to His glory that the little ones should live and be fed, just as the five thousand and their women and children were fed. It would be much more like Him. Only, one never can get past the `But if not' of the three and the fiery furnace. And once the thing is faced it is faced for ever. The mind is at rest, there is no looking back, and no care.

Amy Carmichael

FAITHFUL ALWAYS INVOLVES RISK

Hebrews 11:8-10

Thomas Carlyle once said, "The final question which each of us is compelled to answer is, 'Wilt thou be a hero or a coward?'" This question constantly confronts us in one form or another. *Faith is always confronted with a choice.* We can choose either the high road or the low road. The choice for these young men was no easy one, nor will it be for us. Often it is an agonizing experience. Think of choosing between worshipping the king's image or being incinerated in the king's inferno! Nebuchanezzar did not demand that they deny their faith, only that they bow to his image. In the days of the early church, the mere offering of a pinch of incense to the emperor would have spared many a martyr from being thrown to the lions. Faith always chooses the highest and best even although it be the most costly.

Faith always involves a risk. If there is no risk involved, no faith is necessary. If we can see the path ahead, we are walking by sight. What constituted Abraham the father of the faithful? The key to his whole life of faith is seen at its beginning. "Abraham went out, *not knowing whither* he went." He was willing to risk all on God. We exercise faith only when the way ahead is not clear, when we are so placed that we have no alternative if God lets us down. Not everyone enjoys taking such risks. Many who are bold as lions in taking physical risks are strangely timorous when it comes to taking a step of faith. We like to play safe, to have our plans cut and dried, to have an alternative ready. There is always a risk in the pathway of faith.

J. Oswald Sanders

TO LIVE TO GOD IN SECRET

Hebrews 11:38

The greatest Saints avoided the society of men, when they could conveniently, and did rather choose to live to God in secret.

One said, "As oft as I have been among men, I returned home less a man than I was before."

And this we find true, when we talk long together. It is easier not to speak at all, than not to exceed in speech.

It is easier for a man to lie hid at home, than to be able sufficiently to watch over himself abroad.

He therefore that intends to attain to the more inward and spiritual things of religion, must with Jesus depart from the multitude and press of people!

No man doth safely appear abroad, but he who can abide at home.

No man doth safely rule, but he that is glad to be ruled.

No man doth safely rule, but he that learned gladly to obey.

No man rejoiceth safely, unless he hath within him the testimony of a good conscience.

And yet always the security of the Saints was full of the fear of God.

Neither were they the less anxious and humbler in themselves, for that they shone outwardly with grace and great virtues.

But the security of bad men ariseth from pride and presumption, and in the end it deceiveth them.

Thomas a Kempis

VERY THIN WIRES

John 14:27

I recall a phrase from one of Alexander Whyte's works. It came to mind early this morning. The old biographer wrote of our tendency

" . . . *to hang very heavy weights on very thin wires.* "
We really do. We hang the very heavy weight of our happiness on the very thin wire of our health. High-risk investment! People I know who have that wide, vertical, zipper-like scar down the middle of their chests are living proof that we all are only a pulse beat this side away from that side. Something as tiny as a blood clot, smaller, much smaller than a pea, if lodged in the wrong place, can suddenly turn our speech to a slur and reduce our steps to a shuffle . . . if that.

Two doors away from our home an entire family has been transformed from a life of activity, laughter, and hope to a quiet, introspective group of serious-looking, almost-out-of-touch people. Their only son—a brilliant, alive, bright collegian with a "sky's the limit" promising future—had a head-on collision with a semi.

Snap went the wire. Totaled car. Almost totaled driver. Toppled family. The boy, quasi-conscious, hardly resembles the young man who used to catch my passes on Thanksgiving afternoon and light fireworks with our Curt every Fourth of July. He may never walk again. Or talk. Or think clearly. . . .

We hang the very heavy weight of our peace on the very thin wire of our possessions. We know better, but we still do it. Materialistic to the core, we convince ourselves that life *does* consist in the abundance of things we possess. . . .

Enter brushland fires on the furious wings of Santa Ana winds. Exit Southern California homes and appliances and furniture and beds to sleep in and cars to drive and peace. *Snap goes the wire* when something as heavy as peace is so inseparably linked to something as thin as our possessions.

Charles Swindoll

TARRY TILL IT COMES

Romans 2:10

Whenever you obey God, His seal is always that of peace, the witness of an unfathomable peace, which is not natural, but the peace of Jesus. Whenever peace does not come, tarry till it does or find out the reason why it does not. If you are acting on an impulse, or from a sense of the heroic, the peace of Jesus will not witness; there is no simplicity or confidence in God, because the spirit of simplicity is born of the Holy Ghost, not of your decisions. Every decision brings a reaction of simplicity.

My questions come whenever I cease to obey. When I have obeyed God, the problems never come between me and God; they come as probes to keep the mind going on with amazement at the revelation of God. Any problem that comes between God and myself springs out of disobedience; any problem, and there are many, that is alongside me while I obey God, increases my ecstatic delight, because I know that my Father knows, and I am going to watch and see how He unravels this thing.

Oswald Chambers

This peace is in my case more than a delightful privilege, it is a necessity. I could not possibly get through the work I have to do without the peace of God which passeth all understanding, keeping my heart and mind.

Are you in a hurry, flurried, distressed? Look up, see the Man in the Glory. Let the face of Jesus shine upon you—the face of the Lord Jesus Christ. Is He worried, troubled, distressed? There is no wrinkle on His brow, no least shade of anxiety. Yet the affairs are His as much as yours.

Hudson Taylor

"YOU MAKE IT BY TAKING IT"

Matthew 11:28-30

When hostilities cease in the Second World War—the hour for which multitudes long and pray—it will seem like paradise—for a month or two. Then the heart will tell its own tale. Inward dissatisfaction will wake again, and every honest heart which is strange to Christ will say, "This is not peace."

One's claim to it is established by the surrender of the heart.

Foolish as the statement may seem, anyone who deeply desired it could make peace *now*. You make it by taking it. Inward peace is not made with Germany; it is made with ourselves and the world, and ultimately, with God. If peace were dependent on perfect circumstances, the very dream of it must be abandoned at once so far as this world is concerned. Hostilities will cease, but there is still cancer, bereavement, or human liability to fatal accident, the hurt of waning powers. . . . A treaty can banish bombs, but not these tragic possibilities which are woven into the very fabric of our life and which will always prevent the perfection of conditions.

W.E. Sangster

William Hendriksen says that the Syriac New Testament translates the word *gentle* as "restful" . . . and you shall find *rest* for yourselves." Christ's whole demeanor was such that people were often restful in his presence. This effect is another outworking of the grace of gentleness. People are at rest, or at ease, around the Christian who is truly gentle.

Jerry Bridges

A FENCE CRAWLER

I Timothy 6:6

But in spite of all these attractive attributes this sheep had one pronounced fault. She was restless—discontented—a fence crawler.

So much so that I came to call her "Mrs. Gad-about."

This one ewe produced more problems for me than almost all the rest of the flock combined.

No matter what field or pasture the sheep were in, she would search all along the fences or shoreline (we lived by the sea) looking for a loophole she could crawl through and start to feed on the other side.

It was not that she lacked pasturage. My fields were my joy and delight. No sheep in the district had better grazing.

With "Mrs. Gad-about" it was an ingrained habit. She was simply never contented with things as they were. Often when she had forced her way through some such spot in a fence or found a way around the end of the wire at low tide on the beaches, she would end up feeding on bare, brown, burned-up pasturage of a most inferior sort.

But she never learned her lesson and continued to fence crawl time after time.

Now it would have been bad enough if she was the only one who did this. It was a sufficient problem to find her and bring her back. But the further point was that she taught her lambs the same tricks. They simply followed her example and soon were as skilled at escaping as their mother.

Even worse, however, was the example she set the other sheep.

Philip Keller

ACCEPT THE UNIVERSE

Hebrews 12:7-8

When Carlyle heard that Margaret Fuller had decided to "accept the universe" he roared with laughter. "Well, she'd better!" he shouted good-naturedly. And she had. And so had we.

This idea was once expressed better by a simple-hearted man who was asked how he managed to live in such a state of constant tranquility even though surrounded by circumstances anything but pleasant. His answer was as profound as it was simple: "I have learned," he said, "to cooperate with the inevitable."

The idea here set forth is so wise and practical that it is hard to see how we Christians have managed to overlook it so completely in our everyday living. That we do overlook it is shown by our conduct and conversation. Some of us "kick against the pricks" for a lifetime, all the while believing that we are surrendered to the will of God.

A.W. Tozer

I went to see friends when visiting in their city. At that time one had died, another was in hospital and the third had also begun to show signs of decline. In talking with them and endeavoring to sympathize with them in their sorrow, I found them radiant and victorious.

"It was very difficult to accept this situation at first, but we at last learned that `in acceptance lies peace.' Once we accepted this from the Lord, we experienced peace of heart," said the mother. "And we have learned something else. When once you have fully accepted the discipline of God, *it cannot hurt you any more.*"

Have we yet learned this lesson? The shoulder of the ox is galled only when it resists the yoke.

J. Oswald Sanders

EVEN PAUL HAD TO LEARN

Philippians 4:11-13

Our interest is awakened by words which Paul wrote quite late in his splendid life. "I have learned," declared Paul to the Church at Philippi, "in whatsoever state I am, therewith to be content." A dear friend, wasted by great and long suffering commented smilingly as I read that passage to him. "You see, even Paul had to learn contentment." He was quite right. The ardent, sensitive, energetic, adventurous, combative Paul was not restful by nature. He found it just as difficult as we do, perhaps even more difficult, to live serenely. Yet, in all honesty he made the claim to have achieved a contented spirit even though he wrote from prison with a shackle on his wrist. How often have I looked at a great railway engine throbbing with suppressed power as it waited to commence its long journey, and asked myself whether I had equal efficiency for my own day's task? When we have a disabling sense of inadequacy there is necessarily an absence of repose. Peace is largely a matter of reserves.

Paul faced life with an air of sublime confidence because he was conscious of possessing reserves adequate for meeting any situation whatsoever.

G.H. Morling

Heaven is to be at peace with things.
George Santayana

"IF YOU ARE QUIET"

Psalm 131:2

An old man sat one evening by his door;
His face was tranquil, in his eyes was peace,
His hands were still, his long life work was done,
He had a look about him of release.

And I, who needed much to learn the things
That he had learned, sat down beside him there
On the low doorstep in the scented dusk;
He smiled his gentle smile, he touched my hair,
He said: "My child, I too, was restless once;
I, too, was hurt by life, and blind and dumb
I groped my way; then a wise one said these words:
`If you are quiet, so will help come.'
Twas an old folk saying from an old loved land.
I listened to its teaching, listened long,
And learned its secret: He who trusts in God,
And who goes quietly, he will grow strong.

Grace Noll Crowell

The Quakers practice a method of finding quietness in the midst of turmoil. They call it centering. In your pain you can center down into yourself and insist on times of deep quiet in which you surrender your inner self to God. The contemplatives of the Middle Ages called this *recollection*. It is a time to become still, to enter a recreating silence, to let the fragmentation of your mind be centered on God. This may seem incongruous to your life demands, to the conflict you have passed through. And you may find yourself running from the quiet and from what you will find deep inside you.

Carole S. Streeter

THE GREAT PROBLEM OF LIFE

Psalm 3:5

Take the third and fourth Psalms, for instance. How perfectly they put it all. The great problem in life is, in a sense, how to lay oneself down to rest and to sleep. 'I laid me down and slept,' said the Psalmist. Anybody can lie down, but the question is can you sleep? The Psalmist describes himself surrounded by enemies and by difficulties and trials, and his mighty testimony is that in spite of that, because of his trust in the Lord, he both laid him down and slept, and he awaked safe and sound in the morning. Why? Because the Lord was with him and looking after him.

D. Martyn Lloyd-Jones

In order to have the peace of God it is required: first, that nothing is as important to you as the grace of God, and that you do not become satisfied until you have got assurance of that. Secondly, you need to learn to despair about yourself, that is, to despair of all undertakings, all doings and becomings, and that, just as you are, still an unworthy, lost sinner, you seek all your salvation in Christ alone. Thirdly, it is essential that you do not wait for the assurance in your feelings, or for an inner reply in your heart, but that you take the reply of God where He gives it—in the Word, only in the Word. If only a soul comes so far as to seek this above all, and sighs to himself; "Oh, if I could only have the grace of God, then I would not wish anything higher for myself on earth! Nor would I mind about anything I might suffer. Oh, if I could only believe in Christ alone and be found in Him! If I were only sure that His merits belong to me! And I want to believe in the Word. I do not want to wait for feelings. If I could only believe," and so on, then faith has surely already been kindled. And that soul will surely not remain without the assurance of grace. He *will* have peace. God will see to that.

C.O. Rosenius

THE SWEETEST PART

Hebrews 4:1-3

Said Hudson Taylor in a letter to his sister:

"The sweetest part, if one may speak of one part being sweeter than another, is the *rest* which full identification with Christ brings. I am no longer anxious about anything, as I realize this; for *He*, I know is able to carry out *His Will*, and His will is mine. It makes no matter where He places me, or how. That is rather for Him to consider than for me; for in the easiest positions He must give me His grace, and in the most difficult His grace is sufficient. It little matters to my servant whether I send him to buy a few cash worth of things, or the most expensive articles. In either case he looks to me for the money, and brings me his purchases. So, if God place me in great perplexity, must He not give me much guidance; in position of great difficulty, much grace; in circumstances of great pressure and trial, much strength? No fear that His resources will be unequal to the emergency! And His resources are mine, for He is mine, and is with me and dwells in me. All this springs from the believer's oneness with Christ. And since Christ has thus dwelt in my heart by faith, how happy I have been ! I wish I could tell you, instead of writing about it. . . ."

Some around him could hardly understand this joy and rest, especially when fellow-workers were in danger. A budget of letters arriving on one occasion, as Mr. Nicoll relates, brought news of serious rioting in two different stations. Standing at his desk to read them, Mr. Taylor mentioned what was happening and that immediate help was necessary. Feeling that he might wish to be alone, the younger man was about to withdraw, when, to his surprise, someone began to whistle. It was the soft refrain of the well-loved hymn: "Jesus, I am resting, in the joy of what Thou art. . . ."

Turning back, Mr. Nicoll could not help exclaiming, "How can you whistle, when our friends are in such danger!"

"Would you have me anxious and troubled?" was the long-remembered answer. "That would not help them, and would certainly incapacitate me for my work. I have just to roll the burden on the Lord."

Elizabeth Skoglund

YOU CANNOT REVERSE THE ORDER

Colossians 1:20

Whatever I desire or can imagine for my comfort, I look for it hereafter. For if I might alone have all the comforts of the world and were able to enjoy all the delights thereof (Matt. 16:26), it is certain that they could not long endure.

You cannot be fully comforted (Ps. 77:1-2), nor have perfect refreshment, except in God, the Comforter of the poor and Patron of the humble. Wait a little while, O my soul, wait for the divine promise, and you shall have abundance of all good things in Heaven.

If you desire inordinately the things that are present, you shall lose those which are heavenly and eternal. Let temporal things be used, but things eternal desired.

You cannot be satisfied with any temporal good, because you were not created to enjoy these alone.

Thomas a Kempis

Because you now have peace *with* God, you can experience the fathomless peace *of* God. You cannot reverse the order. As long as one is God's enemy, enduring peace is unattainable. But once a person looks to the Cross and receives its merits by faith, the peace of God is forever his.

When Christ returns to establish his kingdom on earth, peace will reign universally. Until then, the Christian has the awesome privilege of experience and extending the peace of Christ. Still more, he has entered into a personal relationship with Christ marked by a supernatural peace the world cannot duplicate. The right foundation has been laid. Whatever shakes your life may temporarily unsettle you, but it can never disturb your everlasting relationship with the Prince of Peace.

Charles Stanley

TWO OVERWHELMING PROBLEMS

Genesis 1:1

The impersonal beginning, the notion that everything began with an impersonal something, is the consensus of the Western world in the twentieth century. . . .

An impersonal beginning, however, raises two overwhelming problems which neither the East nor modern man has come anywhere near solving. First, there is no real explanation for the fact that the external world not only exists but has a specific form. Despite its frequent attempt to reduce the concept of the personal to the area of chemical or psychological conditioning, scientific study demonstrates that the universe has an express form. One can go from particulars to a greater unity, from the lesser laws to more and more general laws or super-laws. In other words, as I look at the Being which is the external universe, it is obviously not just a handful of pebbles thrown out there. What is there has form. If we assert the existence of the impersonal as the beginning of the universe, we simply have no explanation for this kind of situation.

Second, and more important, if we begin with an impersonal universe, there is no explanation of personality. In a very real sense the question of questions for all generations—but overwhelmingly so for modern man—is "Who am I?" For when I look at the "I" that is me and then look around to those who face me and are also men, one thing is immediately obvious: Man has a mannishness. You find it wherever you find man—not only in the men who live today, but in the artifacts of history. The assumption of an impersonal beginning can never adequately explain the personal beings we see around us, and when men try to explain man on the basis of an original impersonal, man soon disappears.

Francis Schaeffer

THE EERIE EXACTITUDE

Psalm 8:1-9

And then came an experience impossible to describe. It was as if I had been blundering about since my birth with two huge and unmanageable machines, of different shapes and without apparent connection—the world and the Christian tradition. I had found this hole in the world: the fact that one must somehow find a way of loving the world without trusting it; somehow one must love the world without being worldly, I found this projecting feature of Christian theology like a sort of hard spike, the dogmatic insistence that God was personal and had made a world separate from Himself. The spike of dogma fitted exactly into the hole in the world—it had evidently been meant to go there—and then the strange thing began to happen. When once these two parts of the two machines had come together, one after another, all the other parts fitted and fell in with an eerie exactitude. I could hear bolt after bolt over all the machinery falling into its place with a kind of click of relief. Having got one part right, all other parts were repeating that rectitude, as clock after clock strikes noon. Instinct after instinct was answered by doctrine after doctrine. Or, to vary the metaphor, I was like one who had advanced into a hostile country to take one high fortress. And when that fort had fallen the whole country surrendered and turned solid behind me. The whole land was lit up, as it were, back to the first fields of my childhood. All those blind fancies of boyhood became suddenly transparent and sane. I was right when I felt that roses were red by some sort of choice: it was the divine choice. I was right when I felt that I would almost rather say that grass was the wrong color than say it must by necessity have been that color: it might verily have been any other.

G.K. Chesterton

IRRETRIEVABLY GOOD

Genesis 1:31

It is a primordially good world that God creates; only later is it to become distorted by the companionate wills that God permits. Doubtless the world has its dark corners and cruel characters. Ever present is the potential for destructiveness, loss and distortion. It contains people like you and me. But if we could see it as a whole as God sees it, we would see the cosmos as an unimaginably good complexity. God pronounced it good at the outset. It was not Adam or Job or Judas who said of the whole: "It is good" (Gen. 1:4,12,18). God did.

This is a watershed for all Jewish and Christian views of the world. Any world not created good is not God's world. Any bad world, irretrievably evil, is not the Jewish-Christian idea of God's world. Judaism and Christianity have had to fight steadily against alternative pantheistic or dualistic views of the world.

In view of the obvious troubles of human history, some have speculated that there must have been some devilishly evil controlling principle from the beginning in the world, against which the good must struggle ambiguously from beginning to end. Hebraic religion did not characteristically think of God as creating an intrinsically evil or unalterably alien world. To be sure, the world was in due course permitted to fall through the abuse of (primordially good) freedom into something worse than earlier permitted. But even in its worst moments, in its most tragically fallen state, its most wretched condition, something about the world is and remains good. An evil can only emerge out of some good. . . .

Humanity is given dominion and stewardship over the earth. The world, according to the Genesis account, is not given purposelessly, without awareness of potentially harmful contingencies, or without a redemptive plan in mind. The stewardship of creation was entrusted, according to Hebraic religion, to one particular part of it—humanity. "You shall have dominion" (cf. Gen. 1:26, 28) implies: "Take care of it. God entrusts the world to your care."

Thomas C. Oden

"SORRY, I CANNOT USE YOU"

Psalm 51:7-12

Again we must look at the naturalness of the supernatural and the supernaturalness of the natural.

Jesus said, "If anyone does not remain in me, he is thrown aside" (John 15:6, Moffatt). That is an amazing statement: "If you do not remain in me, then life throws you aside." Life says, "Sorry, I cannot use you. You don't fit." Right now before our very eyes that inevitable throwing aside is going on; those who live in hate, selfishness, fear are inevitably thrown aside as unusable. Is that arbitrary? Oh no; the person who holds these things within him becomes unfit. The rest of the verse says, "He withers." Cut off from the source of his true life, he withers, becomes unfit for use. On the other hand, when you remain in Him, you are full of life and life giving.

Again, Jesus says, "He who does not gather with me scatters" (Matt. 12:30, Moffatt). Life is scattered, goes to pieces, breaks down if it is not held together by Christ. On the contrary, he who gathers with Christ gathers up the forces of his own soul into a living unity. He is put together into harmony. "Do not be senseless, but understand what is the Lord's will" (Eph. 5:17, Moffatt). If you know God's will, you have sense; if you don't, you are senseless.

There is a story of a child who couldn't get the jigsaw puzzle of the map of the world together and was well nigh in despair until she looked on the other side of the pieces and found they made a picture of Christ. When she put Him together, then the world on the other side came out all right. Get Christ right in your life, and then all of life will come out with it. For Christ and life are one.

E. Stanley Jones

"SUPPOSE WE HAVE ONLY DREAMED"

Acts 17:24-28

The pain itself made Puddleglum's head for a moment perfectly clear and he knew exactly what he really thought. There is nothing like a good shock of pain for dissolving certain kinds of magic.

'One word, Ma'am,' he said, coming back from the fire, limping because of the pain. 'One word. All you've been saying is quite right, I shouldn't wonder. I'm a chap who always liked to know the worst and then put the best face I can on it. So I won't deny any of what you said. But there's one thing more to be said, even so. Suppose we *have* only dreamed, or made up, all those things—trees and grass and sun and moon and stars and Aslan himself. Suppose we have. Then all I can say is that, in that case, the made-up things seem a good deal more important than the real ones. Suppose this black pit of a kingdom of yours *is* the only world. Well, it strikes me as a pretty poor one. And that's a funny thing, when you come to think of it. We're just babies making up a game, if you're right. But four babies playing a game can make a play-world which licks your real world hollow. That's why I'm going to stand by the play-world. I'm on Aslan's side even if there isn't any Aslan to lead it. I'm going to live as like a Narnian as I can even if there isn't any Narnia. So, thanking you kindly for our supper, if these two gentlemen and the young lady are ready, we're leaving your court at once and setting out in the dark to spend our lives looking for Overland. Not that our lives will be very long, I should think; but that's small loss if the world's as dull a place as you say.'

C.S. Lewis

"MY NAME IS RELIGION"

James 1:26-27

My name is Religion. I am the offspring of Truth and Love, and the parent of Benevolence, Hope, and Joy. That monster from whose power I have freed you is called Superstition; she is the child of Discontent, and her followers are Fear and Sorrow. Thus different as we are, she has often the insolence to assume my name and character, and seduces unhappy mortals to think us the same, till she at length drives them to the borders of despair, that dreadful abyss into which you were just to sink.

Look round and survey the various beauties of the globe, which Heaven has destined for the seat of the human race, and consider whether a world thus exquisitely framed could be meant for the abode of misery and pain. For what end has the lavish hand of Providence diffused such innumerable objects of delight, but that all might rejoice in the privilege of existence, and be filled with gratitude to the beneficent Author of it? Thus to enjoy the blessings he has sent is virtue and obedience; and to reject them, merely as means of pleasure, is pitiable ignorance or absurd perverseness. Infinite goodness is the source of created existence; the proper tendency of every rational being, from the highest order of raptured seraphs to the meanest rank of men, is to rise incessantly from lower degrees of happiness to higher. They have each faculties assigned them for various orders of delights.

Samuel Johnson

If the whole universe has no meaning, we should never have found it has no meaning: just as, if there were no light in the universe and therefore no creatures with eyes, we should never know it was dark. *Dark* would be without meaning. Our looking for real meaning in the universe is one of the facts of nature that must be taken into account!

Kathryn Ann Lindskoog

HOW TO TAKE A WALK

Psalm 104:1-5

A French author has advanced this seeming paradox, *very few men know how to take a walk;* and indeed it is true, that few know how to take a walk with a prospect of any other pleasure than the same company would have afforded them at home.

There are animals that borrow their color from the neighboring body, and consequently vary their hue as they happen to change their place. In like manner, it ought to be the endeavor of every man to derive his reflections from the objects about him: for it is to no purpose that he alters his position, if his attention continues fixed to the same point. The mind should be kept open to the access of every new idea, and so far disengaged from the predominance of particular thoughts as easily to accommodate itself to occasional entertainment.

A man that has formed this habit of turning every new object to his entertainment, finds in the productions of nature an inexhaustible stock of materials upon which he can employ himself without any temptations to envy or malevolence, faults, perhaps, seldom totally avoided by those whose judgment is much exercised upon the works of art. He has always a certain prospect of discovering new reasons for adoring the sovereign Author of the universe, and probable hopes of making some discovery of benefit to others, or of profit to himself. There is no doubt but many vegetables and animals have qualities that might be of great use, to the knowledge of which there is not required much force of penetration or fatigue of study, but only frequent experiments and close attention. What is said by the chemists of their darling mercury is perhaps true of everybody through the whole creation, that if a thousand lives should be spent upon it, all its properties would not be found out.

Samuel Johnson

A RELATIVELY SUCCESSFUL MAN

Ecclesiastes 1:16-17

I suppose I regard myself, or pass for being, a relatively successful man. People occasionally stare at me in the streets—that's fame. I can fairly easily earn enough to qualify for admission to the higher slopes of the Inland Revenue—that's success. Furnished with money and a little fame even the elderly, if they care to, may partake of trendy diversions—that's pleasure. It might happen once in a while that something I said or wrote was sufficiently heeded for me to persuade myself that it represented a serious impact on our time—that's fulfillment. Yet I say to you, and I beg you to believe me, multiply these tiny triumphs by a million, add them all together, and they are nothing—less than nothing, a positive impediment—measured against one draught of that living water Christ offers to the spiritually thirsty, irrespective of who or what they are. . . .

I can never forget reading, when I was a young man, in Tolstoy's Confessions of how, working in his study, he had to hide away a rope that was there, for fear he should use it to hang himself. To me at that time it seemed extraordinary. Here was the greatest writer of modern times; someone whom, as a young aspiring writer myself, I thought of with the utmost veneration; whose work seemed (and seems) to me so marvelous that if in the course of my life I managed to write something even a hundredth part as good as the shortest and most desultory of his short stories I should be well content. And here was this man . . . unable to endure the sight of a rope because it reminded him of how he might end a life which had grown insufferable. Why insufferable? Because he was assailed by the hopes and desires of the world—even more desolating, as he well knew, in realization than in aspiration. Because he seemed to be alone and afraid in an alien universe. Then, as he recounts, he lost himself in Christ's love, from which, St. Paul tells us, nothing can separate us if we hold fast—not tribulation, not distress, neither peril nor sword. Tolstoy, as we know, did hold fast, becoming not only the greatest writer, but also one of the greatest Christians, of modern times.

Malcolm Muggeridge

VAST NEUROTIC MISERY

Ecclesiastes 2:15

I received this letter: "Those psychiatrists who are not superficial have come to the conclusion that the vast neurotic misery of the world could be termed a neurosis of emptiness. Men cut themselves off from the root of their being, God, and then life turns meaningless, goal-less, empty, and sick, and then we get them as psychiatrists."

One psychologist of forty years ago says that without conversion life is "stunted," and another psychiatrist of today says that without it life is "empty" and "sick." What does experience say? The same.

. . . . If someone asks about the "adolescent phenomenon," my reply is that adolescence is an awakening, not merely of the sex urge, but of the total person—physical, mental and spiritual. In that awakening of the total person the spiritual is included and cries out for adjustment, for wholeness, for God.

E. Stanley Jones

Now the Scripture tells us that the state of an unconverted man is this: he seeth no great felicity in the love and communion of God in the life to come, which may draw his heart thither from this present world; but he liveth to his carnal self, or to the flesh; and the main bent of his life is that it may go well with him on earth; and that religion which he hath is but a little by the by, lest he be damned when he can keep the world no longer; so that the world and the flesh are highest in his esteem, and nearest to his heart, and God and glory stand below them, and all their service of God is but a giving him that which the world and the flesh can spare.

Richard Baxter

A STRANGE, MAD, PAINFUL PLACE

Ecclesiastes 4:1-3

As it would be cruel to an Amazonial tribesman to fly him to London, put him down without explanation in Trafalgar Square and leave him, as one who knew nothing of English or England, to fend for himself, so we are cruel to our selfs if we try to live in this world without knowing about the God whose world it is and who runs it. The world becomes a strange, mad, painful place, and life in it is a disappointing and unpleasant business for those who don't know about God. Disregard the study of God, and you sentence yourself to stumble and blunder through life blindfold, as it were, with no sense of direction and no understanding of what surrounds you. This way you can waste your life and lose your soul.

Once you become aware that the main business that you are here for is to know God, most of life's problems fall into place of their own accord. The world today is full of sufferers from the wasting disease which Albert Camus called Absurdism (life is a bad joke!) and from the complaint which we may call Marie Antoinette's fever, since she found the phrase which describes it (`nothing tastes').

J.I. Packer

I noted down some words of Machiavelli which seemed to me very much to the point: `For the great majority of mankind are satisfied with appearances, as though they were realities, and are often more influenced by things that seem than by those that are.' The same notion is expressed by Blake in one of those couplets of his so packed with meaning, so luminous, that you can go on contemplating them to the end of your life without ever exhausting their significance:

They ever must believe a lie
Who see with, not through, the eye.

Malcolm Muggeridge

A VERY INDIVIDUAL THING

Hebrews 11:14-16

With most of us life is a very individual thing. Our salvation and our whole Christian life even are merely personal matters. We do indeed understand that we are members of a whole, but in most cases it hardly interests us. Our work, our service, too, are terribly individualistic. We are concerned, desperately concerned, with the things and people in our own vicinity. We fail, pitifully fail, to see our position in the whole scheme of things, the importance of things to come and our relationship thereto.

Isaac knew well enough that though to most life in this present evil world is but a passing show, yet to the saint of God doing His will, every act and word and thought has a profound significance in relation to future events, and can never be isolated from "things to come." For it is only as we keep our eyes on the future, seeing the relationship of the individual to the whole, that we can properly estimate the value of our life and the service that God has committed to our charge.

The Apostle Paul, though never underrating the importance of the present, the duty of the moment, the value of individualism whether in the person or the group, never lost sight of "things to come"; he saw the future Kingdom and beheld the Church, the Bride, the Body of Christ, as one glorious whole; and with that vision realized the value and importance of every unit that goes to make up that whole.

Abraham also beheld the city, its architect, its builder, and its foundations. He beheld the whole.

A. Paget Wilkes

THE VANITY OF ALL THINGS

Isaiah 26:3

The great remedy against the evil of self-will is to continually remember the vanity of all things and how soon they will come to an end. Thus we shall take off our affections from things that are so earthly and place them on that which shall never end.

This may seem a weak remedy, but it does strengthen the soul greatly. And with regard to trifles, it is useful to take great care when we have an affection for any object. We should turn our thoughts away from it and fix them on God. In this His Majesty assists us and does us a great favor, because in this house the greatest difficulty has already been overcome.

But this separating from ourselves, and this denying and renouncing of ourselves is so difficult. We are closely united to ourselves and love ourselves excessively, also. So here is where true humility must enter. For it is this virtue of humility and that other virtue of mortification which seem always to go together. They seem as two sisters who are inseparable. Indeed, they are.

Teresa of Avila

When the bombers come, they are all fear; when there is something good to eat, they are all greed; when they are disappointed, they are all despair; when they are successful, they can think of nothing else. They miss the fullness of life and the wholeness of an independent existence. Everything subjective and objective is dissolved for them into fragments.

Detrich Bonhoeffer

THE ONLY ANSWER

Romans 13:13-14

I don't think there was ever a dramatic moment when Christian faith came back. I have often thought about this. It's something—well, put it this way—it has always seemed to me that the most interesting thing in the world is to try and understand what life is about. This is the only pursuit that could possibly engage a serious person—what is life about? And of course it is a continuing pursuit. As I have realized the fallacy of all materialist philosophies and materialist utopias, and of the politics of utopianism, so I have come to feel more and more strongly that the answer to life does not lie in materialism. In seeking the other transcendental answer I have inevitably and increasingly been driven to the conclusion, almost against my own will, that for a West European whose life and background and tradition are in terms of Western European Christian civilization, the only answer lies in the person and life and teaching of Christ. Here, and here only, the transcendental answer is expressed adequately and appropriately. Now that is not the kind of conclusion that involves anything like a Damascus Road experience. It is a process of continuing realization. On the other hand, of course, one reaches a point when one comes out into the open about it. For me that was delayed because I felt it was necessary that my personal life should not be a disgrace to the Christian religion when I avowed it. There were certain things which I had to do about my personal life. In my particular case—and I am not laying this down as any kind of a rule—this involved abstemiousness and asceticism, and the mastery of self-indulgence.

Malcolm Muggeridge

A religious person, that liveth not according to discipline, lieth open to great mischief, to the ruin of his soul.

He that seeketh liberty and ease shall ever live in disquiet, for one thing or other will displease him.

Thomas a Kempis

AGONIZED BY A TORMENTING FEELING

Isaiah 55:6-7

The conviction that knowledge of the truth can only be found in life stirred me to doubt the worth of my own way of life. The thing that saved me was that I managed to tear myself away from my exclusive existence and see the true life of the simple working people, and realize that this alone is genuine life. I realized that if I wanted to understand life and its meaning I had to live a genuine life and not that of a parasite; and having accepted the meaning that is given to life by that real section of humanity who have become part of that genuine life, I had to try it out.

At this time the following happened to me: over the course of a whole year, almost every minute I asked myself whether I had not better kill myself with a rope or a bullet. And at the same time as I was experiencing the thoughts and observations I have described, my heart was agonized by a tormenting feeling. I can only describe this feeling as a quest for God.

I say that this quest for God was not a debate but an emotion because it did not arise from my stream of thoughts—it was in fact quite contrary to them—but from my heart. It was a feeling of fear, abandonment, loneliness, amid all that was strange to me, and a sense of hope that someone would help me.

Despite the fact that I was utterly convinced of the impossibility of proving the existence of a God (Kant had shown me this and I had fully understood that it cannot be proven), I nevertheless searched for God in the hope that I might find Him, and reverting to an old habit of prayer, I prayed to Him whom I sought but could not find. In my mind I went over the arguments of Kant and Schopenhauer on the impossibility of proving the existence of God, and I began to refute them. Cause, I told myself, does not belong to the same category of thought as space and time. If I exist then there must be a cause, and a cause of the cause. And the cause of everything is that which we call God. . . . And as soon as I recognized that there is a force with power over me I immediately felt the possibility of life.

Leo Tolstoy

TRANSPARENT SOULS

Ezekiel 36:25-27

The young man was impressed and enquired further what this opaqueness of soul which I had mentioned might be. We turned together to Ezek. 36:25. He was deeply convicted as I pointed out to him the "filthiness of flesh and spirit"; the "idols," objects of beauty, to the unsanctified soul, and yet in God's sight as hideous as the former; and above all a "stony heart" of UNBELIEF incapable of feeling, unimpressionable to the fingerprints of God the Holy Ghost, and utterly unable to believe to the uttermost. As we talked together of these things, and he realized in clearer and more penetrating fashion his need of an inward deliverance, he cried out, "What then shall I do?" I turned again to the prophet's message and pointed out that God had promised to REMOVE this trinity of evil Himself, that His promise was "I will," "I will," reite-rated again and again; and that the only condition to be fulfilled on our part was expressed in the words, "I will yet for this be enquired of to do it for them." In explanation of this enquiry, we turned together to Hebrews 11:6. I endeavored to unfold it somewhat as set forth in a preceding chapter, and urged him at once to get alone with God and seek His favor as therein directed. (1) To come exactly as he was, neither better nor worse, obedient to the call of God. (2) To dare to believe that God is accepting him and fulfilling the promises as found in Ezekiel, here and now. In other words, I urged him to do what that almost inspired couplet bids:
"Before Thy Cross my all I cast,
AND DARE TO LEAVE IT THERE."
He then interrupted, "Is that all I have to do?" With all the earnestness at my command I said, "No." The third and further step was to "diligently seek" God's face, and to listen to "the voice from heaven," not asking for the work to be done, but believing that it is done already. . . . Ten days later received a letter overflowing with praise and thanksgiving for what God had wrought.

A. Paget Wilkes

OUR HUMAN PREDICAMENT

II Timothy 1:10

What, then, did Christ do when he appeared and proceeded to manifest God's eternal purpose of grace? To this Paul gives in II Timothy 1:10 a double answer. First, Jesus `abolished death.' Secondly, he `brought life and immortality to light through the gospel.'

`Death' is, in fact, the one word which summarizes our human predicament as a result of sin. For death is the `wage' sin pays, its grim penalty (Rom. 6:23). And this is true of each form which death takes. For Scripture speaks of death in three ways. There is physical death, the separation of the soul from the body. There is spiritual death, the separation of the soul from God. And there is eternal death, the separation of both soul and body from God forever. All are due to sin; they are sin's terrible though just reward.

But Jesus Christ `abolished' death. This cannot mean that he eliminated it, as we know from our everyday experience. Sinners are still `dead through the trespasses and sins' in which they walk (Eph. 2:1-2) until God makes them alive in Christ. All human beings die physically and will continue to do so, with the exception of the generation who are alive when Christ returns in glory. And some are going to die `the second death,' which is one of the fearful expressions used in the book of Revelation for hell (*e.g.* Rev. 20:14, 21:8). Indeed, Paul has written previously that the final abolition of death still lies in the future, as the last enemy of God to be destroyed (I Cor. 15:26). Not until the return of Christ and the resurrection of the dead shall we be able to shout with joy `Death is swallowed up in victory' (I Cor. 15:54; *cf.* Rev. 21:4).

What is triumphantly asserted in this verse by Paul is that at his first appearing Christ decisively `defeated' or `overthrew' death. The Greek verb *katargeō* is not in itself conclusive, for it can be used with a variety of meanings, which must be determined by the context. Nevertheless, its first and foremost meaning is `make ineffective, powerless, idle' or `nullify.'

John R. Stott

ROUND AND ROUND A BEATEN PATH

Genesis 15:17

To a fellow Missionary.

Beloved Brother:
    I wish you might run down to Tokyo for a day or two, as letters are poor things indeed, when you wish to help a person living four hundred miles distant. I deeply sympathize with you in your soul-trouble, but were I in your place, I would not be eternally dying, but would yield myself right up to God and have done with the consecration forever. It is so easy to keep marching round and round in a beaten path and get nowhere. The reason many Christians have so much fighting to do is because they do not have one sharp decisive battle to begin with. It is far easier to have one great battle than to keep on skirmishing all your life. I know Christians who have actually spent forty years fighting what they term their besetting sin, and on which they have wasted strength enough to have evangelized the world. Have one big battle, one glorious victory, then shout His praises the rest of your life. The height is steep, the way of the Cross is not an easy one, but `let us labor to enter in.'
    The fire cannot consume the gift that is not placed on the altar, but after it is placed there, we can walk through the midst of each smoking sacrifice, and along each path of holy duty, cheerily singing, "I'm free, free, gloriously free."
    God offers us Himself with all of His resources, but to possess them there must be a complete separation from the earthly. The manifestation of His glorious presence is ours only to the extent that we are found willing to withdraw from the world, living, working, and walking alone with God.
    Come down soon if possible. We are having some glorious times in our afternoon services.
                    In the best of bonds,

Charles E. Cowman

ESTABLISHED THROUGH CONFLICT

Ephesians 6:12-13

Every bit of truth we receive, if we receive it willingly, will take us into conflict and will be established through conflict. It will be worthless until there has been a battle over it. Take any position the Lord calls you to take, and, if you are taking it with Him, you are going through things in it, and there will be an element added by reason of the battle. You have taken a position—yes, but you have not really got it yet, the real value of it has not been proved. You have not come into the real significance of it until there has been some sore conflict in relation to it.

As a result of the work of His cross, and as the grand issue of His resurrection, eternal life is received already by those who believe. But while that life is itself victorious, incorruptible, indestructible, the believer has to come by faith to prove it, to live by it, to learn its laws, to be conformed to it. There is a deposit in the believer, which in itself needs no addition, so far as its quality is concerned. So far as its victory, its power, its glory, its potentialities are concerned nothing can be added to it. But the course of spiritual experience, of spiritual life, is to discover, to appropriate, and to live by all that the life represents and means.

T. Austin Sparks

A POWER OF WHICH HE KNEW NOTHING

Acts 1:8

Pierson's dissatisfaction grew as he saw and heard of multitudes converted under the simple preaching of comparatively unlettered evangelists. He realized that there was a power of God of which he knew nothing. There were promises of blessing which were not being fulfilled. He believed in God's Word and in His power, but something must be standing in the way.

While this burden was lying heavily upon him, God sent to Detroit two of His servants, Major D.W. Whittle and his associate, P.P. Bliss, the singing evangelist. They began to hold gospel meetings on Tuesday, October 6, 1874, and continued their Detroit campaign for six weeks. Dr. Pierson gladly sat at their feet, as a learner. He attended the services, studied their methods and observed the results. He learned three things: (1) The power of simple gospel preaching in contrast to that which emphasized literary style; (2) the power of God's Word when used to unfold the great Christian doctrines in contrast to non-Biblical preaching; and (3) the power of gospel song in contrast to elaborate music rendered chiefly for artistic effect.

The evangelists were entertained for a month in the Pierson home and their very presence was a benediction. The calm peace and joy in the Holy Spirit that pervaded their lives spoke even more loudly than their sermons and songs. Their host longed to experience more of the fullness of God's abiding presence and power in his own personal life and ministry.

One night after a meeting of unusual power, the pastor of the Methodist church, in which it was held, entered his lecture room and found Dr. Pierson alone with his head bowed on his hands, deeply moved. On being asked the cause of his distress he replied:

"I feel that I have never been truly converted nor have I preached the Gospel as I ought."

By many external leadings and by the inward "Still small voice" God was calling him to larger, more fruitful service. Just before the evangelists left the city, Major Whittle said to his host, with great earnestness: "Brother Pierson, Bliss and I are firmly convinced that God would mightily use you if you were wholly consecrated to Him. We have agreed to pray for you daily that you may be fully surrendered."

These words were not easy to forget, but for over a year they apparently bore no fruit. Conviction had been growing upon him that before he could be used as he wished for the conversion of men he must be more fully consecrated to God. On November 12, 1875, a day appointed by the Synod of Michigan for fasting and prayer, he was convinced that the great obstacle to his spiritual growth and power was his ambition for literary glory. This conviction had been slowly growing, but he had almost unconsciously fought against it. Now he asked God to deal with ambition in His own way. He was brought to the depths of humiliation and almost despair. The steps by which he began to come out of the slough of despond, he describes as follows:

"I began to pray aloud in private and found this a great help to my realization of the presence of God, and I learned what real prayer meant. Then I was impressed with the necessity for honesty, absolute candour with God in asking what I really wanted, and what I was willing to give up everything else to obtain. I saw that my life had been full of self-seeking and idolatry, such as I had never realized. Next I felt the need of present faith in the sure Word of God which promises answer to such prayer. God gave me this assurance in the preparation of a special sermon to my people. Finally I saw that I must give up every ambition and every idol, and must place myself unreservedly in the hands of God. It was a terrible battle, but at last I said, with all my heart, Lord, let me be nothing, but use me if Thou wilt to save souls and to glorify Thee.

"From that day I was conscious of the presence of the Holy Spirit in my life and work in a way that I had before never known."

ARTHUR T. PIERSON
D.L. Pierson

THE ONLY THING YOU MUST DO

Romans 3:11-12

Jim Kennedy described the experience of conversion in his book: "To this day I have friends from twenty-four years ago who do not know what happened to me. One moment there was a young man managing an Arthur Murray dance studio, his heart and affections fastened entirely upon the things of this world. Then suddenly, overnight, something happened: a new person was born and an old person died. Those things which once to me seemed so desirable, so compelling, now seemed as filthy rags, dead men's bones, things of no interest to me at all.

"Other things, the things of the kingdom of God, those things that are invisible, those things that are eternal, which never occupied my thoughts at all and upon which my heart never dallied, have become exceedingly precious to me. Upon those things my affections have been fastened. There is no other solution than that twenty-four years ago I was born all over again.

"This is the only thing that you must do during your stay on this planet—the only thing you must do. You don't even have to grow up. You don't have to succeed. You don't have to get married. You don't have to have children. You don't have to have a home, a car, and all of the things that people think they must have. The only thing that you must have is a rebirth, because your entire future depends upon it."

In that Tampa apartment, on that remarkable Sunday afternoon, Jim made the transition from presumption to truth. He had presumed that if anybody else got into heaven, he was good enough to make it; he didn't realize that he was calling God a liar—God, who says, "There is none good, no not one. . . ." He had presumed all along that, by performing some good deeds and accumulating an acceptable record of good works, he could reach heaven, at least by a side door or at worst the back entrance.

DR. JAMES KENNEDY,
THE MAN AND HIS WORK
Herbert Lee Williams

MISERABLE FOREVER UNLESS

Romans 3:25-26

For the poet William Cowper, it was Romans 3:25 which opened his spiritual eyes. He said,

"On reading it I immediately received power to believe. The rays of the Sun of Righteousness fell on me in all their fullness; I saw the complete sufficiency of the expiation which Christ had wrought for my pardon and entire justification. In an instant I believed and received the peace of the Gospel."

And there was Martin Luther, the Roman Catholic monk, who suddenly got up off his knees while climbing and kissing the Scala Sancta (sacred stairs) because a single verse of Scripture—"the just shall live by faith"—pierced his mind and convinced him that he could never earn his salvation by such foolishness. There was John Calvin, whose testimony was, "God suddenly converted me unto Himself."

Also there was John Wesley, who wrote in his diary: "It was a quarter to nine, and for the first time in my life I knew that I trusted Jesus Christ alone for my salvation, and I felt my heart strangely warmed and knew that He had delivered me from sin and death unto eternal life." There was Charles Spurgeon, who recalled his visit to a small chapel where an unlettered layman, substituting for the minister, pointed his finger at the young man and said, "You are going to be miserable forever unless you obey my text, Look unto Christ!" Spurgeon later recorded: "In that moment my soul was flooded with the reality of the grace of God as I looked unto the cross of Jesus Christ. I knew that I had received eternal life! My soul was filled with joy. I could have danced all the way home."

Herbert Lee Williams

Augustine wrote:
"I did not choose to read more, nor had I the occasion. Immediately at the end of this sentence Romans 13:12-14, as if a light of certainty had been poured into my heart, all the shadows of doubt were scattered."

SATISFIED WITH THE STATUS QUO

I John 3:1

At other times, there comes upon me certain desires to serve God with such intensity that the experience is indescribable. It is accompanied by certain kinds of pain at seeing how unprofitable I am.

On these occasions, it seems to me that there are no things in this work, neither death, nor martyrdom, that I could not easily endure. This conviction also comes in a flash and is the result of studied reflection. I am wholly changed and know not how I am given such great courage. It makes me feel as if I should shout from the house-tops how terribly important it is that no man should be satisfied with the *status quo*, when we see the marvelous things God is prepared to give us (I John 3:1). . . .

This gentle movement and the interior enlargement of the soul cause it to be less constrained in matters relating to the service of God than it was before; it has much more freedom, also. It is not distressed because of the fear of hell. Although it feels greater fear now for having offended God, yet it is freed from *servile* fear and has a great confidence that it will enjoy Him. The fear that the soul used to have of losing its health by ascetic practice has also ceased, and it thinks it can do all in God. It has more desires for using spiritual discipline than ever. The fear of afflictions which it used to have is also now moderated because it has a more living faith. It knows that if the soul bears them for God's sake, His Majesty will give it grace to bear them with patience. Indeed, sometimes the soul desires them since it has a great desire to do something for God. And as it now understands His greatness better, it accordingly esteems itself more vile.

Having also tried the delights of God, the soul finds those of the world to be in comparison as mere dirt (Philippians 3:8). So the soul separates itself from them little by little, and for doing this the soul has more control over itself.

St. Teresa of Avila

THE BREAKING OF MY INDEPENDENCE

Galatians 2:20

"I am crucified with Christ; nevertheless I live; yet not I, but Christ liveth in me."
These words mean the breaking of my independence with my own hand and surrendering to the supremacy of the Lord Jesus. No one can do this for me, I must do it myself. God may bring me up to the point three hundred sixty-five times a year, but He cannot put me through it. It means breaking the husk of my individual independence of God, and the emancipating of my personality into oneness with Himself, not for my own ideas, but for absolute loyalty to Jesus. There is no possibility of dispute when once I am there. Very few of us know anything about loyalty to Christ—*"For My sake."* It is that which makes the iron saint.

Has the break come? All the rest is pious fraud. The one point to decide is—Will I give up, will I surrender to Jesus Christ, and make no conditions whatever as to how the break comes? I must be broken from my self-realization, and immediately that point is reached, the reality of the supernatural identification takes place at once, and the witness of the Spirit of God is unmistakable—"I have been crucified with Christ."

The passion of Christianity is that I deliberately sign away my own rights and become a bond-slave of Jesus Christ. Until I do that, I do not begin to be a saint.

One student a year who hears God's call would be sufficient for God to have called this College into existence. This College as an organization is not worth anything, it is not academic; it is for nothing else but for God to help Himself to lives. Is He going to help Himself to us, or are we taken up with our conception of what we are going to be?

Oswald Chambers

LITERALLY A NEW LIFE

John 6:63-64

This life-giving in the spirit is not a direct heightening of the natural life in a man, a spontaneous continuation in direct connection with this natural life—blasphemy! How dreadful to take Christianity in vain this way! It is a new life. A new life, yes,—and this is no empty phrase such as we use about this thing and that thing every time something new begins to stir in us. No, it is a new life, literally a new life—for mark this well, death goes between, this *dying to*. The life on the other side of death, yes, that is a new life.

Death goes between; this is the teaching of Christianity. You must die, and the life-giving Spirit is the very one which kills you. The first utterance of the life-giving Spirit is that you must go into death, must die. It is this way so that you shall not take Christianity in vain. A life-giving spirit—that is the invitation. Who would not willingly seize it? But to die first—that is cessation!

It is the Spirit which gives life. Yes, it gives life—through death. In an old hymn designed to comfort the bereaved on the loss of their dead we read "In death we begin life." In this same way, spiritually understood, does the communication of the life-giving Spirit begin in death. Consider that festival day. It was indeed the life-giving Spirit which was poured out over the Apostles that day—that fact is provided by their lives and by their deaths. All this is testified to by the history of the church.

Soren Kierkegaard

TO WEAR OUT IN HIS SERVICE

Psalm 84:1-4

In the forenoon, I felt the power of intercession for precious, immortal souls; for the advancement of the kingdom of my dear Lord and Savior in the world; and withal, a most sweet resignation and even consolation and joy in the thoughts of suffering hardships, distresses, and even death itself, in the promotion of it. Had special enlargement in pleading for the enlightening and conversion of the poor heathen.

In the afternoon, God was with me of a truth. Oh, it was blessed company indeed! God enabled me to so agonize in prayer that I was quite wet with perspiration, though in the shade and the cool wind. My soul was drawn out very much for the world, for multitudes of souls. I think I had more enlargement for sinners than for the children of God, though I felt as if I could spend my life in cries for both. I enjoyed great sweetness in communion with my dear Savior. I think I never in my life felt such an entire weanedness from this world and so much resigned to God in everything. Oh, that I may always live to and upon my blessed God! Amen, amen.

Tuesday, April 20. This day I am twenty-four years of age. Oh, how much mercy have I received the year past! And how poorly have I answered the vows I made this time twelve months ago to be wholly the Lord's, to be forever devoted to His service! The Lord help me to live more to His glory for the time to come. This has been a sweet, a happy day to me; blessed be God. I think my soul was never so drawn out in intercession for others as it has been this night. Had a most fervent wrestle with the Lord tonight for my enemies. I hardly ever so longed to live to God and to be altogether devoted to Him. I wanted to wear out my life in His service and for His glory.

THE LIFE AND DIARY
OF DAVID BRAINERD
Jonathan Edwards

THAT I MAY NOT WEEP

Matthew 25:40

William Osler's work at the bedside was twofold. He brought insight and, in execution, a brilliant ability to cope with disease—and then, when everything that was human had failed, he brought something less tangible but enduring. He would stand at the bedside of a patient for whom he had done all that he could, one hand upon his patient's heart, his watch in the other, counting the slowing, slowing beat—then stillness. An intent, far-off look would come in his eyes, and drawing the cover about the dead as gently as for a sleeping child he would turn away—perhaps whistling. No one who knew him would have thought him unfeeling, and to a physician who did not know him and who had once spoken almost in rebuke of some seeming frivolity in his manner, Osler answered: "If I laugh at any living thing 'tis that I may not weep."

"One day we were walking down the street together," his niece recalled. He found it difficult to walk in the accepted sense of the term. He would dance along humming or whistling. On this day we were dancing along St. Catherine Street hand in hand, when an old and very seedy looking man accosted us and asked for money. Uncle Bill looked at him with his penetrating brown eyes and said with a laugh, `You old rascal, why should I give you money to drink yourself to death?' `Well sir it lightens the road going.' `There is only one thing of value about you and that is your hobnailed liver.' `I'll give it to you, sir. I'll give it to you.' Dr. Osler laughed and gave the old man some silver, saying, `Now, Jehoshaphat, promise me you will get some soup before you start in on the gin.' The old fellow eagerly agreed and went away with infirmity in his step. The doctor looked after him with a thoughtful expression. `Pretty cold for that poor fellow,' he murmured, and then I found we were running after the beggar. `Here, take this. I have a father of my own,' said the doctor, pulling off his overcoat and putting it on the astonished old man. `You may drink yourself to death and undoubtedly will, but I cannot let you freeze to death.'"

THE TREASURY OF GREAT BIOGRAPHIES

"HOW VERY HAPPY WE WERE"

Psalm 43:1-4

Some time ago I held a weekend revival in a small city in Taiwan. Each service, seated toward the back, I noticed a sad-looking old fellow who would frequently get up and leave the service and return later. He was dressed in a faded blue uniform, and I thought perhaps he was the janitor or another workman of some sort. Obviously his mind was dull and the pastor informed me that he was somewhat deficient mentally.

After the Sunday morning service the old fellow insisted that I and the interpreter visit his home. On the way I learned his story. It made an impression on me I will never forget. This man had once been a brilliant young seminary student in our Tokyo Bible Seminary. His record was so outstanding some even claimed that his mind bordered on that of a genius. He returned to his native Taiwan and entered the ministry. From what I could gather, he had financial difficulties; pastors at that time received only a pittance. The allurement of a better paying job was appealing. There was an easier way to make a living, he rationalized, and after all he could still be a Christian; he could still serve the Lord on the side. He took the offering of his life off the altar on which he had placed it and left the ministry. A life chosen for the Holy task became defiled as it was invested in secular work. He found a good position with the railroad, but from that day on life for that young man took an ironic downward twist. I gazed at the saddened old fellow. In his face was written the unmistakable story of disillusionment, heartbreak, spiritual disaster. His movements were slow, his speech childish; everything about him bespoke of hopelessness.

By this time we had arrived at his home. We wandered through a decadent part of town, past piles of litter, into a narrow, muddy lane that marked the entrance to his dwelling. The house was a flimsy, unpainted shack. The mats on the floor were badly frayed and worn and the paper walls were peeling away leaving gaping holes. I saw children about the house dressed in ragged garments, but I wondered that there was no mother present. A bit embarrassed he explained that his wife had left him and lived elsewhere, employed now as a housemaid and prostitute. From a musty, covered closet he extracted a scroll of paper. It was the diploma he had received from the Tokyo Bible Seminary, now yellow with age. He looked at it wistfully and handled it tenderly, as a child would a specially favored toy. He spoke in a distant voice as if recalling an almost forgotten incident. "When I was preaching," he said, "we were always poor but both my wife and I were happy. At that time we had constant peace and joy in our hearts. We worked very hard for almost nothing. Now I realize how very happy we were. Now I have all the money I need but I do not care for money now. What good is it without a wife, without a home, without any peace." He had not read his Bible regularly for years. Prayer had been all but impossible. The curse of disobedience had withered his life. For a moment his face lit up like that of a child with some sudden inspiration. "I could go back and work somewhere in the church again," he suggested. "Perhaps I could start a work of my own." But it was obviously a foolish suggestion. He was now too feeble to begin a new life but more than that he had lost his mental powers. Before we left he brought out some crude picture frames. "I made these myself," he said as he held them up proudly for us to examine. They were poorly constructed indeed. Tenderly he wiped the dust from them and wrapped them up in soiled newspaper saying, "I want to make this gift to you; it is all I can do but I made them myself." We left the old man standing forlornly amid the shambled home with motherless children at his feet. That spoke to me as nothing else of the tragedy of taking the sacrifice off the altar.

Ed Erny

"DO YOU KNOW THAT I HAVE DIED"

Romans 6:1-7

I remember one morning—how can I ever forget it!—I was sitting upstairs reading Romans and I came to the Words: "Knowing this, that our old man was crucified with him, that the body of sin might be done away, so that we should no longer be in bondage to sin." Knowing this! How could I know it? I prayed, "Lord, open my eyes!" And then, in a flash, I saw. I had earlier been reading I Corinthians 1:30: "You are in Christ Jesus." I turned to it and looked at it again. "That you are in Christ Jesus is God's doing!" It was amazing! Then if Christ died, and that is certain fact, and if God put me into Him, then I must have died too. All at once I saw that I had died. My death to sin was a matter of the past and not of the future. It was divine fact that had dawned upon me. Carried away with joy I jumped from my chair and ran downstairs to the young man working in the kitchen. "Brother," I said, seizing him by the hands, "do you know that I have died?" I must admit he looked puzzled. "What do you mean?" he exclaimed, so I went on: "Do you not know that Christ has died? Do you not know that I died with Him? Do you not know that my death is no less truly a fact then His?" Oh, it was so real to me! I felt like shouting my discovery through the streets of Shanghai. From that day to this I have never for one moment doubted the finality of that word: "I have been crucified with Christ; it is no longer I who live, but Christ who lives in me."

Watchman Nee

"DON'T TAKE YOURSELF SERIOUSLY"

Jeremiah 29:13

He *lived*. He walked with God and inspired us all with the fact that `life' was to know God and Jesus Christ Who He had sent, and so greatly did that fact grip us who were long with him that we looked forward to the lectures as opportunities for discerning God, of knowing Jesus Christ, and entering upon `life.' And frequently in our quest he would set our compass with such words as—
"My goal is God Himself . . .
At any cost, dear Lord, by any road."

Nor did he leave us there. He always insisted that that life must be expressed as a bondslave of Jesus Christ and a servant of all men. He used to say—"Don't take yourself seriously; the one thing you have to do is to take God seriously." This he certainly did, and it meant that we saw the Sermon on the Mount lived. He took Jesus Christ seriously always; consequently, there was never any trace of egoism. Conspicuously free from any suggestion of fanaticism, having no peculiar doctrine, holding no particular dogma, having no axe to grind— he had the unhesitating following of every student. We knew that he spake with authority, and every honest seeker after God could follow without the impediment of wondering—What is behind this? There was nothing behind it. It was truth, unshielded, unbolstered, clear and immovable.

OSWALD CHAMBERS,
HIS LIFE AND WORK
Dinsdale T. Young

COMMITTED TO WHAT?

John 1:43

You are not called upon to commit yourself to a need, or to a task, or to a field. You are called upon to commit yourself to God!

Man is not indispensable to God. God is indispensable to man!

I sometimes have an uneasy feeling about certain missionary conventions and the missionary challenge to which we have become accustomed. You hear one speaker after another committing you to the task, claiming your life for this mission field or for that. "The need," all too often it is said, "constitutes the call!" There are a thousand needs, but you are not committed to these. You are committed to Christ, and it is His business to commit you where He wants you. No man or woman on earth has the right to commit any member of the body of Jesus Christ to any task, or to any field; that is to usurp the authority of the Head of the body, Jesus Christ Himself. I Corinthians 12:18— "but now hath God set the members every one of them in the body, as it hath pleased him." The moment I claim the right to commit a man or a woman or a boy or a girl to some field of service, I blaspheme His sovereign place as Lord of the harvest.

Major W. Ian Thomas

If you would be a good Christian, there is but one way—you must live wholly unto God and if you would live wholly unto God, you must live according to the wisdom that comes from God; you must act according to right judgments of the nature and value of things; you must live in exercise of holy and heavenly affections and use all the gifts of God to His praise and glory.

William Law

A TALENT TO BE TRADED WITH

Psalm 118:4-5

As for freedom, according to this analogy, it grows no greater by being wasted, or spent, but it is given to us as a talent to be traded with until the coming of Christ. In this trading we part with what is ours only to recover it with interest. We do not destroy it or throw it away. We dedicate it to some purpose, and this dedication makes us freer than we were before. Because we are freer, we are happier. We not only have more than we had but we become more than we were. This having and being come to us in a deepening of our union with the will of God. Our will is strengthened in obedience to the demands of objective reality. Our conscience is enlightened and it looks out upon a vastly widened horizon. We are able to see far nobler possibilities for the exercise of our freedom because we have grown in charity, and because we are enriched in divine grace we find in ourselves the power to attain ends that had been beyond us before.

All these fruits are meant to be gathered by our freedom when we do the will of God. It is for this that we account ourselves happy when we know His will and do it, and realize that the greatest unhappiness is to have no sense of His purposes or His designs either for ourselves or for the rest of the world. "I walked at large," says the Psalmist, "because I have sought after thy commandments" (Psalm 118:4-5). "I have been delighted in the way of thy testimonies as in all riches. . . . Unless thy law had been my meditation, I had then perhaps perished in my abjection . . ."

Thomas Merton

AN ACCIDENTAL PRODUCT?

Joshua 24:15

But what about human liberty? Is there no spiritual freedom in regard to behavior and reaction to any given surroundings? Is that theory true which would have us believe that man is no more than a product of many conditional and environmental factors—be they of a biological, psychological or sociological nature? Is man but an accidental product of these? Most important, do the prisoners' reactions to the singular world of the concentration camp prove that man cannot escape the influences of his surroundings? Does man have no choice of action in the face of such circumstances?

We can answer these questions from experience as well as on principle. The experiences of camp life show that man does have a choice of action. There were enough examples, often of a heroic nature, which proved that apathy could be overcome, irritability suppressed. Man *can* preserve a vestige of spiritual freedom, of independence of mind, even in such terrible conditions of psychic and physical stress.

We who lived in concentration camps can remember the men who walked through the huts comforting others, giving away their last piece of bread. They may have been few in number, but they offer sufficient proof that everything can be taken from a man but one thing, the last of the human freedoms—to choose one's attitude in any given set of circumstances, to choose one's own way.

Victor Frankl

"THERE IS ONLY ONE THING I DREAD"

II Thessalonians 1:5

There were always choices to make. Every day, every hour, offered the opportunity to make a decision, a decision which determined whether you would or would not submit to those powers which threatened to rob you of your very self, your inner freedom; which determined whether or not you would become the plaything of circumstance, renouncing freedom and dignity to become molded into the form of the typical inmate.

Seen from this point of view, the mental reactions of the inmates of a concentration camp must seem more to us than the mere expression of certain physical and sociological conditions. Even though conditions such as lack of sleep, insufficient food and various mental stresses may suggest that the inmates were bound to react in certain ways, in the final analysis it becomes clear that the sort of person the prisoner became was the result of an inner decision, and not the result of camp influences alone. Fundamentally, therefore, any man can, even under such circumstances, decide what shall become of him—mentally and spiritually. He may retain his human dignity even in a concentration camp. Dostoyevski said once, "There is only one thing that I dread: not to be worthy of my sufferings." These words frequently came to my mind after I became acquainted with those martyrs whose behavior in camp, whose suffering and death, bore witness to the fact that the last inner freedom cannot be lost. It can be said that they were worthy of their sufferings; the way they bore their suffering was a genuine inner achievement. It is this spiritual freedom— which cannot be taken away—that makes life meaningful and purposeful.

Victor Frankl

TRUE FREEDOM

I Corinthians 6:12

We call liberty allowing the other fellow to please himself to the same extent as we please ourselves. True liberty is the ability earned by practice to do the right thing. There is no such thing as a gift of freedom; freedom must be earned. The counterfeit of freedom is independence. When the Spirit of God deals with sin, it is independence that He touches, that is why the preaching of the Gospel awakens resentment as well as craving. Independence must be blasted right out of a Christian, there must be only liberty, which is a very different thing. Spiritually, liberty means the ability to fulfil the law of God.

Oswald Chambers

The sacrifice of selfish privacy which is daily demanded of us is daily repaid a hundredfold in the true growth of personality which the life of the Body encourages. Those who are member of one another become as diverse as the hand and the ear. That is why the worldlings are so monotonously alike compared with the almost fantastic variety of the saints. Obedience is the road to freedom, humility the road to pleasure, unity the road to personality.

C.S. Lewis

RESULTS OR CONSEQUENCES

Isaiah 30:13, 24:4-5

Some people get results, others get consequences. We can see that at work around us. Some people know how to live; they seem to work with the grain of the universe; reality works with them—they get results in harmonious, happy, effective living. Others are not harmonious, not happy, not effective; they are up against it; the nature of reality is not with them; they are working against the grain of the universe—they get consequences.

Is there something here that always has the last word, no matter who has the intermediate word? A great many people don't believe me, "It's all right to do these things [meaning sex license] provided you can get away with it." My reply: "That is a big `provided,' for nobody gets away with it. The results register in you. You have to live with yourself, and the hell of being bad is a bad hell." I used to think that the passage, "Be sure your sin will find you out," meant, "Your sin will find you out"—will register in you, cause deterioration, decay; you will get consequences, in yourself.

An attempt to manipulate the universe and make it do what you want it to do ends in consequences. A young man wrote to the Duke University paper a letter to the older generation in which he said: "I'd like this older generation to get acquainted with this guy called `Kick'—he is a wonderful guy—gives you thrills." I felt like replying: "Young man, may I suggest that you get acquainted with another guy called `Kick-Back.' He is always a little behind the first guy and always has the last kick. You had better get acquainted with him, for everybody does, sooner or later." He overlooked the fact that when you strip off the first three letters of "thrills"—the beginning—you have "ills"—the end. It's not beginning but the end result that counts.

Apparently we are free to choose, but we are not free to choose the results of our choosing. Those results seems to be in hands not our own. There is something here, something with which we must come to terms—or get hurt.

E. Stanley Jones

FREEDOM IN DISCIPLESHIP

II Corinthians 10:5

Jesus himself clearly taught this. He said that whoever commits sin is the slave of sin and that, in contrast to this bondage, he could set men free. What was this freedom which he promised? "If you continue in my word, you are truly my disciples, and you will know the truth, and the truth will make you free" (Jn. 8:31-36). Freedom is found in discipleship, and discipleship is continuing submission to the Word of Jesus, for the Word of Jesus is the truth. No wonder Paul wrote of his resolve to "take every thought captive to obey Christ" (2 Cor. 10:5).

Submission to the authority of Scripture is fundamental to *Christian witness.*

The contemporary world is in great confusion and darkness. Men's hearts are failing them for fear. Has the Christian church any word of assurance for modern man's bewilderment, any light for his darkness, any hope for his fear? One of the greatest tragedies of today is that just when the world is becoming more aware of its need, the church is becoming less sure of its mission. And the major reason for the diminishing Christian mission is diminishing confidence in the Christian message.

We Christians should affirm with great confidence that Jesus is the supreme Lord, to who all authority has been given in heaven and on earth, and that he bids us go and make disciples and teach them all his teaching (Mt. 28:18-19). His commission is that we should proclaim his name as the crucified and risen Savior, and that on the ground of this one and only name forgiveness and new life are available to all who will repent and believe (cf. Lk. 24:44-49). We have no liberty to alter these terms of reference which Christ gave his church in his commission. There is only one gospel. We may neither embellish nor modify nor manipulate it. We are to be the heralds of God's good news. We are charged to lift up our voice with strength, to lift it up without fear and to publish abroad the salvation of God (Is. 40:9; 52:7).

David Howard

THE CULTURAL IMPERATIVE

I Corinthians 9:27

Cultural relativism succeeds in destroying the West's universal or intellectually imperialistic claims, leaving it to be just another culture. So there is equality in the republic of cultures. Unfortunately the West is defined by its need for justification of its ways or values, by its need for discovery of nature, by its need for philosophy and science. This is its cultural imperative. Deprived of that, it will collapse. The United States is one of the highest and most extreme achievements of the rational quest for the good life according to nature. What makes it political structure possible is the use of the rational principles of natural right to found a people, thus uniting the good with one's own. Or, to put it otherwise, the regime established here promised untrammeled freedom to reason—not to everything indiscriminately, but to reason, the essential freedom that justifies the other freedoms, and on the basis of which, and for the sake of which, much deviance is also tolerated. An openness that denies the special claim of reason bursts the mainspring keeping the mechanism of this regime in motion. And this regime, contrary to all claims to the contrary, was founded to overcome ethnocentrism, which is in no sense a discovery of social science.

It is important to emphasize that the lesson the students are drawing from their studies is simply untrue. History and the study of cultures do not teach or prove that values or cultures are relative.

Allan Bloom

If you would find freedom, learn above all to discipline your senses and your soul. Be not led hither and thither by your desires and your members. Keep your spirit and your body chaste, wholly subject to you, and obediently seeking the goal that is set before you. None can learn the secret of freedom, save by discipline.

Detrich Bunhoeffer

THE DISCIPLINE OF SUBMISSION

Ephesians 5:21

Of all the Spiritual Disciplines none has been more abused than the Discipline of submission. Somehow the human species has an extraordinary knack for taking the best teaching and turning it to the worst ends. Nothing can put people into bondage like religion, and nothing in religion has done more to manipulate and destroy people than a deficient teaching on submission. Therefore we must work our way through this Discipline with great care and discernment in order to insure that we are the ministers of life, not death.

Every Disciple has its corresponding freedom. If I have schooled myself in the art of rhetoric I am free to deliver a moving speech when the occasion requires it. Demosthenes was free to be an orator only because he had gone through the discipline of speaking above the ocean roar with pebbles in his mouth. The purpose of the Disciplines is freedom. Our aim is the freedom, not the Discipline. The moment we make the Discipline our central focus we will turn it into law and lose the corresponding freedom.

The Disciplines in themselves are of no value whatever. They have value only as a means of setting us before God so that He give us the liberation we seek. The liberation is the end; the Disciplines are *merely* means. They are not the answer; they only lead us to the Answer. We must clearly understand this limitation of the Disciplines if we are to avoid bondage. Not only must we understand but we need to underscore it to ourselves again and again, so severe is our temptation to center on the Disciplines. Let us forever center on Christ and view the Spiritual Disciplines as a way of drawing us closer to His heart.

Richard J. Foster

A Christian man is the most free lord of all, and subject to none; a Christian man is the most dutiful servant of all, and subject to everyone.

Martin Luther

THE TERRIBLE BURDEN

Philippians 2:6-8

I said that every Discipline has its corresponding freedom. What freedom corresponds to submission? It is the ability to lay down the terrible burden of always needing to get our own way. The obsession to demand that things go the way we want them to go is one of the greatest bondages in human society today. People will spend weeks, months, even years in perpetual stew because some little thing did not go as they wished. They will fuss and fume. They will get mad about it. They will act as if their very life hangs on the issue. They may even get an ulcer over it.

In the Discipline of submission we are released to drop the matter, to forget it. Frankly, most things in life are not nearly so important as we think they are. Our lives will not come to an end if this or that does not happen.

If you will watch these things you will see, for example, that almost all church fights and splits occur because people do not have the freedom to give in to each other. We insist that a critical issue is at stake; we are fighting for a sacred principle. Perhaps that is true. Usually it is not. Often we cannot stand to give in simply because it would mean that we would not get things our own way. Only in submission are we enabled to bring that spirit to a place where it no longer controls us. Only submission can free us sufficiently to enable us to distinguish between genuine issues and stubborn self-will.

If we could only come to see that most things in life are not major issues, then we would hold them lightly. We discover that they are no big deal. So often we say, "Well, I don't care," when what we really mean (and what we convey to others) is that we care a great deal. It is precisely here that the Discipline of silence fits in so well with all the other Disciplines. Usually the best way to handle most matters of submission is to say nothing. There is the need for an all-encompassing spirit of grace beyond any kind of language or action. When we do so we set others and ourselves free.

Richard Foster

VIRTUE AND FREEDOM

Genesis 2:16-17

In 1644 an order had been made that no book should be printed unless approved and licensed by the government. This is part of Milton's great protest against trying to impose a censorship, instead of giving men freedom to choose.

Good and evil we know in the field of this world grow up together almost inseparably. . . . He that can apprehend and consider vice with all her baits and seeming pleasures, and yet abstain, and yet distinguish and yet prefer that which is truly better, he is the warfaring Christian. I cannot praise a fugitive and cloistered virtue, unexercised and unbreathed, that never sallies out and sees her adversary, but slinks out of the race, where that immortal garland is to be run for not without dust and heat. . . .

If every action, which is good or evil in man at ripe years, were to be under pittance and prescription and compulsion, what were virtue but a name, what praise would then be due to well-doing. . . ? Many there be that complain of Divine Providence for suffering Adam to transgress; foolish tongues! When God gave him reason, He gave him freedom to choose, for reason is but choosing. . . . We ourselves esteem not of that obedience or love or gift, which is of force: God therefore left him free, set before him a provoking object, ever almost in his eyes; herein consisted his merit, herein the right of his reward, the praise of his abstinence. Wherefore did He create passions within us, pleasures round about us, but that these rightly tempered are the very ingredients of virtue . . . ?

To be free is the same thing exactly as to be pious, wise, just, temperate, self-providing, abstinent from the property of other people, and in fine, to be magnanimous and brave. To be the opposite of all this is the same as being a slave. And by the judgment of God it comes to pass that a nation that cannot rule and govern itself, but has surrendered itself in slavery to its own lusts, is surrendered also to other masters . . . and made a slave both with and against its own will.

John Milton

REHEARSING HIS BENEFITS

Psalm 103:1-2

As for himself, Epictetus is filled with awe and gratitude by the mystery and splendor of things, and he intones to the Creator a pagan *Magnificat* that is one of the supreme passages in the history of religion:

> What language is adequate to praise all the works of Providence? . . . If we had sense, ought we to be doing anything else, publicly or privately, than hymning and praising the Deity, and rehearsing his benefits? Ought we not, as we dig and plow and eat, to sing a hymn of praise to God? . . . What then?—since most of you have become blind, ought there not to be someone to fulfill this office for you, and in behalf of all sing hymns of praise to God?

Though we have here no word for immortality, and can trace all these ideas back to the Stoics and the Cynics, we find in these pages remarkable parallels to many attitudes of early Christianity. Epictetus, indeed, sometimes advances beyond Christianity: he denounces slavery, condemns capital punishment, and wishes to have criminals treated as sick men. He advocates a daily examination of conscience and announces a kind of Golden Rule: "What you shun to suffer, do not make others suffer;" and he adds: "If a man is reported to have spoken ill of you, make no defense, but say, "He did not know the rest of my faults, else he would not have mentioned only these." He advises men to return good for evil, and to "submit when reviled;" to fast now and then and "abstain from the things you desire." Sometimes he speaks of the body with the blasphemous contempt of an unscoured anchorite: "The body is of all things the most unpleasant and most foul. . . . It is astonishing that we should love a thing to which we perform such strange services every day. I fill this bag, and then I empty it; what is more troublesome?" There are passages that breathe the piety of Augustine and the eloquence of Newman: "Use me henceforward, O God, as thou wilt; I am of one mind with thee. I am thine. I ask exemption from nothing that seems good in thy sight. Where thou wilt, lead me; in what raiment thou wilt, clothe me."

Will Durant

SILENT ADORATION

Psalm 42:1-5

When man in his littleness and God in His glory meet, we all understand that what God says has infinitely more worth than what man says. And yet our prayer so often consists in the utterance *of our thoughts* of what we need, that we give God no time to speak to us. Our prayers are often so indefinite and vague. It is a great lesson to learn, that to be silent unto God is the secret of true adoration. Let us remember the promise, "In quietness and confidence shall be your strength."

"My soul, wait thou only upon God; for my expectation is from Him."

"I will wait for the Lord; my soul doth wait, and in His word do I hope."

It is as the soul bows itself before Him to remember His greatness and His holiness, His power and His love, and seeks to give Him the honor and the reverence and the worship that are His due, that the heart will be opened to receive the Divine impression of the nearness of God and of the working of His power.

O Christian, do believe that such worship of God—in which you bow low and ever lower in your nothingness, and lift up your thoughts to realize God's presence, as He gives Himself to you in Christ Jesus—is the sure way to give Him the glory that is His due, and will lead to the highest blessedness to be found in prayer.

Do not imagine that it is time lost. Do not turn from it, if at first it appears difficult or fruitless. Be assured that it brings you into the right relation to God. It opens the way to fellowship with Him. It leads to the blessed assurance that He is looking on you in tender love and working in you with a secret but Divine power. And as at length you become more accustomed to it, it will give you the sense of His presence abiding with you all the day. It will make you strong to testify for God. Someone has said, "No one is able to influence others for goodness and holiness, beyond the amount that there is of God in him." Men will begin to feel that you have been with God.

Andrew Murray

THE GREAT MEANS

Psalm 96:9

The better we know God the more wonderful becomes our insight into the power of intercession. We begin to understand that it is the great means by which man can take part in the carrying out of God's purpose. God has entrusted the whole of His redemption in Christ to his people to make known and to communicate to men. In all this, intercession is the chief and essential element, because it is in it that His servants enter into the full fellowship with Christ, and receive the power of the Spirit of Heaven as their power for service.

It is easy to see why God had so ordered it. In very deed God desires to renew us after His image and likeness. And there is no other way to do this but by our making His desires our own, so that we breathe His disposition; and in love sacrifice ourselves, so that we may become, in a measure, even like Christ, "ever living to make intercession." Such can be the life of the consecrated believer.

The clearer the insight into this great purpose of God, the more will the need be felt to enter very truly into God's Presence in the spirit of humble worship and holy adoration. The more we thus take time to abide in God's Presence, to enter fully into His mind and will, to get our whole soul possessed by the thought of His glorious purpose, the stronger will our faith become that God will Himself work out all the good pleasure of His will through our prayers. As the glory of God shines upon us, we shall become conscious of the depths of our helplessness; and so rise up into the faith that believes that God will do above all that we can ask or think.

Intercession will lead to the feeling of the need of a deeper adoration. Adoration will give new power for intercession. A true intercession and a deeper adoration will ever be found to be inseparable.

Andrew Murray

PRAISE CAN ROUT THE DEVIL

Psalm 100:4

There are many times when it is more important to praise God than to continue in petition. Praise lifts your eyes from the battle to the victory, for Christ is already Victor, and you have the Victor in your heart that you might have His victory in your life and in your prayer. Normally, all prayer should begin with praise (Ps. 100:4). The Holy Spirit often wants to lead you out of burdened intercession into victorious praise. Burden-bearing is scriptural, but praise is even more so. . . .

Praise renews your strength. Waiting on God and hoping in Him renew you spiritually and often physically also (Isa. 40:29-31). Praising God is often even more effective than prayer in refreshing, reviving, and empowering you. Every Christian at times experiences a sense of spiritual dryness. Certainly, after a spiritual battle, there is mental and emotional exhaustion. Again and again we need an outpouring of the Spirit. Praise brings a change of mood. Praise opens an artesian well of faith and joy. Praise is one of God's means for your inner renewal (2 Cor. 4:6; Ps. 103:1-5). When you are sincere in your praise of God, praise is holy, God-pleasing, and powerful.

You will be far stronger spiritually if you build praise into your daily walk with the Lord. You will be healthier physically by making praise to the Lord a part of your lifestyle. As you praise the Lord, worry flees. Praise drives away frustration, tension, and depression. Praise drives out the darkness and turns on God's light. Praise cleanses the atmosphere of Satan's suggestions of doubt, criticism, and irritation. Praise gives you a heavenly transfusion.

A.B. Simpson called praise both physical tonic and a wholesome stimulant. Praise will change the atmosphere of your life, your home, and your church.

Wesley Duewel

"I HAVE FIXED THE HABIT"

Galatians 6:10

As a Christian, you should go through life blessing others. You can bring streams of blessing, refreshment, and encouragement wherever you go just by punctuating your days with unceasing prayer for others. As time and opportunity permit, you should bless in every possible way as many as you can (Gal. 6:10). Your presence should always bring a blessing. But this will be most true if you are faithfully asking for God's blessing on all about you. You can find opportunities to fill your day with prayers of blessing if you are observant.

General Stonewall Jackson said, "I have so fixed the habit in my mind that I never raise a glass of water to my lips without asking God's blessing, never seal a letter without putting a word of prayer under the seal, never take a letter from the post without a brief sending of my thoughts heavenward, never change my classes in the lecture room without a minute's petition for the cadets who go out and for those who come in."

A beloved English physician of the 1600s, Sir Thomas Browne, was an example of constant prayers of blessing. He said, "I have resolved to pray more and pray always, to pray in all places where quietness inviteth, in the house, on the highway and on the street; and to know no street or passage in this city that may not witness that I have not forgotten God. . . . I purpose to take occasion of praying upon the sight of any church which I may pass, that God may be worshipped there in spirit, and that souls may be saved there; to pray daily for my sick patients and for the patients of other physicians; at my entrance into any home to say, 'May the peace of God abide here;' after hearing a sermon to pray for a blessing on God's truth and upon the messenger; upon the sight of a beautiful person to bless God for His creatures, to pray for the beauty of such an one's soul, that God may enrich her with inward graces.

Wesley Duewel

THE COMMAND OF FAITH

Acts 16:18

Elijah was a mighty man of prayer, but there were times when he was led to use the command of faith. He told the widow at Zarephath to prepare a meal for him first, and she would have a miracle supply of food that would last till the famine was over (I Kings 17:8-16). He told Ahaziah's rude captain, "If I am a man of God, may fire come down from heaven" (2 Kings 1:10). The fire appeared and consumed the captain and fifty men. When Elijah and Elisha reached the Jordan River, Elijah did not pray. Instead, he smote the water and the Jordan rolled back like the Red Sea had done for Moses. When Elisha returned after Elijah's ascension, he also smote the waters of the Jordan, and they parted for Elisha too (2:14).

Jesus repeatedly demonstrated and used the command of faith. In Cana of Galilee, the scene of His first miracle, He simply commanded the servants to fill the water pots with water. He commanded the lepers, "Be clean." He touched blind eyes and said, "Be opened." He commanded deaf ears, "Be opened." To the paralytic, He said, "Get up." He touched feverish bodies, leprous bodies, even dead bodies, the miracle happened. At the grave He commanded, "Lazarus, come forth." He rebuked evil spirits, and they came out. He rebuked the wind and said to the stormy waves, "Quiet, be still!"

The apostles also practiced the command of faith. At the gate of the temple, Peter said, "Get up." To Dorcas, who lay in death, "Get up." To the sorcerer Elymas, Paul said, "You are going to be blind!" And he was. At Lystra Paul called to the man lame from birth, "Stand up on your feet." To the demon enslaving the girl at Philippi, Paul ordered, "In the name of Jesus Christ I command you to come out of her." The spirit instantly left her (Acts 16:18).

Wesley Duewel

PRESERVING THE PRESENCE

Mark 13:33, 37

This poor woman supported her husband and his five children. She had a wonderful gift of prayer, and amidst her great suffering and extreme poverty, preserved the presence of God, and tranquility of mind. There was also a shopkeeper, and one who made locks, very much affected with God. These were close friends. Sometimes the one and sometimes the other read to this laundress; and they were surprised to find that she was instructed by the Lord himself in all they read to her, and spoke divinely of it.

Those friars sent for this woman, and threatened her much if she did not leave off prayer, telling her it was only for churchmen to pray, and that she was very bold to practice it. She replied, "that Christ had commanded all to pray, and that he had said, "What I say unto you I say unto all (Mark 13:33,37), without specifying either priests or friars; that without prayer she could not support her crosses and poverty; that formerly she had lived without it, and then was very wicked; that since she had been in the exercise of it, she had loved God with all her soul; so that to leave off prayer was too renounce her salvation, which she could not do." She added "that they might take twenty persons who had never practiced prayer, and twenty of those who were in the practice of it." Then, said she, "Inform yourselves of the lives of both sorts, and ye will see if ye have any reason to cry out against prayer." Such words as these, from such a woman, one would think might have fully convinced them; but instead of that, it only irritated them the more. They assured her "she should have no absolution till she promised them to desist from prayer." She said, "It depended not on her, and that Christ is master of what he communicates to his creatures, and of doing with it what he pleases."

Madame Guyon

ON TERMS OF FRIENDSHIP

Isaiah 53:5

For prayer is nothing else than being on terms of friendship with God. It is frequently conversing in secret with Him Who loves us.

Now true love and lasting friendship require certain affections; those of our Lord we know are absolutely perfect. Ours are vicious, sensual, and thankless. You cannot, therefore, bring yourselves to love Him as He loves you, because you do not have the same disposition to do so. If you do not love Him, you should be concerned with having His friendship and noticing how great His love is for you. Then you can rise above that pain of being much with Him Who is so different from you.

One day when I went into the oratory to pray, I saw a picture which had been hung there to celebrate a particular feast of the church. It was a representation of Christ so grievously wounded. The very sight of it deeply moved me. For it showed so graphically how much Jesus had loved us by His sufferings for us. So keenly did I feel my part in wounding Him that I thought my heart would break. So I threw myself upon the ground beside it, my tears flowing copiously. I implored Him to strengthen me once and for all, that I might never grieve Him again. . . .

This was then how I prayed. I pictured Christ as being inside me. I used to think about those times when He was most lonely, during those times He must have been most afflicted and alone, like someone in trouble. I then came close to Him.

St. Teresa of Avila

FAR ABOVE ECSTACIES

II Corinthians 11:14

Such was the prayer that was given me at once, which is far above ecstacies, transports or visions. All these gifts are less pure, and more subject to illusion or deceits from the enemy.

Visions are in the inferior powers of the soul, and cannot produce true union—therefore, the soul must not dwell or rely upon them, or be retarded by them; they are but favors and gifts—'tis the Giver alone must be our object and aim.

It is of such that St. Paul speaks, when he says, that "Satan transform himself into an angel of light," 2 Cor. 11:14, which is generally the case with such as are fond of visions, and lay a stress on them; because they are apt to convey a vanity to the soul, or at least hinder it from humbly attending to God only.

Ecstacies arise from a sensible relish, and may be termed a kind of spiritual sensuality, wherein the soul letting itself go too far, by reason of the sweetness it finds in them, falls imperceptibly into decay. The crafty enemy presents such sort of interior elevations and raptures, for baits to entrap the soul; to render it sensual, to fill it with vanity and self-love, to fix its esteem and attention on the gifts of God, and to hinder it from following Jesus Christ in the way of renunciation, and of death to all things.

And as to distinct interior words, they too are subject to illusion: the enemy can form and counterfeit them. Or if they come from a good angel (for God himself never speaks thus), we may mistake and misapprehend them; for they are spoken in a divine manner, but we construe them in a human and carnal manner.

But the immediate word of God has neither tone nor articulation. It is mute, silent, and unutterable; for it is Jesus Christ himself, the real and essential Word—who in the center of the soul, that is disposed for receiving him, never one moment ceases from his living, fruitful, and divine operation.

Madame Guyon

STEEPED IN PRAYER

Daniel 6:10

They were men of prayer. The whole Book of Daniel is steeped in prayer. If you have here the tumult and the shouting of the captains and the kings, you have also the deep calm of the secret place of the Most High. Daniel himself, when death was in the air, flung open his western windows towards Jerusalem, and three times a day knelt praying to his fathers' God. And Shadrach, Meshach, Abednego were men of the same breed.

Today we have lost too much the spirit of prayer. We do not believe in it as Christ believed in it. By prayer, Jesus routed the demons of the desert. By prayer, the apostles shook down the throne of Nero. By prayer, Francis and Luther and Wesley and many another brought from the four winds the breathe upon the dry bones of an effete ecclesiastical institution, and the dead bones sprang to life, an exceeding great army. By real, concentrated, believing prayer the Church today could change the present dangerous situation out of recognition. The real malady of the Church is not theological stagnation nor social indifference: it is prayer paralysis.

All through this story of Daniel you can feel the waft of the supernatural, just because these men were men of prayer. And for ourselves, so apt to get rushed and tired and hectic and despondent, this is the secret— the peace and poise and power of prayer. This can still beat all the Nebuchadnezzars of life, as in the days of old. God can deliver me out of thy clutches, O world, and He will deliver me; but if not, if darkest tragedy and chaos come and what men call disaster, nevertheless, O world, I have fought the fight, I have finished the course, I have kept the faith.

James S. Stewart

PLEASANT, ENJOYABLE EXERCISE

Luke 22:39-45

Do you know anything about spending one costly drop of blood in vicarious intercession? There is nothing worked in the way of result in answer to prayer that does not cost somebody something. "Who in the days of His flesh, having offered up prayers and supplications with strong crying and tears. . . ." When you meet a sick soul, do you cry awhile and then go home and sleep, instead of taking that soul before God and vicariously interceding until by reliance on the Holy Spirit, Jesus Christ is presented to that darkened, difficult life? Blessed be the Name of God, there is no case too hard for Jesus Christ!

Oswald Chambers

If we are simply to pray to the extent of a simple and pleasant and enjoyable exercise, and know nothing of watching in prayer, and of weariness in prayer, we shall not draw down the blessing that we may. We shall not sustain our missionaries who are overwhelmed with the appalling darkness of heathenism. . . . We must serve God even to the point of suffering, by personal self-denial, to the point of pain, the kingdom of Christ. . . . It is ever true that what costs little is worth little.

Hudson Taylor

And now we have told you a little of what is going on. There are days when nothing seems to be done, and then again there are days when the Terrible seems almost visible, as he gathers up his strength, and tears and mauls his prey. And so it is true we have to fight a separate fight for each soul. But another view of the case is a strength to us many a time. "We are not ourselves fighting, but the Powers of Light are fighting against the Powers of Darkness," and the coming of the victory is only a question of time. "Shall the prey be taken from the Mighty or the captives of the Terrible be delivered? But thus saith the Lord, Even the captives of the Mighty shall be taken away and the prey of the Terrible shall be delivered."

Amy Carmichael

AND HE PRAYED AGAIN

James 5:17

Elijah prayed and sent his servant seven times to see if there was evidence of rain; and the seventh time his servant saw a little cloud. Before long, there was a great rain, and the nation was saved.

Do we need "showers of blessing" today? We certainly do!

"But Elijah was a special prophet of God," we might argue. "We can expect God to answer his prayers in a wonderful way."

"Elijah was a man just like us," stated James (5:17, NIV). He was not perfect; in fact, right after his victory on Mount Carmel, Elijah became afraid and discouraged and ran away. But he was a "righteous man," that is, obedient to the Lord and trusting Him. God's promises of answered prayer are for all his children, not just for ones we may call the spiritual elite.

Elijah prayed in faith, for God told him He would send the rain (1 Kings 18:1). "Prayer," said Robert Law, "is not getting man's will done in heaven. It's getting God's will done on earth." You cannot separate the Word of God and prayer, for in His Word He gives us the promises that we claim when we pray.

Elijah was not only believing in his praying, but he was persistent. "He prayed . . . and he prayed again" (James 5:17-18). On Mount Carmel, Elijah continued to pray for rain until his servant reported "a cloud the size of a man's hand." Too many times we fail to get what God promises because we stop praying. It is true that we are not heard "for our much praying" (Matt. 6:7); but there is a difference between vain repetitions and true believing persistence in prayer.

Warren Wiersbe

"I AM GOING TO FIND OUT"

Zechariah 4:6

Upon returning to China in the fall of 1901, after having recuperated from the harrowing effects of the Boxer Rebellion, I began to experience a growing dissatisfaction with the results of my missionary work.

In the early pioneering years I had buoyed myself with the assurance that a seedtime must always precede a harvest, and had, therefore, been content to persist in the apparently futile struggle.

But now thirteen years had passed and the harvest seemed further away than ever. I felt sure there was something larger ahead of me, if I only had the vision to see what it was, and the faith to grasp it. . . .

Of great inspiration to me were the reports of the Welsh Revival of 1904-1905, for they made me to know that revivals were not a thing of the past. Late in the fall of 1905 a pamphlet containing selections from Chas. G. Finney's Autobiography and Revival Lectures was sent to me by a friend in India. It was the final something that set me on fire!

On the front page there was a statement to the effect that a farmer might just as well pray for a temporal harvest without fulfilling the laws of nature, as for Christians to expect a great ingathering of souls by simply asking for it and without bothering to fulfill the laws governing the spiritual harvest.

"If Finney is right," I vowed, "then I am going to find out what those laws are, and obey them, no matter what it costs."

About this time our Foreign Mission Secretary asked me to visit the revival in Korea. Witnessing the Lord at work in the Korean revival was of incalculable significance in my life because it showed me at first-hand the boundless possibilities of the revival method. Korea made me feel, as it did many others, that Revival was God's plan for setting the world aflame.

The missionaries in Korea were just ordinary people. I did not notice any outstanding people among them. It was in prayer that they were different.

Never have I been so conscious of the Divine Presence as I was in these Korean prayer meetings.

Those missionaries seemed to carry us right up in prayer to the Throne of God. One indeed had the feeling they were communing face to face with God.

What impressed me was the practical nature of the revival. It was no wild gust of "religious enthusiasm" dying with the wind upon whose wings it had been borne. There were the usual outward manifestations that accompany such miraculous outpourings of spiritual power.

But beyond that there were tens of thousands of Korean men and women whose lives had been completely transformed by the divine fire.

Every one seemed almost pathetically eager to spread the "Glad Tidings." Even little boys would run up to people on the street and plead with them to accept Christ as their Savior. Everywhere I saw an evident devotion for the Holy Word. Everyone seemed to carry a Bible. And permeating it all was that marvelous spirit of prayer.

On my return to China, I was asked by the missionaries of Kikungshan to tell them the story of the Korean Revival. On Sunday evening as I drew to a close my account of the Spirit's outpouring on the churches of Korea, it seemed the stillness of death pervaded the assembly.

The suppressed sobs became audible here and there. In a little while missionaries were rising to their feet and in tears were confessing their faults to one another.

A conference of prepared addresses had been planned for the ensuing week. But when the missionaries met on Monday morning it was decided that we would throw the prepared scheduled aside and continue in prayer and along whatever line the Lord should move us.

Jonathan Goforth

NOT MEASURED BY THE CLOCK

Isaiah 40:29-31

Our devotions are not measured by the clock, but time is of their essence. The ability to wait and stay and press belongs essentially to our intercourse with God. Hurry, everywhere unseeming and damaging, is so to an alarming extent in the great business of communion with God.

Short devotions are the bane of deep piety. Calmness and strength are never the companions of hurry. Short devotions deplete spiritual vigor, arrest spiritual progress, sap spiritual foundations, blight the root and bloom of spiritual life.

They are the prolific source of backsliding, the sure indication of a superficial piety; they deceive, blight, rot the seed, and impoverish the soil.

It is true that Bible prayers in word and print are short, but the praying men of the Bible were with God through many a sweet and holy wrestling hour.

They won by few words but long waiting. The prayers Moses records may be short, but Moses prayed to God with fastings and mighty cryings forty days and nights.

The statement of Elijah's praying may be condensed to a few brief paragraphs, but doubtless Elijah, who when "praying he prayed," spent many hours of fiery struggle and lofty intercourse with God before he could, with assured boldness, say to Ahab,

"There shall not be dew nor rain these years, but according to my word" (1 Kings 17:1).

To cut short the praying makes the whole religious character short, scrimpy, niggardly, and slovenly.

It takes good time for the full flow of God into the human spirit. Short devotions cut the pipe of God's full flow. It takes time in the secret places to get the full revelation of God. Little time and hurry mar the picture (Psalms 27:14).

Henry Martyn laments that "want of private devotional reading and shortness of prayer through incessant sermon-making had produced much strange-ness between God and his soul."

He judged that he had dedicated too much time to public ministrations and too little to private communion with God. He was much impressed to set apart times for fasting and to devote times for solemn prayer.

Resulting from this he records: "Was assisted this morning to pray for two hours."

Said William Wilberforce the peer of kings: "I must secure more time for private devotions. I have been living far too public for me. The shortening of private devotions starves the soul; it grows lean and faint. I have been keeping too late hours."

Of a failure in Parliament he says: "Let me record my grief and shame, and all, probably, from private devotions having been contracted, and so God let me stumble." More solitude and earlier hours was his remedy.

More time and early hours for prayer would act like magic to revive and invigorate many a decayed spiritual life. More time and early hours for prayer would be manifest in holy living. A holy life would not be so rare or so difficult a thing—if our devotions were not so short and hurried.

E.M. Bounds

SOMETIMES AN AGONY

Acts 16:25

All great soul-winners have been men of much and mighty prayer, and all great revivals have been preceded and carried out by persevering, prevailing prayer in the closet. Before Jesus began His ministry, when great multitudes followed Him, He spent forty days and nights in secret prayer and fasting (Matt. 4:1-11).

Paul prayed without ceasing. Day and night his prayers and pleadings and intercessions went up to God. (Acts 16:25; Phil. 1:3-11; Col. 1:3,9-11).

The baptism of the Spirit, and the three thousand conversions in one day, were preceded by ten days of prayer and praise, heart-searching, and Bible-searching. And they continued in prayer until, on another day, five thousand were converted, and "a great company of the priests became obedient to the faith." (Acts 4:4; 6:4).

Luther prayed three hours a day, and he broke the Roman yoke and the spell of ages, and set captive nations free.

John Knox used to spend nights in prayer, and cry to God, saying, "Give me Scotland, or I die!" and God gave him Scotland.

Baxter stained the walls of his study with praying breath, and sent a tide of salvation through all the land.

Half Nights and Whole Nights of Prayer

Over and over again, John Wesley in his Journals tells us of half and whole nights of prayer in which God drew near, and he and his helpers were empowered to rescue England from paganism, and sent a revival of pure, aggressive religion throughout the whole earth. . . .

The other day a pastor, who prays an hour or more each morning, and a half hour before his evening meeting, and who is very successful in getting souls saved, was lamenting to me that he often has to force himself to secret prayer. But in this he is tempted and tried like his brethren. All men of much prayer have suffered the same (Eph. 6:10-18).

Mr. Bramwell, who used to see hundreds of people converted and sanctified everywhere he went, prayed six hours a day, and yet he said he went to secret prayer reluctantly. He had to sting himself to do it.

And after he got to praying, he would often have dry seasons, but he persevered in faith, and the heavens would open, ad he would wrestle with God until the victory came. Then when he preached the heavens would open and rain down blessings on the people (Isa. 40:29-31).

One man asked another why it was Mr. Bramwell was able to say such new and wonderful things that brought blessings to so many people. "Because he lives so near the Throne that God tells him His secrets, and then he tells them to us," said the other.

Samuel Logan Brangle

IN THE MATTER OF INTERCESSION

I Timothy 2:1

James Fraser now began to assess the size of his task. He wasn't afraid of arduous climbing nor or primitive living, because he loved mountaineering anyway. But the prospect of working alone to build a living church to stand against such a powerful form of spirit-worship was daunting. He knew the hosts of God stood with him. But he also knew that there was no such thing as a solo worker in God's plan. He had, of course, the Mission support behind him, but clearly no-one could be spared to go with him as yet; everyone was involved in Chinese work and stretched to the limit. But he now wrote home about a new kind of partnership.

I know you will never fail me in the matter of intercession (he wrote to his mother), but would you think and pray about getting a group of like-minded friends, whether few or many, whether in one place or scattered, to join in the same petitions? If you could form a small prayer circle I would write regularly to the members.

This was the first suggestion of such partners in his work, and it was acted upon immediately back in Letcheworth. In ones and twos people int he area of his home agreed to share the burden with him. They undertook the task much as a business partnership; it was a clear and definite commitment to the job. They would pray him through.

What a number of earnest, spiritually-minded Christians there are at home and how correspondingly rich are the prayer forces of the Church! How I long for some of this wealth for myself and the Lisu here. Yes, I have had it in measure already . . . but I should very, very much like a wider circle of intercessors.

Our work among the Lisu is not going to be a bed or roses, spiritually, I know enough about Satan to realize that he will have all his weapons ready for determined opposition. He would be a missionary simpleton who expected plain sailing in ny work of God. I will not, by God's grace, let anything deter me from going straight ahead in the path which He leads.

Eileen Crossman

NO PROMINENT NAME

Habakkuk 3:2

The revival that marked the end of the nineteenth century has associated with it the name of Dwight L. Moody. But there was no prominent name connected with the great revival of 1858. One day in that year there appeared a notice in the New York papers announcing that each day at noon one Jeremiah Lamphier would pray in the room at the top of the stair in the old North Dutch Church on Fulton Street. It stated that he would pray for a revival to come to America, and that anyone who was interested was invited to come and pray with him. Lamphier kept his notice running, and for several days nobody came. Then one man came and then another, and in time yet others. Finally, the prayer group overflowed into the sanctuary of the church and, when this became too small to hold the crowds, other groups were formed to meet in adjoining churches. The movement spread to other cities, and by and by all over the land there were groups meeting at noon for prayer. A revival came to the land such as had never come before and as has not come since. The striking fact was that all of it traced back ultimately to one man of faith upon his knees with a great passion in his heart, and that in due time others began to share with him his great concern.

The same thing happened in the case of individuals. One man prays, and another man, perhaps far removed from him, feels the blessed lifting effects of such prayer in his own life. Bishop Seth Ward, after he had been in China for a little while, as a newly elected bishop, received one day a letter from the saintly Bishop O.P. Fitzgerald who was resident in Nashville, saying, "There has not been a day since you left Nashville that I have not carried you up to the throne in my prayers, and I shall continue to bear you up every day for the Father's blessing." Bishop Ward testified that half way around the world he could feel the efficacy of those prayers, and that it was his firm conviction that they made a tremendous difference in the effectiveness of his ministry.

Ray Short

RELIGIOUS VALVES AND PUBLIC ORDER

Matthew 4:23-25

Correlation between religious values and public order was dramatically evident during a religious revival early in this century. The revival began in small Methodist churches in Wales and quickly spilled out into society. During New Year's week in 1905, for the first time ever there was not a single arrest for drunkenness in Swansea County, the police announced. In Cardiff the authorities reported a 40 percent decrease in the jail population while the tavern trade fell off dramatically. Prayer meetings sprang up in coal mines; stores reported stocks of Bible sold out; dockets were cleared in criminal courts; and many police were unemployed. Stolen goods were returned to shocked store owners. One historian reported, "Cursing and profanity were so diminished that . . . a strike was provoked in the coal mines . . . so many men had given up using foul language that the pit ponies dragging the coal trucks in the mine tunnels did not understand what was being said to them and stood still, confused." The revival soon spread throughout the British Isles and much of the English-speaking world. Church attendance rose, and in many areas, as in Wales, public morality was dramatically affected.

Men and women who profess allegiance to the Kingdom of God become models for the rest of society. The role of the City of God, as Augustine said, is "to inspire men and women to organize their communities in the image and likeness of the heavenly city."

Nowhere in modern culture is this more crucial than in the area of the nature and origins of law. In the Kingdom of God, God is King and Lawgiver of all. This does not mean that the Old Testament's civic code should be passed by modern governments. What it does mean, as Plato and Cicero recognized, is that there are moral absolutes that must govern human behavior; there is a law rooted in truth upon which the laws of human society are based.

Charles Colson

EXCHANGING SAFETY FOR HAZZARDS

Matthew 10:1

The dynamic periods are those heroic times when God's people stirred themselves to do the Lord's bidding and went out fearlessly to carry His witness to the world. They exchanged the safety of inaction for the hazards of God-inspired progress. Invariably the power of God followed such action. The miracle of God went when and where His people went; it stayed when His people stopped.

The static periods were those times when the people of God tired of the struggle and sought a life of peace and security. Then they busied themselves trying to conserve the gains made in those more daring times when the power of God moved among them.

Bible history is replete with examples. Abraham "went out" on his great adventure of faith, and God went with him. Revelations, theophanies, the gift of Palestine, covenants and promises of rich blessings to come were the result. Then Israel went down into Egypt, the wonders ceased for four hundred years. At the end of that time Moses heard the call of God and stepped forth to challenge the oppressor. A whirlwind of power accompanied that challenge, and Israel soon began to march. As long as she dared to march God sent out His miracles to clear the way for her. Whenever she lay down like a fallow field He turned off His blessing and waited for her to rise again and command His power.

This is a brief but fair outline of the history of Israel and of the Church as well. As long as they "went forth and preached everywhere," the Lord worked "with them . . . confirming the word with signs following." But when they retreated to monasteries or played at building pretty cathedrals, the help of God was withdrawn till a Luther or a Wesley arose to challenge hell again. Then invariably God poured out His power as before.

A.W. Tozer

MIRACLES FOLLOW THE PLOW

Hosea 10:12

Here are two kinds of ground: fallow ground and ground that has been broken up by the plow. The fallow field is smug, contented, protected from the shock of the plow and the agitation of the harrow. Such a field, as it lies year after year, becomes a familiar landmark to the crow and the blue jay. Had it intelligence, it might take a lot of satisfaction in its reputation; it has stability; nature has adopted it; it can be counted upon to remain always the same while the fields around it change from brown to green and back to brown again. Safe and undisturbed, it sprawls lazily in the sunshine, the picture of sleepy contentment. But it is paying a terrible price for its tranquility: Never does it see the miracle of growth; never does it feel the motions of mounting life nor see the wonders of bursting seed nor the beauty of ripening grain. Fruit it can never know because it is afraid of the plow and the harrow.

In direct opposite to this, the cultivated field has yielded itself to the adventure of living. The protecting fence has opened to admit the plow, and the plow has come as plows always come, practical, cruel, business-like and in a hurry. Peace has been shattered by the shouting farmer and the rattle of machinery. The field has felt the travail of change; it has been upset, turned over, bruised and broken, but its rewards come hard upon its labors. The seed shoots up into the daylight its miracle of life, curious, exploring the new world above it. All over the field the hand of God is at work in the age-old and ever renewed service of creation. New things are born, to grow, mature, and consummate the grand prophecy latent in the seed when it entered the ground. Nature's wonders follow the plow.

A.W. Tozer

A REMARKABLE REVIVAL BEGAN

Acts 8:4-8

During the journey to Palestine McCheyne wrote, "For much of our safety I feel indebted to the prayers of my people, I mean the Christians among them, who do not forget us. If the veil of the world's machinery were lifted off, how much we could find is done in answer to the prayers of God's children." Although extremely weak and ill, McCheyne neglected not his own prayer life. While the tent was being erected at the end of a day's arduous journey, he would lie down on the ground under some tree, completely exhausted by the long ride. After lying almost speechless for half an hour, when the palpitation of his heart somewhat abated, he would propose that his friend Andrew Bonar, who was also a member of the party, and he should pray together. Often, at the point of death in a foreign land, feeling his faculties going, one by one, with every reason to expect that he would soon be with his God, McCheyne devoted himself to prayer for his people. He wrote to them, "When I got better, I used to creep out in the evenings about sunset. I often remembered you all then. I could not write, as my eyes and head were much affected; I could read but very little; I could speak very little, for I had hardly any voice; and so I had all my time to lay my people before God and pray for a blessing on them."

On one of those days when he was stretched on his bed, praying for his flock despite all his own suffering, a very remarkable revival began to be witnessed back in Dundee, under the preaching of Mr. W.C. Burns, who was supplying Mr. McCheyne's place in his absence. Beginning in Kilsyth, a great awakening took place which soon swept over Dundee.

MEMOIRS OF McCHEYNE
Andrew A. Bonar, Editor

A NEW ORTHODOXY

Romans 1:22

At the beginning of the year 1901, the renowned French scholar Berthelot delivered a speech in which he informed his audience that the age of religion has passed and that it must now be replaced by science. I refer to this speech because it was the first to fall into my hands and because it was delivered in the capital of the educated world by a person whom everyone recognizes to be a scholar. The same thought is constantly expressed everywhere, from philosophical treatises to newspaper feuilletons. In his speech Mr. Berthelot says that formerly there were two principles motivating human society: force and religion. Today these principles have become superfluous because *science* has replaced them. By the word science, Mr. Berthelot evidently means, like all who believe in science, a science that embraces every aspect of human knowledge, harmoniously united, assessed according to its degree of importance and in command of such methods that the data obtained is indisputably true. But since there is really no such science, and what is referred to as science is a collection of incidental, totally disconnected items of knowledge which are often completely useless, and not only fail to present the indisputable truth but very often present the most crude delusions, displayed as the truth today and refuted tomorrow, it is obvious that the thing which Mr. Berthelot claims must replace religion does not exist.

Leo Tolstoy

The dogmatism of science has become a new orthodoxy, disseminated by the Media and a State educational system with a thoroughness and subtlety far exceeding anything of the kind achieved by the Inquisition; to the point that to believe today in a miraculous happening like the Virgin Birth is to appear a kind of imbecile, whereas to disbelieve in an unproven and unprovable scientific proposition like the Theory of Evolution, and still more to question some quasi-scientific shibboleth like the Population Explosion, is to stand condemned as an obscurantist, an enemy of progress and enlightenment.

Malcolm Muggeridge

THE FORTRESS IS CRACKING

I Corinthians 1:27

Indeed, we are engaged in a life struggle. I might point out to you that every single anti-Christian system that dominates our world today rests its case on evolution. The two massive non-Christian movements today are: in the East, communism; and in the West, secular humanism. Both of these atheistic systems rest upon the single pillar of evolution.

Yet evolution has not established itself as an irrefutable fact, as its adherents would like people to believe; but rather, it is crumbling on every side. The fortress is cracking; the walls are giving way; the citadel is coming down; there are fissures everywhere! The whole of evolution is in absolute chaos today, and the public does not know it.

For example, does the general public realize that science as we know it today was created by Bible-believing Christians who supported the scriptural account of creation? Their names are recorded in every public library, along with the branch of science which they founded: Joseph Lister, antiseptic surgery; Louis Pasteur, bacteriology; Isaac Newton, calculus; Johannes Kepler, celestial mechanics; Robert Boyle, chemistry, Georges Cuvier, comparative anatomy; Charles Babbage, computer science; Lord Rayleigh, dimensional analysis; John Ambrose Fleming, electronics; James Clark Maxwell, electrodynamics; Michael Faraday, electromagnetics; Lord Kelvin, energetics; Jean-Henri Fabre, entomology of living insects; George Stokes, fluid mechanics; Sir John William Herschel, galactic astronomy; Gregor Mendel, genetics; Louis Agassiz, glacial geology; Blaise Pascal, hydrostatics; William Ramsay, isotopic chemistry; John Ray, natural history; George Bernhard Riemann, non-Euclidian geometry; Matthew Maury, oceanography; David Brewsterm optical mineralogy; the list goes on. Since Christians invented science, the evolutionist argument that "creationists are unscientific" would appear to be—well, unscientific.

James Kennedy

"THE DIVINE WISDOM KNOWETH"

Job 40:1-2

It is a matter of record that science never developed anywhere except where there was Christian influence. In addition, the extension of science has come mainly in areas where the Bible was most freely read.

Galileo, one of the first of modern scientists, believed that he was "thinking God's thoughts after Him." Galileo wrote:

"As to the truth, of which mathematical demonstrations give us the knowledge, it is the same which the Divine Wisdom knoweth; but . . . the manner whereby God knoweth the infinite propositions, whereof we understand some few, is highly more excellent than ours. . . ."

Galileo's faith in a rational universe to which mathematics can be applied is still a basic premise of modern science. Certainly there are those scientists who deny that the universe is rationally organized. But even these men act as if the universe can be understood. They go on making discoveries, but they can give no explanation as to why we should be able to understand things.

Indeed, they become a little ridiculous, for their basic belief, shorn of big words and complicated phrases, is: The universe is orderly because I am orderly; the universe is understandable because I make it understandable.

Fritz Ridenour

The attitude of science toward the notion of a supersensual universe, or series of universes, interacting with the material fabric we know—a concept fundamen-tal to any logical theory of immortality—has ceased to be the hostile or indifferent one it was. On the contrary, it might almost seem that the theory of a universe of finer and infinitely more potent substance is almost ready to be announced by our scientific thinkers as an inevitable conclusion from recent discoveries.

Charles Kassel In Immortality
and the New Physics, "North
American Review," October, 1922

FINDING THE RIGHT TICKET

Job 42:1-2

What chance did Moses have when writing this first chapter of Genesis of getting the thirteen items (geological) all accurate and in a satisfactory order? Using the estimates that we have just suggested, we must multiply them all together, and as a result we find Moses had one chance in 31,135,104,000,000,000,000,000 of getting both the items and the order accurate.

This is an extremely small chance. Let us try to visualize it. Suppose we decide to have a drawing and have this number of tickets printed. In order to get them printed, let us engage more than 8,000,000 presses, each capable of printing 2,000 tickets per minute. And then they would have to run day and night for 5,000,000 years to print this number of tickets. Now let one ticket be marked and the whole mass thoroughly stirred. Then we will blindfold you as we multiply our concept of the power of God, as shown by our sun, by 100 billion. But how many are 100 billion? If you were to count 250 a minute, day and night, it would take you just about one thousand years to count to 100 billion. This gives somewhat of a concept of the power needed for the creation of our galaxy.

Multiply this by a few trillion, the probable number of galaxies, and perhaps you will begin to have a concept of this phase of God's power as demonstrated by the radiation of the stars. If we get this concept, we should understand better what Christ meant when he said, "All power is given unto me."

SCIENCE SPEAKS
Peter W. Stoner

TEN PENNIES IN YOUR POCKET

Psalm 10:3-4

So many conditions are essential to life on our earth that they could not exist in proper relationship by chance. This is proved by the laws of mathematics.

Let me begin by supposing you mark ten pennies from one to ten, put them in your pocket, and give them a good shake. Now try to draw them out in sequence from one to ten, putting each coin back in your pocket after each draw and shuffling them all again. Mathematically, your chance of drawing number one first is one in ten; of drawing one and two in succession, one in 100; of drawing the first three numbers in succession, one in 1,000. The chance that you might draw all of them, from number one through number ten, in that order, would reach the unbelievable figure of one in 10,000,000,000. . . .

The earth rotates on its axis at the rate of about one thousand miles an hour. If it turned at the rate of a hundred miles an hour, our days and nights would be ten times as long, the summer sun would burn up our vegetation every day, and each sprout would freeze in such a long night. The sun, with a surface temperature of 12,000 degrees Fahrenheit, is just far enough away so that this "eternal fire" warms us just enough and not too much. It is marvelously stable, and during millions of years has varied so little that life has survived. But if the temperature on earth had changed so much as fifty degrees, on average, for a single year, all vegetation—and man with it—would be roasted or frozen. The earth travels around the sun at eighteen miles per second. If the rate of revolution had been, say, either six miles or forty miles each second, we would be too far from the sun or too close for our form of life to exist.

SEVEN REASONS WHY
A SCIENTIST BELIEVES IN GOD
A. Cressy Morrison

THICKER OR THINNER

I Chronicles 16:8-12

Had the crust of the earth been ten feet thicker, there would be no oxygen, without which animal life is impossible; and had the ocean been a few feet deeper, carbon dioxide and oxygen would have been absorbed and vegetable life on the surface of the land could not exist. There is a possibility that practically all the oxygen was taken up by the crust of the earth and the seven seas and that the advent of all oxygen-breathing animals had to await the growths of plants which release oxygen. Careful calculation seems to make this source of the oxygen we breathe possible, but, whatever its source, the quantity is exactly adjusted to our needs. If the atmosphere had been much thinner, some of the meteors which are now burned in the outer atmosphere by the millions every day would strike all parts of the earth. They travel from six to forty miles a second and would set fire to every burnable object. If they traveled as slowly as a bullet, they would all hit the earth and the consequences would be dire. As for man, the impact of a tiny meteor traveling ninety times as fast as a bullet would tear him in pieces by the heat of its passage. The atmosphere is just thick enough to let in the actinic rays needed for vegetation and to kill bacteria, produce vitamins, and not harm man.

The great balance wheel is that vast mass of water, the ocean, from which have come life, food, rain, temperate climate, plants, animals, and ultimately man himself. Let him who comprehends this stand in awe before its majesty.

All these facts about our universe could not be the result of chance. The laws of mathematics unerringly prove that they are the design of a Supreme Intelligence.

SEVEN REASONS WHY
A SCIENTIST BELIEVES IN GOD
A. Cressy Morrison

BLUNDERS IN THE BIBLE

Matthew 24:35

Do you know that for years the Science Research Bureau, headed by the late Dr. Harry Rimmer, publicly offered a reward of one thousand dollars to any person who could prove the existence of a scientific blunder in the Bible? Although that offer has been made in twenty-seven different countries, the thousand dollars is still uncollected. But before you attempt to collect the reward, we ought to tell you that in November of 1939, William Floyd of New York City, thinking he had pointed out several bona fide inaccuracies, brought suit against Dr. Rimmer. The case was tried in the Fourth District Municipal Court with the Honorable Benjamin Shalleck on the bench. Mr. Floyd called in his own self-chosen witnesses to prove that the Bible from a scientific standpoint is fallacious. He lost the suit, and Justice Shalleck threw the case out of the Court.

This absence of error in an ancient Book is truly remarkable, for all other ancient books, and even many recent ones, contain scientific blunders and mistakes. In the sacred writings of the Hindus, you find such fantastic nonsense as this: "The moon is 50,000 leagues higher than the sun and shines by its own light; night is caused by the sun's setting behind a huge mountain several thousand feet high, located in the center of the earth; this world, flat and triangular is composed of seven changes—one of honey, another of sugar, a third of butter, and still another of wine, and the whole mass is borne on the heads of countless elephants which in shaking produce earthquakes." Why is it that ridiculous teachings like these are nowhere to be discovered in the Bible, which is much more ancient than the sacred Vedas of India?

Vernon C. Grounds

THE SUPREME AND ONLY ANSWER

I Corinthians 1:30

Jesus Christ is the *supreme answer and the only answer!* He makes the difference between your being bound or free, condemned or pardoned. He is the greatest manifestation of God's power and love on earth; the Head of the Universe and Source of all Wisdom, superseding all philosophy, ritual and law.

Contrary to what some claim, many outstanding men have accepted the facts of the Gospel and testify to the power of Christ. For example, Lambert Dolphin, Jr., Stanford University research physicist, says:

> I wasn't even a true scientist until I met Jesus Christ. I couldn't be, for I was cut off from reality. Life with God is the only reality. And that is possible only through faith in Jesus Christ and His atoning death for our sins. Jesus Christ is the answer to the secret of the universe. In Him I've found the reason for life and the key to everything.

Walter F. Burke, as general manager of Project Mercury and Gemini, acknowledged: "I found nothing in science or space exploration to compel me to throw away my Bible or to reject my Savior, Jesus Christ, in whom I trust."

We cannot fully comprehend how the death of Christ on the cross saves us, but we do know He paid our debt by dying there in our place. If we believe this, we are set free from the guilt and power of sin.

Accepting Christ, or putting faith in Him, not only gains full pardon and forgiveness but it also makes you a new person! This is not the end but the beginning of a new, thrilling life of faith in Jesus Christ. Christ comes not merely to affect your life, but to live it. He has the answers to your problems, doubts, perplexities--and you turn them all over to Him.

David Wilkerson

LORD OF THE MIND

Mark 12:30

God is Lord of the mind, and our worship of Him may not be only with our heart and soul and strength, but also with our mind.

But there are dangers. And the Christian has his duty to point to them. If you start to worship God with your mind, but forget the other three parts of the quartet, it will become terribly easy to elevate yourself and, in effect, deny God. The devil is a very intellectual personage! So, when a German newspaper prints an article with the title 'The Machine is our Savior,' or when Mr. Nehru, on the occasion of the opening of the world's largest dam recently completed in India, spoke of his pleasure at coming to such a place, because 'these are the temples where I worship,' I believe that I can hear a low satanic chuckle. Too great a concentration on the machine can wean us from the fundamentals which the machine should help us to express. This is the greatest temptation of materialism for the average practical Englishman. As Mr. Kitson Clark has put it in his book, *The English Heritage:*

> The practical business of the world takes up so much time; the problems presented by the good which might be procured, or the evil which must be prevented, become so absorbing that direct interest in what is spiritual begins to fade. In due course the importance of spiritual issues seems to be solely derived from their probable effect on the material world; people are to be virtuous that they may better serve the needs of your policy, not because virtue has any inherent value in itself.

C.A. Coulson

"DONE NOTHING FOR US"

Genesis 1:1

If science has mesmerized our age by its miracles of practical achievements, it cannot be too strongly stressed that in the arena of our deepest and most desperate need it has done nothing for us. That is why religion is never out of date and why it speaks just as cogently to our space-minded generation as it did to Abraham when he struck his tents in Ur of the Chaldees long ago.

Murdo Macdonald

Butler never had any literary ambition, though he was a born writer. . . . He himself put the secret of his greatness into a single sentence of six words, which he addressed to me as we were crossing the courtyard of the British Museum together. He said, with the most intense emphasis, "Darwin banished mind from the universe." He added, "My grandfather quarrelled with Darwin's grandfather; my father quarrelled with Darwin's father; I quarrelled with Darwin; and my regret for having no son is that he cannot quarrel with Darwin's son." As a matter of fact Darwin had converted [Samuel] Butler for six weeks because in those days all we clever people who called ourselves Secularists, Freethinkers, Agnostics, Atheists, Positivists, Rationalists, or what not, and were called Infidels doomed to eternal damnation, were all anti-Clericals snatching at any stick big enough to whack the parsons; and the biggest stick was the Natural Selection of Darwin and Wallace, carried to absurdity. . . . We all, Butler included, grabbed it joyously. Butler alone thought it out deeply and quickly enough to grasp the horror of its banishment of mind from the universe.

The ensuing controversies only obscured this fundamental issue. They did not affect me because I had read the Patmos Evangelist's "In the Beginning was the Thought" and came up against the neo-Darwinist shallowness. . . . (Darwin, by the way, was no more a Darwinist than I am a Shavian.)

AUTOBIOGRAPHY OF
GEORGE BERNARD SHAW

"I HAD MOTIVES"

Colossians 2:8

In his book *Ends and Means* Huxley said, "I had motives for not wanting the world to have a meaning, consequently I assumed that it had none and was able without any difficulty to find satisfactory reasons for this assumption—for myself, as no doubt, for most of my contemporaries, the philosophy of meaninglessness was essentially an instrument of liberation. The liberation we desired was simultaneously liberation from a certain political and economic system and liberation from a certain system of morality. We objected to the morality because it interfered with our sexual freedom."

What about that? To satisfy their own lust, without sense of guilt these men actually led thousands of mixed-up youth down the path to emotional and moral destruction.

G. Campbell Morgan

First, Reason cannot explain everything; it is good enough as far as it goes, but it is not enough. There is man, there is the mystery of human life in its origins and destiny, there is the soul. Reason can fathom none of these. They are reached through Christianity, not Cartesian mechanics and logic. Second, scientific theism like all rational theology, turns God into a mere philosophic abstraction—in this case a geometer and convenient initial motive force and saver of mechanics. This God lets a Descartes or Newton be, and in so doing justifies His existence; thereafter His further self-perpetuation is quite unimportant. On the contrary Pascal's God is, as he says in the amulet he carried with him, the "God of Abraham, God of Isaac, God of Jacob. Not of the philosophers and the scholars." He remarks, "I cannot forgive Descartes. In all his philosophy he would have been quite willing to dispense with God. But he could not help granting Him a flick of the forefinger to start the world in motion. Beyond this he has no further need of God." Pascal saw, as some modern proponents of the scientific justification of religion have failed to see, that scientific pensees.

INTRODUCTION TO PENSEES
Blaise Pascal

CLOTHED HIM WITH OMNIPOTENCE

James 4:7

Let us boldly take our stand in Christ and as we submit to God and in His name and strength resist the Devil he will flee (James 4:7). He must retreat and fall back, for God says, he must. Some one has said that our unbelief has clothed the Devil with an omnipotence which he does not rightly possess and that he has no power over us if we do not fear him. This is certainly true, for he is a conquered foe.

Do we believe it, and do we treat him as if he was? We are told to "put on the complete armor of God with a view to having power to stand against the strategies of the adversary, to have power to withstand in the evil day and all things having accomplished, to stand, taking up the shield of faith in which ye shall have power all the ignited darts of the evil one to quench" (Roth. trans. Eph. 6:11-17).

Let us meet the Devil as a conquered foe and use the authority given to us by Christ to tread upon the serpents and scorpions and over all the power of the enemy, yes, the enemy, when he even comes as an angel of light, or the wicked spirits in the heavenlies. The Devil is the prince of the power of the air (Eph. 2:2). How often we feel the very atmosphere around us heavy and oppressive with the powers of evil and especially do the missionaries realize this in the heathen countries.

Physicians say that disease is produced by a germ life that floats in the air. Might it not be that Satan and the rulers of darkness and principalities and power and evil spirits in the heavenlies are very busy at work in this way? God is the giver of life and health, and is the devil the author of disease?

We must not be afraid of him but meet him with "It is written," and sing even when the fight is hard, "Victory." And always remember that he is a conquered foe, and we can then sing victory and believe it too.

"Thanks be unto God who at all times leads us in triumph to the Christ, and the fragrance of the knowledge of Him makes manifest, through us, in every place."

John Kimber

A SENSIBLE SOMETHING

Ephesians 1:13-14

He gives assurance of salvation in the form of an `earnest,' He gives us `foretastes' of that glory, samples of it, installments of it in order to make it real to us.

We do not `take it by faith;' we know; we have tasted it, we have felt it. It is the love of God being made real by means of this impression upon the mind and the heart by the Spirit. It is a sensible something; it is experimental; it affects the emotions and feelings; it is direct and immediate, not indirect and mediate. There is surely nothing more precious in the whole of Scripture, and yet how little we hear about it today. It seems to have dropped out of evangelical teaching. It is because of that `psychological' teaching about `taking it by faith and not worrying about your feelings.' What if Henry Venn had been in that position! He says himself that he does not know what he would have done, had not God made His love so plain and clear to him directly and immediately. He is so sure and certain of it in the depth of his soul. He was not `taking it by faith;' he knew it had been given to him by God Himself to prepare him for the grievous trial that was to come to him. And he was able to shout `Hallelujah!' No man has ever had the love of God `shed abroad' in his heart without knowing it; and it always leads to the shout!

D. Martyn Lloyd-Jones

IT COMES AND GOES

Matthew 4:10

All is not lost if sometimes you have less affection which you sometimes feel is the effect of grace present, and a sort of foretaste of your native land of Heaven; but hereon you must not lean too much, for it comes and goes. But to strive against evil motions of the mind and to reject (Matt. 4:10) immediately a suggestion of the Devil is a notable sign of virtue and shall have great reward.

. . . . Know that the ancient Enemy strives by all means to hinder your desire to do good, and to keep you void of all religious exercises, particularly from devout remembrance of My passion and from profitable calling to mind of sins, from the guard of your own heart, and from the first purpose of advancing in virtue. Many evil thoughts he forces on you, that he may cause a weariness and horror, to call you back from prayer and holy reading. Humble confession is displeasing to him and if he could he would cause you to cease from holy communion. . . .

My son you are not able always to stand in the more fervent desire of virtue, nor to persist in the highest stage of contemplation. But you must sometimes by reason of original corruption descend to inferior things, and bear the burden of this corruptible life, though against your will and with weariness. As long as you carry a mortal body, you shall feel weariness and heaviness of heart. You ought therefore in the flesh oftentimes to bewail the burden of the flesh; for you cannot employ yourself unceasingly in spiritual studies and divine contemplation.

Then it is expedient to fall to humble and outward works and to refresh yourself with good actions; to expect with firm confidence My coming and heavenly visitation.

Thomas A. Kempis

ONE OF HIS CONVERTS

I Peter 2:2

Dawson picked up a hitch-hiker whose speech indicated he was not a believer. Within moments he discovered this man was one of his "converts" of the previous year whose decision had not been followed up and who had virtually died on the vine. Shaken, Dawson reasoned that there must be countless such persons who had sincerely, perhaps with tears, called on the name of the Lord, but whose lives had not been changed. What was wrong?

From that time on Dawson resolved to follow up anyone he led to Christ—a work more difficult than soulwinning—and to encourage others to give their converts the rightful opportunity to grow in Christ. The truth had come into focus, and he made an axiom of it: "You can lead a man to Christ in twenty minutes to a couple of hours, but it takes twenty weeks to a couple of years to adequately follow him up." The hitch-hiker convert startled him into realigning his ministry—less emphasis on getting the decision and more on growing up into Christ.

The conviction of the need to build laborers and the conviction of the imperative of follow-up for the new Christian began to shape the course of Dawson's ministry and figure prominently in his preaching. He became a pest on the subject until follow-up became a staple of Christian ministry.

"Don't bring spiritual babes to birth and leave them to die for lack of nourishment," he exhorted his audiences. Giving them a Bible was not enough. They must be fed. "Don't just set the baby in the pantry with a can opener. Mix his formula and heat it to the right temperature; then hold the bottle for him." The hit-and-run evangelism he and others had practiced for years, resulting only in the "survival of the fittest," he now condemned as dead wrong.

THE STORY OF DAWSON TROTMAN
Betty Skinner

NOT A SPARK OF HOLINESS

I John 1:3

That ye may have fellowship with the Father—O beloved, this is so wonderful, that I could not have believed it, if I had not seen it! Shall a hell-deserving worm come to share with the holy God? Oh the depth and the length of the love of God, it passeth knowledge!

A natural man has not spark of God's holiness in him. There is a kind of goodness about you. You may be kind, pleasant, agreeable, good-natured, amiable people; there may be a kind of integrity about you, so that you are above stealing or lying; but as long as you are in a natural state, there is not a grain of God's holiness in you. You have not a grain of that absolute hatred against all sin which God has; you have none of that flaming love for what is lovely, pure, holy, which dwells in the heart of God. But the moment you believe on a manifested Christ, that moment you receive the Spirit, the same Spirit which dwells in the infinite bosom of the Father dwelleth in you; so you become partakers of God's holiness, you become partakers of divine nature. You will not be as holy as God; but the same stream that flows through the heart of God will be given you. Ah! does not your heart break to be holier? Look then to Jesus, abide in Him, and you will share the same spirit with God Himself.

Andrew A. Bonar

The soul is lost in God with Jesus Christ. All *around* it is God. It is now so "rooted and fixed in God" that it is an immovable rock, not to be shaken by trials or blows of any kind (Acts 20:24). God puts it to strange testings and He does not leave it the shadow of anything to cling to, or rest upon, out of *Himself.*

Jessie Penn-Lewis

THE ONLY ULTIMATE DISASTER

Hebrews 11:8-10

Every day is rich with new aspects of Him and His working. As one makes new discoveries about his friends by being with them, so one discovers the "individuality" of God if one entertains Him continuously.

One thing I have seen this week is that God loves beauty. Everything He makes is lovely. The clouds, the tumbling river, the waving lake, the soaring eagle, the slender blade of grass, the whispering of the wind, the fluttering butterfly, this graceful transparent nameless child of the lake which clings to my window for an hour and vanishes forever. Beautiful craft of God! And I know that He makes my thought-life beautiful when I am open all the day to Him. If I throw these mind-windows apart and say "God, what shall we think of now?" He answers always in some graceful, tender dream.

I know that God is love-hungry, for He is constantly pointing me to some dull, dead soul which He has never reached and wistfully urges me to help Him reach that stolid, tight-shut mind. Oh God, how I long to help You with these Moros. And with these Americans! And with these Filipinos! All day I see souls dead to God look sadly out of hungry eyes. I want them to know my discovery! That any minute can be paradise, that any place can be heaven! That any man can have God! That every man *does have God* that moment he speaks to God, or listens for Him!

Frank Laubach

The only ultimate disaster that can befall us, I have come to realize, is to feel ourselves to be at home here on earth. As long as we are aliens we cannot forget our true homeland, which is that other kingdom You proclaimed.

Malcolm Muggeridge

KEEPING GOD IN MIND

Psalm 5:1-2

As I analyze myself I find several things happening to me as a result of these two months of strenuous effort to keep God in mind every minute. This concentration upon God is *strenuous*, but everything else has ceased to be so. I think more clearly, I forget less frequently. Things which I did with a strain before, I now do easily and with no effort whatever. I worry about nothing, and lose no sleep. I walk on air a good part of the time. Even the mirror reveals a new light in my eyes and face. I no longer feel in a hurry about anything. Everything goes right. Each minute I meet calmly as though it were not important. Nothing can go wrong except one thing. That is that God *may slip from my mind* if I do not keep on my guard. If He is here, the universe is with me. My task is simple and clear.

And I witness to the way in which the world reacts. Take Lanao and the Moros, for illustration. Their responsiveness is to me a continuous source of amazement. I do nothing that I can see excepting to pray for them, and to walk among them, thinking of God. They know I am a Protestant. Yet two of the leading Moslem priests have gone around the province telling everybody that I would help the people to know God.

Frank Laubach

THE SOUL IN UNION

Hebrews 4:1

The soul in union rests from all disquieting fears.
It is delivered from fear of want; fear of suffering; fear of man; and guilty fear of God. The fear which is based upon guilt is very different to that fear which is synonymous with reverence.

The soul in union rests from conflict with Providence.
The soul united to God is necessarily united with Him in all the movements and arrangements which He makes. He rests from the perplexities of making his choice, by accepting the choice his Father makes for him in all circumstances. God's choice is only another name for His Providence.

Moreover God's Providence is internal as well as external. He is the Inspirer of the feelings of the heart, as well as the Director of outward events. The renewed soul therefore rests from all anxiety as to the wandering imaginations, and from recurring to other scenes and situations in unholy discontent. He rests from feelings of envy which supposes the existence of superiority in others, in position or aught else. He rests from easily offended feelings; if injured by another, he knows his Father (without originating the unholy impulse) has seen fit for some wise reason, to direct its application against himself. He receives the blow with a quiet spirit, while he has sorrow for him who inflicts its.

The soul in union rests from labor.
The term labor implies effort. There is life and activity in heaven, but not labor, which involves pain and effort. The soul renovated does not cease to be active, he finds and knows no idle moments; but the work which he does ceases to possess the ordinary attributes of labor.

Jessie Penn-Lewis

REFUSING TO BE HUMILIATED

Mark 9:29

"Why could not we cast him out?" The answer lies in a personal relationship to Jesus Christ. This kind can come forth by nothing but by concentration and redoubled concentration on Him. We can ever remain powerless as were the disciples, by trying to do God's work not in concentration on His power, but by ideas drawn from our temperament. We slander God by our very eagerness to work for Him without knowing Him.

You are brought face to face with a difficult case and nothing happens externally, and yet you know the emancipation will be given because *you* are concentrated on Jesus Christ. This is your line of service—to see that there is nothing between Jesus and yourself. Is there? If there is, you must get through it, not by ignoring it in irritation, or by mounting up, but by facing it and getting through it into the presence of Jesus Christ, then that very thing, and all you have been through in connection with it, will glorify Jesus Christ in a way you will never know till you see Him face to face.

We must be able to mount up with wings as eagles; but we must also know how to come down. The power of the saint lies in the coming down and living down. "I can do all things through Christ which strengtheneth me," said Paul, and the things he referred to were mostly humiliating things. It is in our power to refuse to be humiliated and to say—"No, thank you, I much prefer to be on the mountain top with God." Can I face things as they actually are in the light of the reality of Jesus Christ, or do things as they are efface altogether my faith in Him, and put me into a panic?

Oswald Chambers

SOMETHING TO WRITE HOME ABOUT

John 15:2

In the whole plant world there is not a tree to be found so specially suited to be the image of man in his relation to God, as the vine. There is none of which the fruit and its juice are so full of spirit, so quickening and stimulating. But there is also none of which the natural tendency is so entirely evil—none where the growth is so ready to run into wood that is utterly worthless except for the fire. Of all plants, not one needs the pruning knife so unsparingly and so unceasingly. None is so dependent on cultivation and training, but with this none yields a richer reward to the husbandman.

Andrew Murray

We would like to get to know this exalted person (The Duke of Edinburgh), but we fully realize that this is a matter for him to decide, not us. If he confines himself to courteous formalities with us, we may be disappointed, but we don't feel able to complain; after all we had no claim on his friendship. But if instead he starts to take us into his confidence, and tells us frankly what is in his mind, on matters of common concern, and if he goes on to invite us to join him in particular undertakings he has planned and asks us to make ourselves permanently available for this kind of collaboration whenever he needs us, we shall feel enormously privileged, and it will make a world of difference to our general outlook. If life seemed boring and dreary hitherto it will not seem so any more, now that the great man has enrolled us among his personal assistants. Here's something to write home about and something to live up to.

KNOWING GOD
J.I. Packer

"OF COURSE YOUR HEART IS DEAD"

Colossians 3:3

The secret of this great blessing is to be found by abiding in Christ. Dr. Gordon used to tell a little circumstance which came beneath his eyes in New England, which presents to us a figure of it all. Two little saplings grew side by side. Through the action of the wind they crossed each other. By and by the bark of each became wounded and the sap began to mingle, until in some still day they became united to each other. This process went on more and more until they were firmly compacted. Then the stronger began to absorb the life from the weaker; it grew stronger while the other grew weaker and weaker, until finally it dropped away and then disappeared. And now there are two trunks at the bottom and only one a the top. Death has taken away the one, life has triumphed in the other.

J. Wilbur Chapman

At the end of this convention a dear child of God cried, "Lord, give me Thy heart of love for sinners. Thy broken heart for their sins. Thy tears with which to admonish night and day. O Lord, I feel so cold! My heart is so hard and dead. I am so lukewarm!"

A friend had to interrupt him: "Why are you looking down at your poor self, brother? Of course your heart is cold and dead. But you have asked for the broken heart of Jesus. His love, His burden for sin, His tears. Is He a liar? Has He not given what you asked for? Then why look away from His heart to your own?"

John used to say, "When we keep near to Jesus it is He who draws souls to Himself through us, but He must be lifted up in our lives; that is, we must be crucified with Him. It is self in some shape that comes between us and Him.

PRAYING HYDE
Francis Mc Graw

WHOLLY GIVEN UP TO HIM

James 5:16

My beloved sons and daughters:

Nothing has been made more plain to me since leaving home than that in cultivating morals and truth in the inward parts, I have too much neglected to exhibit outwardly a winning manner. I have never meant to be abrupt or discourteous but have often impressed others as unsympathetic and taciturn or even cynical it may be. . . . I am sure that Truth is not to be at the cost of Love and that is selfishness not to restrain the inner feelings from needless exposure in face and manner.

I want to ask forgiveness for any offenses against love which I have committed in the home, and to remove all stumbling-blocks out of your way, my beloved children.

God's infinite loveliness grows on me. To an extent hitherto unknown every detail has been committed to His hands and He has shown Himself marvelously faithful. I can only testify and exhort you more and more to commit to Him every matter however small in perfect trust. Let us be in a very uncommon sense wholly given up to Him. Time is short; eternity is long; and Christ is near. May God keep you on His shoulder for supporting strength, on His bosom for cherishing love, and cheer you Himself and hold you in His embrace.

With tenderest love,
Father

ARTHUR T. PIERSON
D.L. Pierson

"I WILL TELL YOU THE SECRET"

Ephesians 4:29-32

Undoubtedly resentment and bitterness and unforgiveness not only poison the thought life, but they can play havoc with the body as well, for they are deadly destructive things. Whether they were the whole cause, or only weakened my bodily defenses against infection, at any rate after a time I became really ill, and one day while I was in bed, feeling very wretched indeed, a stranger walked into my room, saying that she had heard from mutual friends that I was ill, and that she had felt led to come and see me.

And as we walked together, somehow it all came out again, and I found myself telling her the old familiar story with all its bitter details. And at the end I added despairingly, "The awful part is that I can't forgive and forget. I just long to do so because it comes in between the Lord and me the whole time, but I can't."

She said, "I will tell you the secret of how to forgive and forget. As long as you talk about this thing and discuss it with others, just so long will you never get free from it. But if you take this wrong done to you to the cross of our Lord, and confess it to him exactly as though it was a wrong done against himself, and ask him to forgive it completely and to forget it, just as you ask him to forgive and forget your own sins against him, and if you will leave it there at the cross and promise him never to touch it again, namely, that you will never speak of it to anyone else, but act as though the wrong had never been committed at all, and if you refuse to listen to anyone who mentions it, you will go free and forget it altogether."

Take it to the cross and leave it there, and promise never to touch it again. That is the secret. I found it worked absolutely perfectly and at once.

Hannah Hurnard

NO WITNESS, NO LIMELIGHT

Matthew 5:16

The wonder of the Incarnation slips into the Life of ordinary childhood; the marvel of the Transfiguration descends to the valley and demon-possessed boy, and the glory of the Resurrection merges into our Lord providing breakfast for His disciples on the seashore in the early dawn. The tendency in early Christian experience is to look for the marvelous. We are apt to mistake the sense of the heroic for being heroes. It is one thing to go through a crisis grandly, but a different thing to go through every day glorifying God when there is no witness, no limelight, and no one paying the remotest attention to you. If we don't want medieval halos, we want something that will make people say—What a wonderful man of prayer he is! What a pious, devoted woman she is! If anyone says that of you, you have not been loyal to God.

Oswald Chambers

But the one thing that the "modern thinker" ought to learn first is the one thing from which he is probably farthest away, namely, that he can learn more about God and the mysteries of His government through his conscience and his heart and actual obedience to the Word of God than he ever can with all his brains when these things are forgotten.

William E. Biederwolf

LEARNING TO WALK

Romans 6:4

The New Testament calls the Christian life a "walk." This *walk* begins with a step of faith when we trust Christ as our Savior. But salvation is not the end—it's only the beginning—of spiritual life. "Walking" involves progress, and Christians are supposed to advance the spiritual life. Just as a child must learn to walk and must overcome many difficulties in doing so, a Christian must learn to "walk in the light." And the fundamental difficulty involved here is this matter of *sin*.

Warren Wiersbe

Finish every day and be done with it. You have done what you could. Some blunders and absurdities no doubt have crept in; forget them as soon as you can. Tomorrow is a new day; begin it well and serenely and with too high a spirit to be cumbered with your old nonsense. This day is all that is good and faith. It is too dear, with its hopes and invitations, to waste a moment on yesterdays.

Ralph Waldo Emerson

THE ALL-IMPORTANT PROCESS

Philippians 3:10

We must not discount a Spirit-fostered experience, blessing, or even a crisis; but it is to be remembered that these simply contribute to the overall, and all-important process. . . . It takes time to get to know ourselves; it takes time and eternity to get to know our Infinite Lord Jesus Christ. Today is the day to put our hand to the plow, and irrevocably set our heart on His goal for us—that we "may know him, and the power of his resurrection, and the fellowship of his sufferings, being made conformable unto his death" (Phil. 3:10).

"So often in the battle," says Austin-Sparks, "we go to the Lord, and pray, and plead, and appeal for victory, for ascendancy, for mastery over the forces of evil and death, and our thought is that in some way the Lord is going to come in with a mighty exercise of power and put us into a place of victory and spiritual ascendancy as in an act. We must have this mentality corrected. What the Lord does is to enlarge us to possess. He puts us through some exercise, through some experience, takes us by some way which means our spiritual expansion, and exercise of spirituality so we occupy the larger place spontaneously. `I will not drive them out from before thee in one year; lest the land become desolate, and the beast of the field multiply against thee. By little and little I will drive them out before thee, until thou be increased' (Ex. 23:29-30)."

One day in the House of Commons, British Prime Minister Disraeli made a brilliant speech on the spur of the moment. That night a friend said to him, "I must tell you how much I enjoyed your extemporaneous talk. It's been on my mind all day." "Madam," confessed Disraeli, "that extemporaneous talk has been on my mind for twenty years!"

Miles J. Stanford

A SAINT OR A BRUTE

I Corinthians 1:2

We are familiar with the thought that our bodies are like machines, needing the right routine of food, rest, and exercise if they are to run efficiently, and liable, if filled up with the wrong kind of fuel—alcohol, drugs, poison—to lose their power of health functioning and ultimately to 'seize up' entirely in physical death. What we are, perhaps, slow to grasp is that God wishes us to think of our souls in a similar way. As rational persons, we were made to bear God's mortal image— that is, our souls were made to run on the practice of worship, law keeping, truthfulness, honesty, discipline, self control and service to God and our fellows. If we abandon these practices, not only do we incur guilt before God, we also progressively destroy our own souls. Conscience atrophies, the sense of shame dries up, one's capacity for truthfulness, loyalty, and honesty, is eaten away, one's character disintegrates. One not only becomes desperately miserable; one is steadily being de-humanized. This is one aspect of spiritual death. Richard Baxter was right to formulate the alternatives as 'A Saint or Brute.' That, ultimately is the only choice, and everyone, sooner or later, consciously or unconsciously opts for one or the other.
J. I. Packer

Then there is meditation and taking time to think. Throw the newspaper on one side and think about God and about your soul and about all these things. We do not talk enough to ourselves. We must tell ourselves that we are in His presence, that we are His children, that Christ has died for us and that He has reconciled us to God. We must practice the presence of God, and realize it, we must talk to Him, and spend our days with Him. That is the method.
D. Martyn Lloyd-Jones

THE SHRIMP THAT GREW

II Corinthians 12:9-10

"My strength is made perfect in weakness" was God's message to Paul. "When I am weak, then am I strong" was Paul's testimony (II Cor. 12:9-10). Of God's heroes it is recorded that it was "out of weakness they were made strong" (Heb. 11:34).

William Wilberforce, the great Christian reformer who was responsible for the freeing of the slaves in the British Empire, was so small and frail a creature that it seemed even a strong wind might knock him down. But once Boswell heard him speak in public in advocacy of his great cause, and afterwards said, "I saw what seemed to me a shrimp mount the table, but as I listened he grew and grew until the shrimp became a whale."

"It is a thrilling discovery to make," writes J.S. Stewart, "that always it is upon human weakness and humiliation, not human strength and confidence, that God chooses to build His kingdom; and that He can use us not merely in spite of our ordinariness and helplessness and disqualifying infirmities, but precisely because of them. . . . *Nothing can defeat a church or soul that takes, not its strength but its weakness, and offers it to God to be His weapon.* It was the way of Francis Xavier and William Carey and Paul the apostle. 'Lord, here is my human weakness. I dedicate it to Thee for Thy glory.' This is the strategy to which there is no retort. This is the victory which overcomes the world."

J. Oswald Sanders

DRAWN AWAY

I Corinthians 10:12

We are drawn away from watchfulness by over-confidence. We come to believe we are beyond a particular temptation. We look at someone else's fall and say, "I would never do that." But Paul warned us, "If you think you are standing firm, be careful that you don't fall" (I Corinthians 10:12). Even when helping a fallen brother, we are to watch ourselves lest we also be tempted (Galatians 6:1).

We are often drawn away from obedience by the abuse of grace. Jude speaks of certain men "who change the grace of our God into a license for immorality" (Jude 4). We abuse grace when we think we can sin and then receive forgiveness by claiming I John 1:9. We abuse grace when, after sinning, we dwell on the compassion and mercy of God to the exclusion of His holiness and hatred of sin.

We are drawn away from obedience when we begin to question what God says in His Word. This was Satan's first tactic with Eve (Genesis 3:1-5). Just as he said to Eve, "You surely shall not die" so he says to us, "It is just a little thing!" or "God will not judge that sin."

So we see that though sin no longer has dominion over us, it wages its guerrilla warfare against us. If left unchecked, it will defeat us. Our recourse against this warfare is to deal swiftly and firmly with the first motions of indwelling sin.

Jerry Bridges

A VAST COMMANDING SENSE OF GRACE

Psalm 107:8-15

One of the beloved teachers of a former generation was that profound theologian and humble man of God, Professor Hugh R. Mackintosh. There is a sentence of his—a golden, piercing, challenging sentence—which often comes back to mind: `I fancy that as we grow older, as we think longer and work harder and learn to sympathize more intelligently. The one thing we long to be able to pass on to men is a vast commanding sense of the grace of the Eternal. Compared with that, all else is but the small dust of the balance.'

To these words I expect that many of us here today would say Amen with all our heart. For when all is said and done—the tumult and the shouting, the theological debate and ecumenical conferring, the variations of life's experience bright and dark, the argument this way and that—there still emerges for you, for me, for all of us, the one thing needful: a vast commanding sense of the grace of the Eternal.

Now clearly, it was to convey and communicate some such sense that this Hebrew poet wrote his psalm. Here is a man who knows how difficult life can be, the strains and stresses that our sensitive, vulnerable nature has to bear. He knows it, because he has tasted it in his own mature experience. But this also he knows, and this is the great thing he sets himself to herald and proclaim: that for every possible predicament of man there is corresponding grace of God, for every particular human need the requisite particular supernatural resource. If this is true, then the whole world is suddenly different. And the Christian faith exists to assure us that it is literally, absolutely true. May God make us sure of it today!

James S. Stewart

OUR ADVANTAGE AND GOD'S GLORY

John 7:17

Shall I be content to do God's will for my own advantage?

It is better to do His will with a weak, but deliberate co-operation than to do His will unconsciously, unwillingly, and in spite of myself. But let me not confine my idea of perfection to the selfish obedience that does God's will merely for the sake of my own profit. True happiness is not found in any other reward than that of being united with God. If I seek some other reward besides God Himself, I may get my reward but I cannot be happy.

The secret of pure intention is not to be sought in the renunciation of all advantage for ourselves. Our intentions are pure when we identify our advantage with God's glory, and see that our happiness consists in doing His will because His will is right and good. In order to make our intentions pure, we do not give up all idea of seeking our own good, we simply seek it where it seeks its joy in God's own will to do good to all men in order that He may be glorified in them.

And, therefore, a pure intention is actually the most efficacious way of seeking our own advantage and our own happiness.

Thomas Merton

In seeking to know God better we must keep firmly in mind that we need not try to persuade God. He is already persuaded in our favor, not by our prayers but by the generous goodness of His own heart. "It is God's nature to give Himself to every virtuous soul," says Meister Eckhart. "Know then that God is bound to act, to pour Himself out into thee as soon as ever He shall find thee ready." As nature abhors a vacuum, so the Holy Spirit rushes in to fill the nature that has become empty by separating itself from the world and sin. This is not an unnatural act and need not be an unusual one, for it is in perfect accord with the nature of God. He must act as He does because He is God.

A.W. Tozer

TWO KINDS OF GREATNESS

Matthew 20:20-28

It is vitally important that we know what Christ meant when He used the word *great* in relation to men, and His meaning cannot be found in the lexicon or dictionary. Only when viewed in its broad theological setting is it understood aright. No one whose heart has had a vision of God, however brief or imperfect that vision may have been, will ever consent to think of himself or anyone else as being great. The sight of God, when He appears in awesome majesty to the wondering eyes of the soul, will bring the worshiper to his knees in fear and gladness and fill him with such an overwhelming sense of divine greatness that he must spontaneously cry, "Only God is great!"

All this being true, still God Himself applies the word great to men, as when the angel tells Zacharias that the son who is to be born "shall be great in the sight of the Lord," or as when Christ speaks of some who shall be great in the kingdom of heaven. No greater born of woman.

Obviously there are two kinds of greatness recognized in the Scriptures—an absolute, uncreated greatness belonging to God alone, and a relative and finite greatness achieved by or bestowed upon certain friends of God and sons of faith who by obedience and self-denial sought to become as much like God as possible. It is of this latter kind of greatness that we speak.

To seek greatness is not wrong in itself. Men were once made in the image of God and told to subdue the earth and have dominion. Man's very desire to rise above his present state and to bring all things under subjection to him may easily be the blind impulse of his fallen nature to fulfill the purpose for which he was created. Sin has perverted this natural instinct as it has all others. Men have left their first estate and in their moral ignorance invariably look for greatness where it is not and seek to attain it in ways that are always vain and often downright iniquitous.

A.W. Tozer

HUNGER IN HOSTILITY

Genesis 3:9

The problem of the Bible is not that of finding God; it is getting right with the God who is there.

I think this is our great hope against all totalitarian systems of men. Jesus is the essential image. He *is* Lord of all creation. That image is lodged at the root of reality.

In his book *Mission Control*, John Wesley White cites the fact that Mao Tse-Tung was deep in reflection during a rather tedious meeting. He was doodling on a piece of paper. This paper got into the hands of reporters. This was the exposure of his inner mind: "Alone in the desolate vastness, I say to this ageless earth, `Who is the Maker of the universe?'" Here is another doubter having his doubts, trying to put down this inner witness that gets to a man in his solitude. We wonder how much hunger there is in man's hostility. Why do all the rebel poets, existential philosophers, and sick dramatists keep dragging God into their theme? They are like the Unitarians who have been defined as "those who can't take it, but can't quite leave it alone."

A cartoon appeared in a school paper, showing two pretty high school girls crossing the campus. The one girl said to her friend, "Look, there's Gregory!" Whereupon the other girl replied, "Oh, I really don't care. We're not on speaking terms any more. I've lost all interests in him. We haven't spoken for 2 days, 6 hours, and 48 minutes."

A little girl, Linda, became angry with her parents. Wanting to punish them, she wrote her mother a letter: "Dear Mom, I hate you. I'm running away from home. Love, Linda."

Roy C. Putnam

A NERVOUS INGRATIATING GOD

Isaiah 40:28

How much of our Christian service is like the frantic challenging of Joshua, "Art thou for us or for our enemies?" How many of us have forgotten to stand still, to be still and know that God Is with His answer for all our problems. Jean Paul Sartre, speaking of his drift into atheism, said, "I did not recognize in the fashionable God who was taught me, Him who was waiting for my soul. I needed a creator, I was given a big bigness man." Christian people themselves do a disfavor to the faith which they preach because they have forgotten how to tremble in awe before God Himself. "Almighty God," writes Dr. Tozer, "just because He is almighty, needs no support. The picture of a nervous, ingratiating God, fawning over men to win their favor, is not a pleasant one. Yet, if we look at the popular conception of God, that is precisely what we see. Too many missionary appeals are based upon the fancied frustration of Almighty God. I fear that thousands of young people enter Christian service with no higher motive than to help deliver God from the embarrassing situation His love has gotten Him into, and His limited abilities seem to be unable to get Him out of."

The true drive for much Christian activity today is a fear that God is embarrassed, finding Himself in a dilemma in which His love wants to save and His power is unable to do so.

David Mckee

"THIS COULD BE A TURNING POINT"

Psalm 145:9

Viewed against the whole awful mystery of human suffering and existence, viewing this mystery against the greater mystery of Calvary's strange design, the soul can say, "The Lord is good to all and His tender mercies are over all His works." "His mercy is everlasting; His truth endureth to all generations."

Man views himself fallen from such goodness, looks with suspicion and fear toward God. Dr. Tozer writes, "The whole outlook of mankind might be changed if we could only believe that we dwell under a friendly sky, under the God of heaven who though exalted in majesty is eager to be friends with us."

Dr. Helmut Theliche, writing in his book, *How the World Began,* says, "When someone says to me, `There is a supreme intelligence that conceived the creation of the world, devised the laws of causality, and maneuvered the planets into their orbits,' then all I can say to them is, `You don't say so!', and then I go on reading my newspaper or turn on the television, for this is not a message that I could live by. But when someone tells me that there is One who knows me, One who cares a lot when I go my own way, One who paid a great price in order to be the star you can gaze on and the stay you can rest upon; when someone says *that* to me, I stop and listen, for if it is true that there is One who is interested in me, then this could mean a turning point in my life. The whole outlook on life might be changed by such a conviction."

David McKee

NO LASTING VALUES

Hebrews 13:8

Universities . . . became both centers of political activism and defenders of relativism. But just as the influence of the university was expanding, it suddenly had very little to teach. The very idea of truth had been called into question as early as 1940, when Reinhold Niebuhr warned that America was a victim of "an education adrift in relativity that doubted all values, and a degraded science that shirked the spiritual issues."

Universities responded by simply changing the goal of education. Where once the object of learning had been the discovery of truth, now each student must be allowed to decide truth for himself. Dogma, not ignorance, became the enemy.

The youth culture of the universities took what they were taught to heart, developing what scholar James Hitchcock calls "a visceral sense that all forms of established authority, all rules, all demands for obedience, were inherently illegitimate."

Influenced by existential writers such as Jean-Paul Sartre and Albert Camus, the generation of the sixties made autonomy its god and sought meaning in the pleasures of easy sex and hard drugs. The consequences were felt not only in private standards of morality, but in the literature and art of the times. Take for example the work of Andy Warhol, who on his death in early 1987 was hailed by *Newsweek* as "the most famous American artist of our time." Warhol was responsible for the rise of "pop art" in the early sixties, gaining international fame for his two hundred Campbell soup cans, an oil painting of row after row of those familiar red and white labels.

Inspired by the mass production techniques of industrial societies, pop art deliberately denied the distinctions between high culture and popular culture. Implicitly and explicitly it asserted relativism's principal tenet that all values are equal; the distinction between bad taste and good taste is elitist; all notions of bad and good are merely one class's way of snubbing another. There are no lasting values, no timeless truths, only artifacts of the moment.

Charles Colson

UTILITARIAN INDIVIDUALISM

Ecclesiastes 1:16-18

One popular T-shirt and bumper-sticker slogan says, "He who dies with the most toys wins."

Pascal said, "separated from God, men seek satisfaction in their senses." This is more than mindless hedonism; it is a world view in which, according to professor Allan Bloom, "the self has become the modern substitute for the soul."

A 1985 study titled *Habits of the Heart* calls this attitude "utilitarian individualism," arguing that the two primary ways Americans attempt to order their lives are through "the dream of personal success" and "vivid personal feeling." This was reinforced as those interviewed consistently defined their ultimate goals in terms of self-fulfillment or self-realization. Marriage was seen as an opportunity for personal development, work as a method of personal advancement, church as a means of personal fulfillment.

What this study reflects is simply the inevitable consequences of four decades of the steady erosion of absolute values. As a result we live with a massive case of schizophrenia. Outwardly, we are a religious people, but inwardly our religious beliefs make no difference in how we live. . . .

This cultural revolution, rendering God irrelevant, has permeated the Western media, the instrument that not only reflects, but often shapes societal attitudes. God is tolerated in the media only when He is bland enough to pose no threat. One national columnist, annoyed by what she regarded as religious zealots, wrote longingly of ancient Rome, where "the people regarded all the modes of worship as equally true, the intellectuals regarded them as equally false, and the politicians regarded them as equally useful. What a well-blessed time. . . . I think we could try to emulate the laid-back spirit it reveals."

More often, however, the media reflect something less than this laid-back spirit and at times even seems infected with a "brooding and pervasive devotion to the secular and . . . hostility to the religious," a view confining religion to a "neutral status, devoid of any inherent meaning."

Charles Colson

"THEY LOVE MORALITY"

Jude 16

"Men, although they are individually rascals, are collectively a most decent lot: they love morality." This is the formula for Tartuffe. The student moralism was a species of the Tartuffe phenomenon, but a wholly new mutant of it. Unlike other revolutionary movements, which tended to be austere and chaste—beginning with the first revolution, 1688, in England, which was really puritan—this one was antipuritanical. The slogan was "Make love, not war." Although the similarity of language was exploited, this is very different from "Love thy neighbor," which is an injunction very different to fulfill. "To make love" is a bodily act, very easy to perform and thought to be pleasant. The word "obscene" was transferred out of sex into politics. Somehow the students had touched on a whole set of desires previously thought to be questionable, which had hardly dared to name themselves but which were ripe for emancipation and legitimation. The ideology for the revolution was already in place. Moderation of the infinite bodily desires had become "repression" of nature, one of the forms of *domination*, the buzzword of the advanced thinkers and consciousness raisers. All that was needed were the heroes willing to act out the fantasies the public was now ready to accept as reality: the hero, as hedonist, who dares to do in public what the public wants to see. It was *épater les bourgeois* as a bourgeois calling. The practices of the late Roman empire were promoted with the moral fervor of early Christianity and the political idealism of Robespierre. Such a combination is, of course, impossible. It is playacting, a role, and the students knew it. But that haunting sentiment was assuaged by the fact that this was the first revolution made for TV. They were real because they could see themselves on television. All the world had become a stage, and they were playing leads. The cure proposed for the bourgeois disease really was its most advanced symptom.

Allan Bloom

A ROTTENNESS BEGINS

Luke 11:43

Government remains the paramount area of folly because it is there that men seek power over others—only to lose it over themselves.

Thomas Jefferson, who held more and higher offices than most men, took the sourest view of it. "Whenever a man has cast a longing eye on [office]," he wrote to a friend, "a rottenness begins in his conduct." His contemporary across the Atlantic, Adam Smith, was if anything more censorious. "And thus *Place* . . . is the end of half the labors of human life; and is the cause of all the tumult and bustle, all the rapine and injustice which avarice and ambition have introduced into this world." Both were speaking of moral failure, not of competence. When that comes into question, it gains no higher rating from other statesmen. In the 1930s, when a chairman was being sought for the Senate investigation of the munitions industry, a leader of the peace movement asked the advice of Senator George Norris. Ruling himself out as too old, Norris went down the list of his colleagues crossing off one after the other as too lazy, too stupid, too close to the Army, as moral cowards or overworked or in poor health or having conflict of interest or facing re-election. When he had finished he had eliminated all but Senator Gerald Nye, the only one out of the 96 whom he deemed to have the competence, independence and stature for the task. Much the same opinion in different circumstances was pronounced by General Eisenhower in discussing the need for inspired leaders to create a United States of Europe as the only way to preserve Europe's security. He did not think it would happen, because "Everyone is too cautious, too fearful, too lazy, and too ambitious (personally)." Odd and notable is the appearance of lazy in both catalogues.

Barbara Tuchman

A HEARTY ADMIRATION

Romans 10:14-15

Schweitzer wrote, "I feel a hearty admiration for missions. It has produced among the natives human and Christian characters which would convince the most decided opponents of missions as to what the teaching of Jesus can do for primitive man." He found that, far from the spread of the Gospel being harmful to primitive character, it build upon native good nature and enriched it. Dr. Schweitzer did not deny the good qualities of the primitive man, of whom he said that "with Christianity added to his good qualities wonderfully noble characters can result." Perhaps the greatest boon which the Christian mission brings to the African is that, in many instances, he is liberated from a tribal rite and introduced to a universal ethic.

The criticism which is based upon cultural relativity is the most confused of all contemporary attacks upon the missionary idea because the critic who reveals himself as being one who thinks that all positions are merely relative, inevitably falls into self-contradiction. If there is no objective moral order, and therefore no real right, then there is likewise no real wrong. How, then, can the critic claim that the promotion of foreign missions is wrong? All that he can say, in intellectual honesty, is that he does not like it, but that is too trivial to be worth repeating.

If there is any justification of our contemporary concern about the state of the nation and about the evils, such as those of war and poverty, which are almost universally attacked, it is only on the basis that objective right and wrong actually exist. No sensible person gets worked up over his own subjective preferences.

Elton Trueblood

ITS ALL-EMBRACINGNESS

Matthew 8:19

The individual personality of Christ becomes all-embracing, just as a great leader of men may be said to carry them in himself and his will governs their action, not by hypnotism but by their voluntary allegiance to him. So in this case the same principle is carried to the utmost possible limit; because His love, as shown, is infinite, therefore there can be no barriers set to its all-embracingness. Christ, the individual man, necessarily becomes the all-embracing personality, because through Him all-embracing love is made known.

We have lately become familiar with the psychology of crowd-consciousness. We do not as yet know very much about it, but we know enough to be aware that we are on the threshold of immensely important discoveries concerning human nature and the laws of its development; and we know broadly that the moral level of crowd-consciousness is always higher or lower than the average of the individuals composing the crowd. If the crowd is met together in the pursuit of an ideal end, then in the crowd there will be greater forces of idealism than in the average members composing it, taken separately; and quite equally, if it is met together for a selfish end or in hatred and antagonism, those spirits will be more potent than they are with the average members of the crowd.

William Temple

ASKING FOR SERENITY OF SOUL

Colossians 3:5

Do we then, if we are covetous, value our earthly treasures for their pleasantness alone? No such luck. The covetous man may begin with that, and at least there is some delight in it, something that comes from God. But he doesn't keep it long. " . . . covetousness, which is idolatry!" said Saint Paul. Almost at once the coveter makes a god of his possessions, asks more than pleasure from them, asks that serenity of soul which only God can give. And Saint Paul might have said, "Covetousness, which is hate." For the man soon learns to value what he gets chiefly because his fellows can't have it; to desire his neighbor's wife, not because she is beautiful, but because she is another's. And Paul might have ended with, "Covetousness, which is pride." Before long the gold and elephants, the convertibles and chinchillas, are no use at all to the coveter in themselves; he will drop them the instant they go out of fashion, he even resents them a little as responsibilities; but he must have them to convince himself that he is all-powerful, all-successful, all-important—in fact, God. For a while he may tolerate the existence of his neighbors, since it reassures him to have somebody to envy him; but in the end he will covet their very lives, for he cannot be satisfied as long as anything exists in all eternity that he does not possess. A thousand sayings in a hundred languages testify to the insatiability of covetousness— "He will never have enough," goes the grim Scottish proverb, "till his mouth is filled with mould."

So much, the Christian world has always known. How it has *lived* is another story. Almost from the beginning men wanted the Church to be a strong organization, and then saw that it would be stronger if it could grow rich. An order of friars would be founded dedicated to poverty—and would end by owning half the countryside. The temptation was very natural. But the Middle Ages did at least know that it was a temptation; did at least reject covetousness in theory and regard poverty as a necessary part of holiness.

Joy Davidman

IT MUST FIND ITS NUTRIMENT

Psalm 139:23

My point is that those who stand outside all judgments of value cannot have any ground for preferring one of their own impulses to another except the emotional strength of that impulse. We may legitimately hope that among the impulses which arise in minds thus emptied of all 'rational' or 'spiritual' motives, some will be benevolent. I am very doubtful myself whether the benevolent impulses, stripped of that preference and encouragement which the *Tao* teaches us to give them and left to their merely natural strength and frequency as psychological events, will have much influence. I am very doubtful whether history shows us one example of a man who, having stepped outside traditional morality and attained power, has used that power benevolently.

C.S. Lewis

I indulge in no mere figure of speech when I say that our nation, the immortal spirit of our domain lives in us—in our hearts, and minds, and consciences. There it must find its nutriment or die. This thought more than any other presents to our mind the impressiveness and responsibility of American citizenship. The land we live in seems to be strong and active. But how fares the land that lives in us? Are we sure we are doing all we ought to keep it in vigor and health?

Grover Cleveland

A CERTAIN MORAL DEMAND

Colossians 3:23

Every religion is an answer to the question of the meaning of life. And the religious answer includes a certain moral demand which sometimes follows and sometimes precedes the explanation of life's meaning. It is possible to reply to the question as follows: the meaning of life lies in personal well-being, therefore make use of any good fortune available to you. Or, the meaning of life lies in the well-being of an aggregate of people, therefore serve this group with all your strength. Or, the meaning of life lies in the fulfillment of the will of Him who gave you life, therefore strive as hard as you can to know that will and fulfil it. Or the same question can be answered in this way; the meaning of your life lies in your own personal enjoyment and that is the purpose of man's life. Or, the meaning of your life lies in the service to that group of people of which you count yourself a member, therefore that is your purpose; or, the meaning of your life lies in the service to God, therefore that is your purpose.

Morality is included in the explanation of life given by religion and can in no sense be separated from religion. This truth is especially evident in those attempts made by non-Christian philosophers to deduce a doctrine of high morality from their philosophy. These philosophers realize that Christian morality is essential and that it is impossible to live without it; moreover, having realized that it exists, they wish to merge it with their non-Christian philosophy and even to present things in such a way that Christian morality appears to emerge from their pagan, or social, philosophy. They try to do this, but it is precisely these attempts that show more clearly than anything else that not only is Christian morality independent of pagan philosophy, but it is directly opposed to both social philosophy and to the philosophy of personal well-being, or personal liberation from suffering.

Leo Tolstoy

NO NEED OF FICTITIOUS SUPPORTS

John 3:21

The Christian ethic—that which we acknowledge as a consequence of our world outlook—demands not just the sacrifice of the individual to the individuality of the group, but demands the renunciation of both personal and group individuality for service to God. Pagan philosophy only explores the means of acquiring the greatest well-being for the individual, or for a group of individuals, and the contradiction is inevitable. The only method of concealing this contradiction is to accumulate abstract conditional concepts one on top of the other, and to avoid departing from the nebulous sphere of metaphysics. This is what the majority of philosophers have done since the time of the Renaissance, and it is to this circumstance—the impossibility of reconciling the previously accepted demands of Christian philosophy with a moral philosophy based on paganism—that one must attribute the peculiar abstraction, lack of clarity, unintelligibility and irrelevance to life, of modern philosophy. With the exception of Spinoza, whose philosophy, despite the fact that he did not consider himself a Christian, is derived from religious foundations that are sincerely Christian, and of Kant, who presented his ethics as being quite independent of his metaphysics, all other philosophers, even the brilliant Schopenhauer, evidently invented artificial links between their ethics and their metaphysics.

It seems that the Christian ethic is something we have always had and that it stands quite firmly and independently of philosophy, with no need of fictitious supports to hold it up, while philosophy merely invents certain clauses which cannot be contradicted by ethical data and binds itself to the ethic as if that is where it originates. All such clauses appear to justify the Christian ethic, but only so long as they are being examined in the abstract. The moment they are applied to problems concerning practical life, not only does disagreement arise but a blatant contradiction between the philosophical premises and what we regard as morality emerges in full force.

Leo Tolstoy

"MANKIND IS MAD"

Psalm 69:14

In a sermon at Harvard University Chapel, David H. C. Read told of his World War II experience as a POW. Standing next to a German guard as a destructive allied air raid took place nearby, they commiserated over the horror of war. "Die menscheit ist verrueckt!" the guard said. "Mankind is mad." And he went on, "The good God should destroy us all and begin again."

But God did not destroy us all. He set in motion the act of repentance: the way back, the way of rebuilding a broken world. I have never forgotten the words of the chief of a small Brazilian jungle tribe who told me of his view of God before he ever heard of Jesus Christ. "We always assumed that our Maker was so disappointed with us that He went off and left us. Now we know that He came to us and made a way for us to come back to Him."

Gordon MacDonald

From the Orient comes the story of a man who dreamed that he had stumbled into a deep pit where he lay in helpless despair. A Confucianist, passing by, leaned over the edge of the hole and shouted down, "Friend, let me give you some good advice. If you ever get out of your trouble, see to it that you never get into it again." Shortly afterwards a Buddhist passing by leaned over the edge of the hole and shouted down, "Friend, if you manage to climb up so that I can grab your hand, I will help you out." Then in the dream Christ passed by and, hearing the groans of despair, descended into the pit and climbed out with the man on His shoulders. That is the difference between mere religion and faith in the Lord Jesus. Religion may offer you sage advice and make an ineffectual effort to help you help yourself, but Christ, descending to the level of your wretchedness and impotence, lifts you up into liberty and joy. That was why when challenged by a Chinese statesman, "What right have you Christians to bring your gospel to this country where we have our own religions?" the missionary answered, "The right to give to others something too good to keep."

Vernon C. Grounds

INCALCULABLE RESOURCES

Galatians 2:16

It is wonderful to be alive, because in Christ *something has happened to man's struggle.* `By the deeds of the law,' he writes to the Romans, `shall no flesh be justified . . . But now the righteousness of God without the law is manifested.'

`By the deeds of the law'—that means, by the old method of struggling to keep the commandments. By laboring grimly at the cultivation of character. By trying to build a new world from beneath. By adopting a creed of scientific self-salvation. By imagining we can eliminate the corporate evils of the body politic by better social planning, or fight down temptation by naked resolution, suppressing our own particular private devil by main force. It is gallant and heroic warfare, no doubt, but it is not the gospel.

There is a moving moment in Scott's *Ivanhoe,* where Rebecca is facing her most difficult renunciation. `I will tear this affection from my heart,' she cries, `though every fibre bleed as I rend it away.' Noble, indeed. We bow before the nobility of such a spirit. But is that the best? On the battlefields where men struggle for their souls and for the soul of the world, is there no better way? Are we thrust back upon the resources of a stoic resolution? Is the world, seeking salvation, thrown back on man's ethical energies? A heartbreaking business. `By the deeds of the law shall no flesh be justified.' That way lies only disenchantment and defeat.

But now! Now in Christ the new dynamic has appeared. Now there are incalculable resources for the fight. Surely the most wrong-headed psychology in the world is that which speaks of you and me as closed personalities, with just so much strength and no more, with strictly limited reserves of power. For what Christ has done is to make us feel, at all the gateways of our nature, the pressure and bombardment of the infinite energies of a world unseen.

James S. Stewart

SHORT-SIGHTED PREACHMENT

Romans 6:23

Another doctrine which hinders God's work, and one which is heard almost everywhere, is that sinners are not lost because they have sinned, but because they have not accepted Jesus. "Men are not lost because they murder; they are not sent to hell because they lie and steal and blaspheme; they are sent to hell because they reject a Savior." This short-sighted preachment is thundered at us constantly, and is seldom challenged by the hearers. A parallel argument would be hooted down as silly, but apparently no one notices it: "That man with a cancer is dying, but it is not the cancer that is killing him; it is his failure to accept a cure." Is it not plain that the only reason the man would need a cure is that he is already marked for death by the cancer? The only reason I need a Savior, in His capacity as Savior, is that I am already marked for hell by the sins I have committed. Refusing to believe in Christ is a symptom of deeper evil in life, of sins unconfessed and wicked ways unforsaken. The guilt lies in acts of sin; the proof of that guilt is seen in the rejection of the Savior.

If anyone should feel like brushing this aside as mere verbal sparring, let him first pause: the doctrine that the only damning sin is the rejection of Jesus is definitely a contributing cause of our present weakness and lack of moral grip. It is nothing but a neat theological sophism which has become identified with orthodoxy in the mind of the modern Christian and is for that reason very difficult to correct. It is, for all its harmless seeming, a most injurious belief, for it destroys our sense of responsibility for our moral conduct. It robs all sin of its frightfulness and makes evil to consist in a mere technicality. And where sin is not cured power cannot flow.

A.W. Tozer

THE MYSTERIOUS DEPTHS AND
CONVOLUTIONS

Romans 7:23-24

The dominant themes in Pascal's disconnected, sometimes obscure, and occasionally undecipherable passages of this always fascinating and often spontaneous stream of thoughts is that man is miserable and lost without God; that "true" religion (i.e. Christianity) explains this condition of wretchedness, explains man, and clarifies the soul as to what it is and what it longs for; and that faith in God completes man. The doctrines of man's Fall and original sin, says Pascal, "may shock us, striking us as utterly incomprehensible, but without this mystery we are incomprehensible to ourselves. Christianity reveals man to himself; its mysteries illumine the mysterious depths and convolutions of the otherwise inscrutable and rationally incomprehensible cavern of the soul."

INTRODUCTION TO PENSEES
Blaise Pascal

Late have I loved Thee, O Beauty so ancient and so new; late have I loved Thee! For behold Thou wert within me, and I outside; and I sought Thee outside and in my unloveliness fell upon those lovely things that Thou hast made. Thou were with me and I was not with Thee. I was kept from Thee by those things, yet had they not been in Thee, they would not have been at all. Thou didst call and cry to me and break open my deafness; and Thou didst send forth Thy beams and shine upon me and chase away my blindness. Thou didst breathe fragrance upon me, and I drew in my breath and do now pant for Thee. I tasted Thee, and now hunger and thirst for Thee. Thou didst touch me, and I have burned for Thy peace.

St. Augustine

A MORAL MIRACLE

Galatians 2:20

The heredity of the Son of God is planted in me by God, a moral miracle. Pseudo-evangelism has gone wildly off the track in that it has made salvation a bag of tricks whereby if I believe a certain shibboleth, I am tricked out of hell and made right for heaven—a travesty of the most tremendous revelation of the Redemption of the human race by Jesus Christ. The New Testament's teaching about Christianity is that the Son of God is formed in me on the basis of His marvelous regeneration until, as Paul says, "the life which I now live in the flesh"—not the life I am going to live when I get to heaven, but the life I now live in this flesh, the life that all see and know—"I live by the faith of the Son of God who loved me, and gave Himself for me."

Oswald Chambers

By trying to pack all of salvation into one experience, or two, the advocates of instant Christianity flaunt the law of development which runs through all nature. They ignore the sanctifying effects of suffering, cross carrying and practical obedience. They pass by the need for spiritual training, the necessity of forming right religious habits and the need to wrestle against the world, the devil and the flesh.

Undue preoccupation with the initial act of believing has created in some a psychology of contentment, or at least of non-expectation. To many it has imparted a mood of disappointment with the Christian faith. God seems too far away, the world is too near, and the flesh too powerful to resist. Others are glad to accept the assurance of automatic blessedness. It relieves them of the need to watch and fight and pray, and sets them free to enjoy this world while waiting for the next.

A.W. Tozer

September 21

IN THE SCHOOLHOUSE OF REPENTANCE

Romans 8:28-30

One of the martyr reformers has wisely remarked that we need not go about to trouble ourselves with curious questions of the predestination of God, but let us endeavor ourselves that we may be in Christ. For when we be in Him then are we well, and then we may be sure that we are ordained to everlasting life. When you find these three things in your heart— repentance, faith, and a desire to leave sin, then you may be sure your names are written in the Book, and you may be sure also that you are elected and predestined to everlasting life. Again, 'If thou art desiring to know whether thou art chosen to everlasting life thou mayest not begin with God, for God is too high, thou canst not comprehend Him; begin with Christ and learn to know Christ and wherefore He came, namely, that He came to save sinners and made Himself subject to the law and a fulfiller of the law, to deliver us from the wrath and danger thereof. If thou knowest Christ then thou mayest know further of thy election.' Illustrating this idea by his own personal experience Octavius Winslow says, 'If I believe in Christ alone for salvation I am certainly interested in Christ, and interested in Christ I could not be if I were not chosen and elected.' In all those quotations Winslow has been quoting the great English Protestant Father, Hugh Latimer, who was a great preacher of all these doctrines. That is how Latimer dealt with this particular matter.

Now let me quote from John Bradford, a contemporary of Latimer and a fellow-martyr for this great faith and the Protestant confession. He was burnt at Smithfield. This is how he writes, 'If ye feel not faith then know that predestination is too high a matter for you to be disputers of until you have been better scholars in the school-house of repentance and justification, which is the grammar-school wherein we must be conversant and learned before we go to the university of God's most holy predestination and providence.'

Martyn Lloyd-Jones

THE MORAL REQUIREMENTS

John 3:19-21

Some time ago during a question-and-answer session at Harvard Divinity School, a student stood up and asked me, "Can you tell me in plain and clear language what I must do to be saved?" Over and over again, as I lecture at colleges and universities, I am asked that question. Can the alcoholic, the thief, the murderer, the sex pervert, be changed radically and made a new man? At a West Coast university a professor of science came to see me in my room at the Student Union, and he said: "You are going to be amazed at the ultimate question I am here to ask you." The he told me a long story of his own inward struggle with moral, spiritual and intellectual issues. "More and more," he said, "I have come to realize that my problem with Christianity is really not intellectual at all. It is moral. I have not been willing to meet the moral requirements of Christianity." And he added, "Here is my question: What can I do to receive Jesus Christ?"

When the Governor of one of our states entertained us in his home, he asked to talk to me privately. We went into a back room, where he locked the door. I could see that he was struggling with his emotions, but finally he said to me: "I am at the end of my rope. I need God. Can you tell me how to find him?"

On another occasion, when I visited the men on death row in a prison, a strong, intelligent-looking man listened intently to what I had to say. Then I asked the men if they would be willing to kneel down while I prayed. Just before we knelt there, the man said: "Can you explain once again what I must do to be forgiven of my sins? I want to know that I am going to heaven."

We make it so complicated. Twentieth-century man asks the same question that man has always asked. It is old, but it is ever new. It is just as relevant today as in the past. Just what must one do to be reconciled to God?

Billy Graham

THE OTHER TRANSCENDENTAL ANSWER

Romans 2:7

R.T.: When did this business about religion and the possible truth of what Jesus Christ was teaching, when did this come back to you in a big way?

M.M.: I don't think there was ever a dramatic moment when it came back. I have often thought about this. It's something—well, put it this way—it has always seemed to me that the most interesting thing in the world is to try and understand what life is about. This is the only pursuit that could possibly engage a serious person—what is life about? And of course it is a continuing pursuit. As I have realized the fallacy of all materialist utopias, and of the politics of utopianism, so I have come to feel more and more strongly that the answer to life does not lie in materialism. In seeking the other transcendental answer, I have inevitably and increasingly been driven to the conclusion, almost against my own will, that for a West European whose life and background and tradition are in terms of Western European Christian civilization, the only answer lies in the person and life and teaching of Christ. Here, and here only, the transcendental answer is expressed adequately and appropriately. Now that is not the kind of conclusion that involves anything like a Damascus Road experience. It is a process of continuing realization. On the other hand, of course, one reaches a point when one comes out into the open about it. For me that was delayed because I felt it was necessary that my personal life should not be a disgrace to the Christian religion when I avowed it. There were certain things which I had to do about my personal life. In my particular case—and I am not laying this down as any kind of a rule—this involved abstemiousness and asceticism, and the mastery of self-indulgence.

Malcolm Muggeridge

A NEGATIVE MESSAGE NEEDED

Jeremiah 3:20-21

First, we may say that there is a time, and ours is such a time, when a negative message is needed before anything positive can begin. There must first be the message of judgment, the tearing down. There are times, and Jeremiah's day and ours are such times, when we cannot expect a constructive revolution if we begin by overemphasizing the positive message. People often say to me, what would you do if you met a really modern man on a train and you had just an hour to talk to him about the gospel? I would spend forty-five or fifty minutes on the negative, to show him his real dilemma—to show him that he is more dead than even he thinks he is; that he is not just dead in the twentieth-century meaning of dead (not having significance in this life) but that he is morally dead because he is separated from the God who exists. Then I would take ten or fifteen minutes to tell him the gospel. And I believe this usually is the right way for the truly modern man, for often it takes a long time to bring a man to the place where he understands the negative. And unless he understands what is wrong, he will not be ready to listen to and understand the positive. I believe that much of our evangelistic and personal work today is not clear simply because we are too anxious to get the answer without having a man realize the real cause of his sickness, which is true moral guilt (and not just psychological guilt feelings) in the presence of God. But the same is true in a culture. If I am going to speak to a culture, such as my culture, the message must be the message of Jeremiah. It must be the same in both private and public discourse.

Francis Schaeffer

A KNOT WHICH BAFFLES HUMAN SKILL

Romans 5:6

The central and most glorious truth of the Christian Gospel is that God, in the Person of Jesus Christ, bent to man's dilemma and did for him what he could not do for Himself. It was, indeed, a problem for God alone. Horace, in his *Ars Poetica*, laying down the rules for young dramatists, warned them against the too ready use of a device employed by playwrights in that period. When their characters were entangled in difficult situations, a god would be introduced to extricate the hero or elucidate the plot. The young playwrights overdid it. Horace laid it down that, in tragedy, a god should never be introduced save to untie a knot which baffled all human skill.

That describes our human situation; it was a knot which baffled all human skill. But Christ bent to our need. He as born among us, lived our life, was tempted in all points, like as we are, suffered at the hands of sinners, and offered, as Man, a perfect repentance for our race. He exposed sin, accepted God's righteous judgment which makes punishment its consequence, sacrificed Himself in willing acceptance of the price, in some mysterious way bore the entail on our behalf. And it was *God* who did it. Love, not vindictiveness, is at its heart. Sin demands punishment in any righteous world, and God in Christ bears the dreadful cost. It was no pathetic, beaten figure who cried from the Cross: `It is finished!' It was God's own Son, Royal, and Priestly, and Sovereign. He alone could do it. No one else could see sin for what it was. No one else could bear the heaped-up wickedness of our race.

Nor was this all. In His death, the Bible teaches, He broke the *power* of sin. In a way we do not fully comprehend, He devitalized it; He took the life out of death (if the paradox can be allowed) and opened the Kingdom of Heaven to all believers. Something was done on Calvary which needs never to be done again.

W.E. Sangster

HE FIRST BUILDS A MAN

James 1:4

"If I take care of my character," said Moody, "my reputation will take care of itself." The mature man knows that the most important part of his life is the part that only God sees. What he is in the closet is much more important than what he is in the pulpit. The man who fails in the secret place will ultimately fail in the public place. The mature man majors on building Christian character; he saturates himself with the Word; he spends time in prayer; he battles sin. He lets patience have her perfect work so that he can become still more mature in Christ (James 1:4). He is not quick to jump into the spotlight; like Joseph he knows that God has His purposes and His times.

The immature man covets praise and success in the eyes of men. He revels in statistics and in comparing his work with the work of others. He forgets the warning of Paul about those who, "measuring themselves by themselves, and comparing themselves among themselves, are not wise" (II Cor. 10:12). He belongs to a "mutual admiration society" and is very unhappy if someone is not praising him and his work. He is unmindful of the counsel in II Corinthians: "Not he that commendeth himself is approved, but whom the Lord commendeth" (10:18).

When God wants to build a ministry, He first builds a man, a man of character and faithfulness. He tests him with a few things; if he proves faithful, He promotes him to many things (Matt. 25:21). But if He sees that popularity is the governing force of a man's life, God abandons him just as He abandoned King Saul and Demas. The mature pastor majors on being a success in the eyes of God, no matter what others say.

Warren Wiersbe

BETWEEN EASTER AND PENTECOST

Hebrews 6:1

The apostle John . . . addressed himself to his readers as little children, fathers, and young men (I John 2:12-14). He took note of the fact that there are different stages of growth in the Christian life, attained by different students in the school of Christ.

The important thing is that we must "press on to maturity" (Heb. 6:1). Keep on growing. Too many Christians become stuck in their Christian lives—"stuck between Easter and Pentecost," as Dr. Graham Scroggie put it.

A godly Christian lady known to the author was dying of cancer. She knew she had only a few days to live. Her husband was attending to her needs, trying to make things as easy as possible for her. She said to him, "You must not make things too easy for me. I must keep growing, you know." Her life of intimacy with God had brought her to a state of spiritual maturity in which she was more concerned about growing up into Christ than about her own very real pain and discomfort. We too need to be ambitious to increase in our knowledge of God.

The writer of the letter to the Hebrews urged his readers to cultivate such an ambition, in these words: "Therefore leaving the elementary teaching about the Christ, let us press on to maturity" (6:1). Dr. Alexander Smellie pointed out that the King James Version renders it, "Let us go on." The Revised Version renders it, "Let us go on." Bishop Wescott prefers to render it, "Let us be borne on."

"The truth is that it needs all three to disclose the verb's significance and wealth. Put them together, and they speak to us of three dangers which beset us as we look to the perfection front. There is the danger of stopping too soon. There is the danger of sinking into discouragement. And there is the danger of supposing that we are alone." How gracious God is to make provision through the ministry of the Holy Spirit, for our being "borne on to maturity."

J. Oswald Sanders

"BUT NOT THROUGH ME"

Exodus 3:7-11

"Come now, I will send *thee* and *thou* wilt deliver My people." Moses was replying, "I believe You can and will do it, but not through *me*." God's almightiness was not the point in question. It was Moses' appropriation and obedience of faith that hung in the balance. Thus when Moses did set forth to carry out the commission, the Holy Spirit rightly says it was done "by faith." The same difference in the quality of believing makes the dividing line between Elijah and the other 7000 true believers who had not bowed the knee to Baal, and yet who had so little influence on the lives of their generation that Elijah did not know of their existence.

If we trace our weakness in the exercise of authoritative faith to the source, we shall find that our spiritual vitality is sapped at the roots through failure to take a bold grasp of the truth of "Christ in you," sufficient to shatter the illusion and consequent weakening effects of a false sense of separation. We know God only at a distance. We know touches of His power and grace, visitations which come and go. We are sure about the past through trust in His atoning work, and of the future through the promise of eternal life. But we have only a variable consciousness of His daily presence with us.

The transforming truth is that of our inward fusion with Him. "He that is joined to the Lord is one spirit." Can anything describe actual union more realistically than that? We *have* His mind. We *have* His power. If all power is in Him, all power is in us. This was the transforming revelation to the men of faith of old. Moses had the call and the seal as a young man, but at a critical moment he felt himself alone, and fled. Forty years later he was baptized at the burning bush into realized union with the "I AM," and from that time spoke forth the word of authority and was unconquerable.

Norman Grubb

THESE ARE THE FACTS

Psalm 91:1-2

If one lived on *facts*, and not on feelings, even the feelings would respond in time to the facts. These are the facts!

God is on the throne. Behind those rain-heavy clouds the sun is shining, and, behind the God-denying look of this mad world, God is always there: the Father of Jesus, whose love is as great as His power.

This is the day that He has made. I will rejoice and be glad in it. I will think on His light, His joy, His power . . . and myself as His beloved child. I will *run* on His errands—still *His*, though so ordinary and so same. Done for Him they will be *extra*-ordinary. I will make them as perfect as possible.

And, as I meditate, though it be but for five or seven unhurried minutes in the morning, it will bless me in the moment, and sink down into my subconsciousness to bless me a hundredfold when it rises again in an hour of special need.

Fancy having a subconscious stored with treasure like that, richly accumulating from a daily deposit! Fancy being ready to turn the mind over to meditation whenever one is kept waiting: not fuming and fretting for the bus which doesn't come (and getting worse for doing it!) but dwelling on the peace which will seep into me at any moment by the turning of a thought. Holiness, freedom, power, peace, light, joy, beauty, wisdom, love . . . all are key words for meditation.

W.E. Sangster

I know your secret thoughts, and that it is very expedient for your welfare that you be left sometimes without a taste of spiritual sweetness, lest you should be puffed up with your prosperous state and desire to please yourself in that which you are not. . . . That which I have given I can take away; and I can restore it again when I please. When I have it, it is Mine; and when I withdraw it, I have not taken anything that is yours; for mine is ever the good and perfect gift.

Thomas A. Kempis

A PRECARIOUS SWITCHBACK RIDE

Philippians 4:4

They rely on feelings. . . . Their Christian life becomes a precarious switchback ride as they soar to the heights of elation, only to plunge again into the depths of depression. This is not good at all. Do learn to mistrust your feelings. They are so variable. They change with the weather and vacillate with our health. We are fickle creatures of whim and mood and our fluctuating feelings very often have nothing whatever to do with our spiritual progress.

John R. Stott

Don't bother much about your feelings. When they are humble, loving, brave, give thanks for them; when they are conceited, selfish, cowardly, ask to have them altered. In neither case are they you, but only a thing that happens to you. What matters is your intentions and your behavior. (I hope all of this is not very dull and disappointing. Write freely again if I can be of use to you.)

P.S. Of course God does not consider you hopeless. If He did He would not be moving you to seek Him (and He obviously is).

C.S. Lewis

Yesterday you may have been perfectly happy and you went to sleep anticipating another great and glorious day, but you find yourself in the morning waking up depressed and in a wrong mood. Suddenly, without any explanation, you just find yourself like that. Now this is the essence of the problem. In other words, our feelings are variable, and I would emphasize the danger of being controlled by them.

D. Martyn-Lloyd Jones

TELL HIM THAT YOU DELIGHT IN HIM

Psalm 6:2-4

Accustom yourself to commune with God, not with thoughts deliberately formed to be expressed at a certain time, but with the feelings with which your heart is filled. If you enjoy His presence, and feel drawn by the attraction of His love, tell Him that you delight in Him, that you are happy in loving Him, and that He is very good to inspire so much affection in a heart so unworthy of His love. But what shall you say in seasons of dryness, coldness, weariness? Still say what you have in your heart. Tell God that you no longer find His love within you, that you feel a terrible void, that He wearies you, that His presence does not move you. Say to Him, "O God, look upon my ingratitude, my inconstancy, my unfaithfulness. Take my heart, for I cannot give it; and when Thou hast it, oh, keep it, for I cannot keep it for Thee; and save me in spite of myself."

Fénelon

If we are so led by the Spirit, where we go and what we do is of comparatively little moment; we may be forced by the circumstance of our life into surroundings that seem full of peril, but if God sent us there, such surroundings can do us no harm, though they may dull our *feeling* of happiness. Only let us remember that if, by God's mercy, we are free agents and can choose our own way of life, then it is simple mockery to talk of aspirations for the higher life, if we deliberately indulge our lower nature, by living in an atmosphere of worldliness, or by doing something which is, perhaps, quite innocent for others but consciously works us harm.

George H. Wilkinson

No one who has not tried it would believe how many difficulties are cleared out of a man's road by the simple act of trying to follow Christ.

Alexander Maclaren

LITTLE MORE THAN GUT FEELING

Romans 7:5-6

Feelings, passions, and emotive flow cannot substitute for analysis, observation, logical consistency, and historical awareness. Uncritical emotion may mislead, as Amos recognized in the irony of those who without reason *"feel* secure on the mountains of Samaria" (Amos 6:1). Modern psychological conscious-ness often finds it easier to talk about inner feelings than to provide a reasonable analysis of the motives of emotive life. One need not deny the importance of the emotive life in order to affirm the need for reason.

The plague of personalistic pietism has been the unconstrained notion that what is really important about God is only "what I feel about it right now." As a result, what one must finally trust comes down to little more than "gut feelings" and changeable, often self-assertive, emotive states—not the manifestation of God, not Scripture, not the historical experience of a community. Feeling disclosure is a primary objective in the intensive group experience. However useful, that in itself is incomplete; one's feelings may emerge out of cruelty, deception, or inordinate anxiety, for example. Classical Christian teaching asked for more than feeling-disclosure. It asked for rigorous, critical reflection, within the bounds of humble contrition, concerning the self-disclosure of God and its relevance for everything human.

Classical Christian teaching sought to nurture and assist this capacity for careful analytical reflection to avoid Christians becoming "slaves to passions and pleasures" (Titus 3:3; John Chrysostom). Without the constraint of sound moral reasoning, the passions are prone to become "licentious" (2 Pet. 2:18), "ungodly" (Jude 18), "worldly" (Titus 2:12), or "dishonorable" (Rom. 1:26). Even the law, which is good, is prone to awaken "sinful passions," as Paul knew: "While we lived on the level of our lower nature, the sinful passions evoked by the law worked in our bodies, to bear fruit for death" (Rom. 7:5).

Thomas Oden

GOD SEEMS TO HAVE WITHDRAWN

Job 23:3

Then again one often finds in the Christian life that there are variations in feelings and in sentiments. That is a matter that often troubles and perplexes God's people. We have all known something about it. You find that for some reason or another the experience you have been enjoying, suddenly comes to an end and you say with Job: 'O that I knew where I might find Him.' You are not conscious of having done anything wrong, but God seems to have withdrawn Himself and you feel yourself to be deserted. These desertions of the Spirit, that seem to take place from time to time, are again but parts of God's way of chastising His children, part of His great process of training and preparing us for the grand end and object He has in view for us.

D. Martyn Lloyd-Jones

Thanks very much for your kind letter. My own progress is so very slow (indeed sometimes I seem to be going backwards) that the encouragement of having in any degree helped someone else is just what I wanted. Of course the idea of not relying on emotion carries no implication of not rejoicing in it when it comes; you may remember Donne's Litanie—'that our affections kill us not—nor die.' One of the minor rewards of conversion is to be able at last to see the real point of all the old literature which we were brought up to read with the point left out.

C.S. Lewis

If one fights for good behavior, God makes one a present of the good feelings.

Juliana H. Ewing

UNDERTAKE THE DUTY

Psalm 63:1-6

Make allowance for infirmities of the flesh, which are purely physical. To be fatigued, body and soul, is not sin; to be in "heaviness" is not sin. Christian life is not a feeling; it is a principle: when your hearts will not *fly*, let them *go*, and if they "will neither fly nor go," be sorry for them and patient with them, and take them to Christ, as you would carry your little lame child to a tender-hearted, skillful surgeon. Does the surgeon, in such a case, upbraid the child for being lame?

Elizabeth Prentiss

When you feel ill and indisposed, and when in this condition your prayer is cold, heavy, filled with despondency and even despair, do not be disheartened or despairing, for the Lord knows your sick and painful condition. Struggle against your infirmity, pray as much as you have strength to, and the Lord will not despise the infirmity of your flesh and spirit.

Father John

God calls us to duty, and the only right answer is obedience. If it can be glad and willing and loving obedience, happy are we; but, in any case, whether we ourselves get enjoyment and blessing from the task or not, the call must be obeyed. The will of God must be done for the sake of ourselves. Undertake the duty, and step by step God will provide the disposition. We can at least obey. Ideal obedience includes the whole will and the whole heart. We cannot begin with that. But we can begin with what we have. God calls. It is better to obey blunderingly than not to obey at all.

George Hodges

The test of love is not feeling, but obedience.

William Bernard Ullathorne

NOT DEPENDENT ON FEELINGS

John 21:15-19

But, Lord, now that we are come so near Thee, and on right terms with Thee, we venture to ask Thee this, that we that love Thee may love Thee very much more. Oh! since Thou hast been precious, Thy very name has music in it to our ears, and there are times when Thy love is so inexpressibly strong upon us that we are carried away with it. We have felt that we would gladly die to increase Thine honor. We have been willing to lose our name and our repute if so be Thou mightiest be glorified, and truly we often feel that if the crushing of us would lift Thee one inch the higher, we would gladly suffer it.

For oh! Thou blessed King, we would set the crown on Thy head, even if the sword should smite our arm off at the shoulder blade. Thou must be King whatever becomes of us; Thou must be glorified whatever becomes of us.

But yet we have to mourn that we cannot get always to feel as we should this rapture and ardour of love. Oh! at times Thou dost manifest Thyself to us so charmingly that heaven itself could scarce be happier than the world become when Thou art with us in it. But when Thou art gone and we are in the dark, oh! Give us the love that loves in the dark, that loves when there is no comfortable sense of Thy presence. Let us not be dependent upon feeling, but may we ever love Thee, so that if Thou didst turn Thy back on us we would think none the less of Thee, for Thou art unspeakably to be beloved whatsoever Thou doest, and if Thou dost give us rough words, yet still we would cling to Thee, and if the rod be used till we tingle again, yet still will we love Thee, for Thou are infinitely to be beloved of all men and angels, and Thy Father loved Thee. Make our hearts to love Thee evermore the same. With all the capacity for love that there is in us, and with all the more that thou canst give us, may we love our Lord in spirit and in truth.

C.H. Spurgeon

NOT FEELING BRIGHT NOW

I Timothy 4:14

"Neglect not the gift that is in thee." We have to be careful not to neglect the spiritual reality planted in us by God. The first thing that contact with reality does is to enable us to diagnose our moods. It is a great moment when we realize that we have the power to trample on certain moods. Moods never go by praying, moods go by kicking. A mood nearly always has its seat in the physical condition, not in the moral, and it is a continual effort to refuse to listen to those moods which arise from a physical condition; we must not submit to them for a second. It is a great thing to have something to neglect in your life; a great thing for your moral character to have something to snub. "The expulsive power of a new affection"—that is what Christianity supplies. The Spirit of God on the basis of Redemption gives us something else to think about. Are we going to think about it?

Oswald Chambers

I feel very strongly that some of us are thinking in terms such as these: "Today I have been a little more careful; today I have been doing a little better; this morning I have been reading the Word of God in a warmer way, so today I can pray better! Or again today I have had a little difficulty with the family; I am not feeling too bright now; it seems that there must be something wrong; therefore I cannot approach God."

What, after all, is your basis of approach to God? Do you come to Him on the uncertain ground of your feeling, the feeling that you may have achieved something for God today? Or is your approach based on something far more secure, namely the fact that the Blood has been shed and that God looks on that Blood and is satisfied?

The reason we listen so readily to the accusations of Satan is that we are still hoping to have some righteousness of our own to offer God (to sort of make for bargaining power).

Watchman Nee

IN A MISERABLE, DEAD CONDITION

Philippians 4:6

Wed., Jan. 17, 1723 Dull. I find by experience that if I make resolutions and do what I will, with never so many inventions, it is all nothing, and to no purpose at all without the motions of the Spirit of God; . . . our resolutions may be at the highest one day, and yet, the next day we may be in a miserable, dead condition, not at all like the same person resolved. So that it is no purpose to resolve, except we depend on the grace of God. For, if it were not for His mere grace, one might be a very good man one day and a very wicked one the next.

Sat., Jan. 5 A little redeemed from a long dreadful dullness about reading the Scriptures. This week have been unhappily low in the weekly account and what are the reasons for it?—Abundance of listlessness and sloth; and if this should continue much longer, I perceive that other sins will begin to discover themselves. It used to appear to me that I had not much sin remaining; but now, I perceive that there are remainders of sin.

Jonathan Edwards Diary

We need to guard against being over-anxious about the subjective side of things, and so becoming turned in upon ourselves. We need to dwell upon the objective—"abide in me"—and to let God take care of the subjective. And this He has undertaken to do.

You are in a room and it is growing dark. You would like to have the light on in order to read. There is a reading lamp on the table beside you. What do you do? Do you watch it intently to see if the light will come on? Do you take a cloth and polish the bulb? No, you get up and cross the room and turn on the switch. You turn your attention to the source of power and when you have taken the necessary action there the light comes on.

Watchman Nee

MORBID SELF-ANALYSIS

Matthew 17:8

The idea that the Bible is full of commands to self-examination is prevalent—many of us think this is the truly pious thing to do. In view of this idea many will be surprised to find that there are only two texts in the whole Bible that speak of self-examination, and that neither of these can at all be made to countenance the morbid self-analysis that results from what we call self-examination. . . .

Said Adelaide Proctor, "For one look at self take ten looks at Christ. . . ."

Let us try God's fast. Let us lay aside all care for ourselves and care instead for our needy brothers and sisters. Let us stop trying to do something for our own poor miserable self-life, and begin to try to do something to help the spiritual lives of others. Let us give up our hopeless efforts to find something in ourselves to delight in and delight ourselves only in the Lord and in His ways. If we do this, our misery will be ended.

We sing sometimes 'Thou O Christ are all I want,' but as a fact we want many other things. We want good feelings, we want fervor and earnestness, we want realizations, we want satisfying experiences; and we continually examine ourselves to try to find out why we do not have these things. . . .

Fenélon says that we should never indulge in any self-reflected acts, either of mortification at our failures, or of congratulation at our successes; but that we should continually consign self and all self's doings to oblivion and should keep our interior eyes upon the Lord only.

Hannah Whithall Smith

DEAD ENDS

Matthew 14:29-31

We have seen in our quest that there is the Way and not-the-way, and we have marked out the steps in finding the Way. Having our feet upon the Way— firmly, I trust—we may now look at some roads with dead ends. For many people starting upon the way get side-tracked into roads that lead nowhere. We shall look at sixteen roads that lead to the Never-Never Land. The signs that we shall put up over these roads that lead to dead ends are commandments: "Thou shalt not enter." That sounds dogmatic and authoritarian, but in reality these commandments are simply the distilled experience of the race. We shall look at some ways humanity, by the method of trial and error, is finding out how *not* to live.

The first road with a dead end is *Fear*. When fear is spelled with a small *f* it may be contributive. For fear may have useful biological ends. Fear makes the frightened deer alert and fleet; it makes the surgeon skillful, for he sees the dangers that beset him if he does the wrong thing; it makes the soul alert lest it hurt itself through wrong choices. Fear harnessed to constructive ends may be constructive. When we use fear and control it, then it is good. When fear uses us and controls us, then it is bad. When fear becomes Fear, then it becomes master and runs us into roads with dead ends. Then Fear becomes fearsome.

Fear has three things against it: (1) It is disease producing. (2) It is paralyzing to effort. (3) It is useless.

If these three things are true, then to conquer fear is one of the first conquests of life. Without that conquest we limp through life. I asked a doctor, "Is fear Enemy No. 1?" "Enemy No. 1? It's Enemy No. 1½," he replied. If it is Enemy No. 1, then we must face it first of all and get it out of the way before we can walk upon the Way with heads up and our hearts released and unafraid. The first word of the gospel was the voice of the angel, "Fear not." The first word of Jesus after His resurrection was, "Have no fear!" (Matt. 28:10, Moffatt). Between that first word and the last word the constant endeavor of Jesus was to get men released from fear. We must learn His secret.

E. Stanley Jones

READY TO GIVE UP

I John 3:19-21

I hope you enjoy more religion than I do. This heavy affliction does not have that salutary effect on my heart which I anticipated. Mercies and judgments seem to be thrown away on me, and I am afraid that I shall never make much advance in the divine life. I had such a view and sense of my depravity this morning as made me ready to give up all for lost—not I mean as it regards my interest in Christ—there I feel strong—but as it regards any attainments in holiness, while remaining in this state of sin.

LETTER TO HIS WIFE
Adoniram Judson

There are two kinds of condemnation, namely, that before God and that before myself and the second may at times seem to us even more awful than the first. When I see that the Blood of Christ has satisfied God, then I know my sins are forgiven and there is for me no more condemnation before God. Yet I may still be knowing defeat, and the sense of inward condemnation on this account may be very real, as Romans 7 shows. But if I have learned to live by Christ as my life, then I have learned the secret of victory and praise God! "There is therefore now no condemnation." The mind of the spirit is life and peace (Rom. 8:6) and this becomes my experience as I learn to walk in the Spirit. With peace in my heart I have no time to feel condemned, but only to praise Him who leads me on from victory to victory.

Watchman Nee

ENORMOUS SACRED SELF-CONFIDENCE

Philippians 4:13

Mark the mingling of profound humility with the tone of absolute confidence. When the Apostle looked at himself he was filled with shrinkings and timidities, but when he thought about his acceptance and his endowment he was possessed by confident triumph. Whatever shrinking he had about himself, he had no shrinking that he was the elect of God, endowed with the grace of God, in order to proclaim the evangel of God. It was just because he was so perfectly assured of his acceptance and of his vocation that he felt so perfectly unworthy. Did not Cromwell say of George Fox that an enormous sacred self-confidence was not the least of his attainments? I am not quite sure that Oliver Cromwell correctly interpreted George Fox. I would be inclined to withdraw the word "self" and insert the word "God," and then we have got, not only what George Fox ought to be, but what the Apostle Paul was.

J.H. Jowett

Some time ago, using the familiar Gallup procedure, a number of questions were addressed to young people, particularly students. One of these questions was: "What is the basic feeling you have toward life?" Sixty percent of them replied with a shocking unanimity: fear. Why is it that persons who do not by any means impress one as being anxious or depressed should give such a strange answer?

Helmut Thielicke

How do we find a way to handle fear and worry? Many people say action will kill fear. That's true. I believe it, teach it, and practice it.

Carole C. Carlson

AFRAID OF LIFE

Psalm 23

In the first place, science most certainly does not free man from fear. Modern man is as full of fear as was his primitive ancestor. On this all the psychologists are agreed. Dr. Oscar Forel, whom nobody can accuse of having a Christian bias, declares roundly that "metaphysical anguish" remains the fundamental human problem. The scientists are as much afraid as the rest. I have already referred to a remark made by Harold Urey, Nobel Prize winner for Physics, one of the inventors of the Atomic bomb: "I write in order to make you afraid. I am myself a man who is afraid. All the scientists I know are afraid. The men of science are clearly becoming conscious of the limitations of science; that it is no more than a representation of things—a representation that is most fruitful in practical deductions—but that it tells us nothing of things themselves, not even of matter or energy. It can never then have an answer for the problems that haunt the heart of man.

Tournier

During those last days Amy Carmichael kept by her side the last stanza of an old hymn which epitomized her source of comfort:

> Green pastures are before me
> Which yet I have not seen,
> Bright skies will soon be o'er me
> Where the dark clouds have been.
>
> My hope I cannot measure,
> My path to life is free,
> My Savior has my treasure,
> And He will walk with me.

In all of her endeavors Christ was her motivation, her source of power, her lifetime goal. That made all the difference in her suffering.

THE LIFE OF AMY CARMICHAEL
Elizabeth Elliot

WILLINGLY IN SUBJECTION

Hebrews 11:38

If you will withdraw yourself from speaking vainly and from gadding idly, as also from hearkening after new things and rumors, you shall find time enough and suitable for meditation on good things.

The greatest saints avoided, when they could, the society of men (Heb. 11:38) and did rather choose to live to God in secret.

A certain one has said: "As oft as I have been among men, I returned home less a man than I was before." And this we often find true, when we talk long together. It is easier altogether to hold one's peace, than not speak more words than we ought. It is easier for a man to keep himself well at home than when he is abroad.

He therefore who intends to attain to the more inward and spiritual things of religion must with Jesus depart from the multitude (Matt. 5:1).

No man safely appears abroad, but he who gladly hides himself. No man safely speaks, but he who willingly holds his peace (Eccles. 3:7). No man safely rules, but he who is willingly in subjection. No man safely commands, but he who has learned well to obey. No man safely rejoices, unless he has within him the witness of a good conscience (Acts 23:1).

And yet always the security of the saints was full of the fear of God. Neither were they the less anxious and humble in themselves, for they shined outwardly with great virtues and grace. But the security of bad men arises from pride and presumption, and in the end it turns to a man's own deceiving.

Thomas A. Kempis

The recognition of that empty space can come very early. Amy Carmichael says, `My first memory as a tiny child is this: after the nursery light had been turned low and I was quite alone, I used to smooth a little place on the sheet, and say aloud to our Father, "Please come and sit with me."'

Isabel Kuhn

THE MOST DREARY WILDERNESS, PARADISE

Psalm 119:97

Henry Martyn's spiritual life did not stop short at gratitude for the forgiveness of sins. We find in his writings increasing and deepening longings after God, numerous instances of delight and satisfaction in prayer, and many indications of his intense love of the Word of God. He felt he could not live one happy hour without having communion with God; even the most dreary wilderness would become paradise with His presence. At times, when he began to pray in much dejection, he could feel only a great darkness; but soon the Lord would pour into his heart light, joy and comfort. Nothing in the weak words used could bring such an astonishing change of heart; it could only be through God's fulfilling His promises made to those who seek Him. `If there be anything I do, if there be anything I leave undone, let me be perfect in prayer,' was his cry. His love of the Bible was equally intense; he called it `a precious and wonderful book,' and later his translation work led him increasingly to appreciate its wisdom. `What I have learnt from the Word of God is satisfying,' he wrote, `which nothing else in the whole world is.'

HENRY MARTYN
Constance Padwick

As I analyze myself I find several things happening to me as a result of these two months of strenuous effort to keep God in mind every minute. This concentration upon God is *strenuous*, but everything else has ceased to be so. I think more clearly, I forget less frequently. Things which I did with a strain before, I now do easily and with no effort whatever. I worry about nothing, and lose no sleep. I walk on air a good part of the time. Even the mirror reveals a new light in my eyes and face. I no longer feel in a hurry about anything. Nothing can go wrong excepting one thing. That is that *God may slip from my mind* if I do not keep on my guard. If He is there, the universe is with me. My task is simple and clear.

Frank Laubach

IN THE NOISE AND CLUTTER

Exodus 33:14

Many find it more difficult to worship in a kitchen than before an altar. Some feel themselves serving God better through preaching to crowds than in washing pots and pans. But it was different with Nicholas Herman (called Brother Lawrence 1611-1691): "The time of business," he said, "does not with me differ from the time of prayer; and in the noise and clutter of my kitchen, while several persons are at the same time calling for different things, I possess God in as great tranquility as if I were upon my knees at the blessed sacrament." It took ten years of careful spiritual discipline before he was able to achieve the practice of the presence of God in the duties of daily living.

Brother Lawrence was a soldier and a household servant who became a lay member of the Barefooted Carmelites. Without formal education, outside elegant cathedrals, and void of elegant ritual, he was able to have a personal union of himself and God. This was for him the highest goal of living: "I cannot imagine how religious persons can live satisfied without the practice of the presence of God. For my part, as I can, I keep myself retired within Him in the very center of my soul, and when I am so with Him, I fear no evil." His conversion began at eighteen, when on a mid-winter day he saw a leafless tree. As he reflected that spring would soon bring blossoms and leaves to the tree, his thoughts turned to the wonders of God in His world. From that time he endeavored to walk constantly "as in His presence."

Brother Lawrence wrote that he had learned "to persevere in His holy presence wherein I keep myself by a simple attention and an absorbing passionate regard to God, which I may call an actual presence of God. As I apply myself to prayer, I feel my whole spirit lifted up without any trouble or effort of mine; and it remains as it were in elevation, fixed firm in God as in its center and resting place."

Thomas Kepler

A COMMUNING HEART

Psalm 63:6-8

How about your life? How important is your life to God? What holy satisfaction do you bring to God each day? Your service is important to God, but your communion is much more important. Service that flows from a communing heart has tremendous power and is tremendously effective in the sight of God.

It seems that God can find a thousand people eager to serve Him before He finds one whose great hunger is to commune with Him. Communion does not make you a recluse. Communion does not make you impractical or of little earthly use to others. It qualifies you to carry the presence of God with you and make all of your life a holy and fragrant blessing to others.

You don't lose time spent in communing with God! You invest it in the very heart of God. You invest it with the supreme Being of the universe. You can become one of earth's privileged few if you really commune with God. You can become one of the princes or princesses of eternity if now you will truly give yourself in daily communion with God.

A communing heart almost unconsciously becomes an interceding heart. Why? Because your communion is with Jesus and He is the great High Priest/Intercessor. As you commune with Jesus, He shares with you His holy heartbeat, His hunger for a whole world.

Wesley Duewel

MEDITATION NOT MYSTICAL

Psalm 1:2-3

Peace and quiet. They go together, don't they? That is why consistent quiet times alone with God are so indispensable to experiencing the abiding peace of Christ. Yet I must confess that these times of fellowship with the Lord are occasionally dry and uneventful. Out of a desire to see God work more effectively and personally in my life has come a discovery that has enlivened my quiet times and made them more rewarding than ever.

I begin my quiet time with the reading of Scripture. There really is no other way to know God than through the revelation of his Word by the illumination of the Holy Spirit. If Scripture is not the centerpiece of your quiet time, then it will not impart the supernatural life that every word of God contains. After reading (usually one chapter in a book of the Old Testament and another chapter in the New Testament), I pray. God has answered many, many of my prayers. I have come to know Christ intimately. Yet I thirst for something more—something deeper.

I have come to realize that my thirst is quenched as I spend time meditating on the Word of God. Meditation is not mystical. Rather, it is the extremely practical and nourishing exercise of pondering and thinking on what God is saying through his Word. It is the art of asking questions of the Scriptures and then of yourself and discovering how the truth examined can be applied to your life and the particular problems you face.

Until I gave my quiet time the added dimension of meditation, I never received its rich fullness.

Charles Stanley

"THEY'RE HUNGRY FOR GOD"

Psalm 42:1

Thoughts are like flowers; those gathered in the morning keep fresh the longest.

André Gide

Yesterday a sister was telling me about some sisters who go to the prison. They take the Blessed Sacrament, and the prison chaplain has started daily adoration for half an hour. To see those prisoners, young boys and men, adoring. They are preparing some of those boys for First Communion. They're hungry for God—they are very hungry for God. That man who we picked up from the streets said, "I have lived like an animal in the street but I'm going to die like an angel." I can tell you that of the eighteen thousand that have died in Calcutta alone, I've not seen one of them die in distress. Nobody has died in despair. It is so beautiful. We feel this is the fruit of our vocation, of our oneness with Christ. We need that continual feeding; that is why we begin the day at half past four in the morning and then we have Mass, Holy Communion, and meditation.

Mother Theresa

In the morning fix thy good purpose; and at night examine thyself what thou hast done, how thou hast behaved thyself in word, deed, and thought; for in these perhaps thou has oftentimes offended both God and thy neighbor.

Thomas A. Kempis

AN EXHORTATION TO LISTEN

Psalm 27:14

Whoever will listen will hear the speaking Heaven. This is definitely not the hour when men take kindly to an exhortation to *listen*, for listening is not today a part of popular religion. We are at the opposite end of the pole from there. Religion has accepted the monstrous heresy that noise, size, activity and bluster make a man dear to God. But we may take heart. To a people caught in the tempest of the last great conflict God says, "Be still, and know that I am God," and still He says it, as if He means to tell us that our strength and safety lie not in noise but in silence.

It is important that we get still to wait on God. And it is best that we get alone, preferably with our Bible outspread before us. Then if we will we may draw near to God and begin to hear Him speak to us in our hearts. I think for the average person the progression will be something like this: First a sound as of a Presence walking in the garden. Then a voice, more intelligible, but still far from clear. Then the happy moment when the Spirit begins to illuminate the Scriptures, and that which had been only a sound or at best a voice, now becomes an intelligible word, warm and intimate and clear as the word of a dear friend. Then will come life and light, and best of all ability to see and rest in and embrace Jesus Christ as Savior and Lord and All.

A.W. Tozer

It is common knowledge that in doing something 21 times, a habit is formed. If no other good comes from this journal, we want to help you start the habit of consistently meeting God in fellowship each day. In these 15 days you will be well along in establishing the best habit we know. Imagine—fifteen times—the Lord will have had first place in your life. We are sure you will continue the rest of your life.

DeVern Fromke

THE VALUE OF QUIETNESS

Psalm 46:10

"The *sadhu* is more like Jesus than anyone we have ever known." They quickly discovered that the secret which lay behind these qualities was something he also shared with Jesus. Like his Master, he knew the value, the compelling necessity, of quietness and meditation. . . .

Sundar seldom talked publicly of his devotional life, though his addresses were the product of much meditation and prayer. Now and again he opened his heart to his friends, however.

"Rising early, I begin by reading a chapter of the Bible. I make a mental note of the verses which seem suggestive," he told his friends who asked about his methods of meditation. "Then when I have quietly read the whole chapter, I return to each of these verses and meditate on them, one at a time. After I have exhausted all that God can say to me through those verses at that time I spend a quarter of an hour `collecting myself' for prayer.

"I have no special posture for prayer. I may sit, or kneel, or stand. I use no words. I think only of those things that I have been reading, of the things I have been doing or intend to do, of the people I know, of myself and of Jesus—such thought *is* prayer. And, in such prayer, *God* speaks, not man."

THE STORY OF SADHU SUNDAR SINGH
Cyril Davey

THE HARDEST MISSION FIELD

II Corinthians 2:16

Dinapore, Dec. 6, 1806

To the Rev. J. Chamberlain, Katwa,

I find myself here in a sphere so vast that I cry out with unfeigned astonishment, "Who is sufficient for these things?" I am somewhat dispirited at finding myself at a standstill; not knowing what course to take to acquire the language of the people—for the fine language of my Mussulman (Muslim) mûnshi is as unintelligible as English to the country people, and I have very limited opportunities of being much with them. I cannot be absent a night from this station without permission from the commander-in-chief. However, these are small difficulties. Our great obstacle is the dominion which Satan has obtained over the hearts of men. Yet through the support and power of God, I think I am willing to continue throwing in the net at the Lord's command through all the long night of life, though the end may be that I have caught nothing.

Henry Martyn

Dr. Samuel Zwemer met a young medical student who said he would go to Arabia if he could be convinced that it was the hardest mission field in the world. Dr. Zwemer sat down and wrote, "Arabia is the hardest mission field in the world for the following reasons: 1. The climate is the most unbearable. One hundred degrees in the shade is common. . . . It stays hot all night. 2. Arabic is the hardest language of which I know anything. 3. You probably cannot expect any converts to Christianity in your lifetime. All you can do is serve and love and let the results come as God sends them. 4. In addition, our mission has no money. We're not supported by any church board and we have to raise our own funds. 5. New missionaries must promise not to marry for five years. Life here at this time is too primitive for women and children. Let me know what you decide.

The young medical student read the letter and replied, "I am your man." His name was Paul Harrison.

Selected

REMEMBERING WILLIAM CAREY

John 4:35

`Come in, and sit down,' said a soft, welcoming
voice in response to my knock. `My husband is busy, but he
will be glad to see you presently.'

I sat down in the homely inglenook, quite close to
an open window. A gentle breeze stirred the spotless chintz
curtains, and carried with it into the room the perfume of
flowers. It was a delightful room, just like those low-
ceilinged apartments you see sometimes in old country
houses. A solemn old grandfather clock in one corner of the
room looked very dignified, and a home-made map and
some interesting prints of foreign scenes were hung upon the
walls. I saw several books lying open upon the table, the
learned character of which rather surprised me.

`You see how busy he has been,' said his wife,
returning to her work-basket. `School was dismissed only
an hour ago, and he has already mended one pair of shoes
and made some patterns. So he goes on, day after day,
hammering and reading, reading and hammering.'

Presently a little maid pushed open the door. In her
hands were a pair of heavy boots. `If you please,' she said,
`can father have them back tomorrow?'

`If it's possible,' answered the shoemaker's wife; and
she patted the curly head as the child turned to go,
seemingly quite satisfied with the promise. Then she called
out to her sons, who were playing in the sunny lane, `Felix,
don't play so roughly, but look after William.'

A moment later the shoemaker came out of the
inner room: a short young man with the unmistakable stoop
of a student. His leathern apron did not hide the threadbare
breeches and faded hose; and his wig badly fitted. His quick
glance took in at once the broken boots on the bench.
`Another pair!' he murmured, with a curiously patient little
smile. Then he turned to welcome me, and I became aware
of the wonderful light in his eyes. Presently he went over
and touched with a

tenderness remarkable for such clumsy hands—hands seared and stained with toil—the flowers that grew in his window box. It seemed to me that they had something to do with his look of happiness, for he said as he touched them, `I see God's hand in each petal, and His smile in every glowing heart.'

Whilst his wife prepared a meal, we went together up a tiny winding staircase that led to a room above. There the shoemaker-schoolmaster showed me some more of his treasured books, for he had many, and presently took up the Book he loved most of all. With this held reverently in his hand, he went on to talk of a great dream of his, of which I had already heard from others, and of the sermon he was shortly to preach at Nottingham. `Here is the manuscript,' he said fervently. `God spoke to me as I wrote it. I am praying that it will end in the founding of a society in our denomination for the spreading of the light of the Gospel to the heathen peoples.' He put it away, and walked over to the open window, and I stood beside him. The sky was a lovely blue, and the setting sun shone on wide fields, through which a river flowed on its gentle course. Birds sang in the trees and I could hear the distant merriment of children at their play. And I spoke of these. But he said, `What I see ever are the fields of vast heathendom, and I believe they are "white unto harvest." And for their reaping I am ready and eager to go.'

Memories of William Carey

WHY DID YOU WAIT SO LONG?

John 9:4

I was reminded recently of how most of today's church is, tragically, preoccupied with lesser matters. Father Vincent J. Donovan, in *Christianity Rediscovered*, reports his experience of 19 years as a missionary to the Masai tribes of eastern Africa. When he arrived, he observed that the established mission station had thriving schools, hospitals, and other institutions and services for the Masai, and that the relations between the missionaries and the Masai were excellent. Nevertheless, no Masai had become Christians.

Donovan wrote to his bishop: Masai kraals are visited very often. . . . But never, or almost, is religion mentioned on any of these visits. . . . The relationship with the Masai, in my opinion, is dismal, time consuming, wearying, expensive, and materialistic. . . . It looks as if such a situation will go on forever.

I suddenly feel the urgent need to . . . simply go to these people and do the work among them for which I came to Africa.

I would propose cutting myself off from the school and the hospital, as far as these people are concerned—as well as the socializing with them—and just go and talk to them about God and the Christian message. . . .

That is precisely what I would propose to do. I know what most people say. It is impossible to preach the gospel directly to the Masai. They are the hardest of all the pagans, the toughest of the tough.

But I would like to try. I want to go to the Masai on daily safaris—unencumbered with the burden of selling them our school system, or begging for their children for our schools, or carrying their sick, or giving them medicine.

Outside of this, *I have no theory, no plan, no strategy, no gimmicks*—no idea of what will come. I feel rather naked. *I will begin as soon as possible.*

When Donovan explained to the first Masai chief what he proposed to do and why it was so important, the chief asked, understandably, "If that is why you came here, why did you wait so long to tell us about this?"

George Hunter

THE END OF INDIA

II Thessalonians 2:7-8

We have come to the end of India
Where the rocks run into the sea,
The wonderful, blue-green, boundless sea,
That moves and murmurs constantly
About the rocks at the end of the land
That is greater than we can understand,
And dark with a terrible mystery—
The mystery of iniquity.

For at the end of India
A temple stands on a rock,
As if set there to block
The way of the God of the sea
From entering in at His gate;
But He is patient to wait
Till the towering temple wall
Shall shiver and totter and fall
With a plunge into the sea,
And the land shall be cleansed from iniquity.

So, at the end of India
Where the rocks run into the sea,
The wonderful, blue-green, boundless sea,
Mystery touches mystery;
And every thud of the waves on the shore
As they break in might,
And leap in white.

Amy Carmichael

SHE IS A TOY, A SLAVE

Galatians 3:28

One of the chief characteristics of most non-Christian religions is the degradation of women. . . . It is equally established that in the religion of Jesus Christ where "there is neither male nor female" she has reached her highest sphere.

"In the history of humanity as written," says Herbert Spencer, "the saddest part concerns the treatment of women . . . I say the saddest part, because though there have been many things more conspicuous-ly dreadful—cannibalism, the torturing of prisoners, the sacrificings of victims to ghosts and gods—these have been occasional, whereas the brutal treatment of women has been universal and constant."

The position of the wife of ancient Egypt is strikingly illustrated by two statues uncovered in the Temple of Luxor at Karnak. They are statues of the great Rameses and his wife. Rameses is standing, chiseled, according to Egyptian sculpture, in heroic size. The wife of Rameses stands properly beside him, but she reaches only as high as the knee of her royal husband. Though in many lands now the woman stands as high as her husband's heart, she of Egypt under the Mohammedan religion is still like the wife of Rameses, no higher than her husband's knee. She is a toy, a slave subjected to the whims of her husband.

The woman of highly civilized Greece had no share in the intellectual life of men. . . . Nor was she permitted to visit the athletic games at Olympia. Her main duties were to cook and spin, and to oversee the domestic slaves of whom she herself was practically one.

Even the famed Greek philosophers were bitter against women. Plato presents a state of society wholly disorganized when slaves are disorganized, when slaves are disobedient to their masters, and wives are on an equality with their husbands. Aristotle characterized women as beings of an inferior order, and the great Socrates asks the pathetic question: "Is there a human being with whom you talk less than with your wife?"

Aaron J. Kligerman

LITTLE HELL

Matthew 11:28

Cowman's first attempt at giving a Gospel message was made some months after his conversion. He thought it might be well to get in touch with various classes. One Sabbath evening he attended a service in a district in Chicago known as "Little Hell." The leader, mistaking him for a minister, invited him to preach for them on the following Sabbath evening. With the conviction that every opportunity which presented itself should be "bought up," the invitation was accepted.

Hours were spent in prayer and the study of the Word. Sabbath evening came and the walk of a mile and a half was made in silence. The hall was crowded to its limit with men and women of the worst class. Some came reeling down the aisle in a drunken stupor; others were soon fast asleep from the effect of strong drink. The friendless were there, the homeless, the penniless. What a number of sin-marred faces looked up at the speaker! The carefully prepared sermon was forgotten and he talked to the hearts of that motley crowd, begging them with tears to give up their lives of sin and come to Jesus; and they came, a long altar full—weeping their way to Zion. He was there until midnight praying with them, and thus a definite work began with a limited amount of knowledge in the divine art of soul-winning. What a great encouragement he received from his labors in "Little Hell," where he spent every Sabbath evening thereafter. In the after years when he went to Japan as a missionary, many of these "down-and-outs" whom he had led to Christ became his faithful supporters in his new field of labor. . . .

He disarmed men by trusting them. He dealt with hundreds in the crises of their lives. Thus when but a young man among men he saw all sides of life, learned the secrets of hundreds of characters and was trusted and loved. Men felt that he was not a voice merely, but a friend, and in his arms they were lifted up.

CHARLES COWMAN,
MISSIONARY WARRIOR
Lettie Cowman

RECKLESS, DEFIANT ABANDONMENT

Deuteronomy 1:21

One of the choicest traits of Charles Cowman's character was that of his unfailing optimism. He always saw the sun when it did not shine and was

> One who never turned his back but marched breast forward. Never doubted clouds would break.

A search through his manuscripts and papers for texts that would hint at discouragement has been in vain, for a note of victory rings through every letter, every sentence. His simple trust in God made him always confident of His care. Only once can I recall his giving away to anything like discouragement and that was during the days when he first broke down in health and was laid aside. His sister called to see him and found him helplessly ill. He lay quite still, a tear trickled over his cheek as he said to her, "It is so very difficult to lie here absolutely helpless, when so much work remains to be done." After she had left the room he said to me, "Oh forgive me for saying what I did. It sounded as if I were murmuring and God knows I did not mean it that way."

As we trace his life, let us notice the wonderful persistence of the faith that God had given him. Where others might have turned aside, he seemed to be more directed of God than ever; where others would have been cast down, he seemed to be carried along by a power from above.

Said the Rev. Oswald Chambers of Scotland; "The thing that strikes you about Charles Cowman is not his holiness, but his absolutely reckless, careless, defiant abandonment to Jesus Christ."

CHARLES COWMAN,
MISSIONARY WARRIOR
Lettie Cowman

"I AM GOING TO PREACH TONIGHT"

Ephesians 5:14

During his waking hours Charles exhorted us as he had never exhorted before and in the delirium of sleep he would break out in the most impassioned appeals to the church to awaken from her sleep, and stand by the cause of foreign missions. When we did not know whether he was with the angels or with us, with one foot on the other shore, he shouted back to us, "Tell the people not to let the warmth go out of their hearts." One night in a delirium he spoke for a full hour on the need of God's children taking advance ground in sending the Gospel to the heathen. He said to me, "Help me to get up, I am going to preach tonight." Asking him to what church he was going, he replied, "I am speaking at Christ Church at a missionary meeting and my text is Eph. 5:14, `Awake thou that sleepest, arise from the dead, and Christ shall give thee light.'"

He then added, "From now on in every meeting where I shall speak, I expect to combine foreign missions and the Lord's coming." He loved His appearing and said on that particular night, "Mother, are you ready for the coming of our Lord?" She replied in the affirmative. The nurses were then questioned, and he finally said to me, "My dearest, is His coming more than a doctrine to you? Is His coming a living hope? Assuring him that it was, he then requested me to sing his favorite hymn,

> It may be at morn when the day is
> awaking,
> When sunlight thro' darkness and
> shadow is breaking,
> That Jesus will come in the fullness
> of glory
> To receive from the world His own.

CHARLES COWMAN,
MISSIONARY WARRIOR
Lettie Cowman

WHOSE CHILDREN?

Psalm 71:16-19

When Katharine was fourteen years old she raised her hand at a youth conference to signify her desire to become a Christian, and seven years later she raised her hand at another conference to indicate her willingness to become a missionary. Soon after that she married Phil Howard and they sailed to Belgium to work with the Belgian Gospel Mission. During their first furlough, however, Phil was asked to join the staff of the Sunday School Times, and his acceptance signaled an end to their foreign missionary service. But this was not the end of their commitment to foreign missions. Indeed, the new ministry offered an expanded opportunity for involvement in world missions.

In the years that followed, while they raised their six children, their home became a crossroads for Christian workers and missionaries. . . .

It was this environment and commitment to prayer that propelled the children into missionary work themselves. Katharine tells how on one occasion a verse kept going over and over in her mind: "Pray ye, therefore, the Lord of the harvest, that he will send forth laborers into His harvest." She vowed to pray for more missionaries. But, she writes, "One day the thought struck me, whose children are you asking God to send? I backed away from the implications, but it was no use. Finally I was willing to pray that he would send my children if that was His will for them."

It was. . . . She later wrote of the result of her prayer: "Our son Phil and his wife [were] in the bush of Canada's Northwest Territories. . . . In that same year, 1958, our daughter Elisabeth Elliot and her three-year-old Valerie went to live with the Auca Indians, the tribe that had killed her husband, Jim. Our second son, Dave, was teaching in the Seminario Biblico in San Jose, Costa Rica. . . . Virginia and her husband [were] in the Sulu Sea of the Philippines, contacting remote villages with the gospel. . . . Tom was criss-crossing the U.S. that year as Foreign Mission Fellowship staff member for Inter-Varsity Christian Fellowship."

Ruth Tucker

WEDDED TO THE CHARTER

I John 2:2

The key to the missionary message is the propitiation of Christ Jesus. Take any phase of Christ's work—the healing phase, the saving and sanctifying phase—there is nothing limitless about those. "The Lamb of God which taketh away the sin of the world!"—that is limitless. The missionary message is the limitless significance of Jesus Christ as the propitiation for our sins, and a missionary is one who is soaked in that revelation.

The key to the missionary message is the remissionary aspect of Christ's life, not His kindness and His goodness, and His revealing of the Fatherhood of God; the great limitless significance is that He is the propitiation for our sins. The missionary message is not patriotic, it is irrespective of nations and of individuals, it is for the whole world. When the Holy Ghost comes in He does not consider my predilections, He brings me into union with the Lord Jesus.

A missionary is one who is wedded to the charter of his Lord and Master; he has not to proclaim his own point of view, but to proclaim the Lamb of God. It is easier to belong to a coterie which tells what Jesus Christ has done for me, easier to become a devotee to Divine healing, or to a special type of sanctification, or to the baptism of the Holy Ghost. Paul did not say "Woe is unto me, if I do not preach what Christ has done for me," but "Woe is unto me, if I preach not the gospel." This is the Gospel—"The Lamb of God, which taketh away the sin of the world!"

Oswald Chambers

"SPEAK HIS LANGUAGE, SHARE HIS SORROW"

Philippians 2:7

As we develop the characteristics of biblical leadership, we begin to identify with those to whom we minister. Missionaries soon learn this is vital for compassionate, intimate ministry. Like the Baptist missionary couple who went to Sri Lanka a few years ago, taking with them four rooms of furniture. When they set up their home in Colombo, it looked just like the one they had left in America, including a deep freezer, television, and microwave. After two years and many urgent appeals for funds from the faithful in the States, they had two or three converts. Disillusioned, they shipped themselves and their possessions home.

William Booth, founder and first general of the Salvation Army, sent a command to all of his missionaries in India: "Go to the Indian as a brother, which indeed you are, and show the love which none can doubt you feel . . . eat and drink and dress and live by his side. Speak his language, share his sorrow."

And Count Zinzendorf, the great reformer, sent missionaries around the world with the same instruction: Do not lord it over the unbelievers but simply live among them; preach not theology, but the crucified Christ.

Those are good instructions for all of us. For in a post-Christian culture, the church in America is not unlike a missionary outpost.

As Dietrich Bonhoeffer put it: "The church is herself only when she exists for humanity. . . . She must take her part in the social life of the world, not lording it over men, but helping and serving them."

If the church can only be the church when it exists for others, then the Christian can only be truly Christian when he or she is willing to be emptied out for others. There are no harder words in all of Scripture than Jesus' commandment that we love one another as He loved us—which means love that lays down its life for another.

Sometimes that is a commandment we must take literally.

Charles Colson

LET IT PASS

I Peter 2:20

Humility and patience in adversity more please me,
      my son,
    than much comfort and devotion in prosperity.
And why should a little thing spoken against thee make
      thee sad?
    had it been greater, thou shouldst not have been
      disturbed.
But now let it pass: 'tis nothing strange; it hath happed
      before;
    and if thou live longer, it will happen again.
Thou art manly enough while there is nought to oppose
      thee:
    thou canst give good counsel, and hast
      encouraged others with words:
But when suddenly the trouble cometh to thine own
    door, thou lackest to thyself both in
      courage and counsel.
Consider thy great weakness, which thou discoverest
      often in trifling concerns:
    and yet it is all for thy good, when these or such
      like things befall thee.
Put the matter as well as thou canst out of thy mind;
    and if the tribulation hath touched thee, let it
      not cast thee down nor entangle thee.
Bear it patiently, if gladly thou canst not:
    or even if thou resent this saying and feel
      indignation, yet govern thyself;
    nor suffer an unchastened word to escape thee,
      whereby the little ones may stumble.
The storm that hath arisen will quickly subside:
    and thy hidden pain will be soothed by
      returning grace.
I still Am, saith the Lord, ready to aid thee and console
      thee more than ever,
    if thou but trust me, and beseech me with all
      thy heart.
Be more tranquil in mind, and brace thyself to better
      fortitude;
    All is not lost, even though again and again thou
      feel thyself broken or well-nigh spent.

Thomas A. Kempis

"THERE GOES MY PRIDE"

I John 5:13

We come to another rung in our ladder: *Surrender to Christ*. That sounds simple—after it is done! But before, it seems vague and unreal. You are now so near that all you will have to do is to say "Yes," and the relationship is set up. Christ has already said His Yes. All His barriers are down.

A student sat on a log bridge over a mountain stream and made his life decision. As she sat there, she took twigs of wood and one by one threw them into the stream and watched them float away. She named those twigs: "There goes my pride." "There goes my fear." "And there goes my self." That self was the last thing she threw in, and the decisive thing. When she threw in that last twig, she rose radiant. I have been laughing ever since, ever since I got my self off my hands. . . .

That surrender is important, for there can be no love between persons unless there is mutual self-surrender. If either one withholds the self, then love simply will not spring up. It cannot spring up, for love by its very nature is mutual self-surrender. In inmost depths of your being whisper to Him: "You have me and all I have—forever."

You now come to the next step: *Acceptance of the self of the other person—Christ*. Your very surrender of yourself will give you an inner boldness and confidence that you, having surrendered your self, have a right to take the very Self of Christ into yourself.

Someone has said, "We don't make friends; we recognize them. You don't make Christ a Friend, a Savior; you recognize Him as such. He has always been and is your Savior and Friend; now you are recognizing Him as such. That is receptive faith.

The last step is: *A continuous, mutual adjustment of being to being, of purpose to purpose*. This is the stage of continuous growth and this will go on forever.

But one thing is settled, and settled forever: You belong to Christ, Christ belongs to you. You are forever each other's. The eternal pact has been made.

E. Stanley Jones

SINKING TO PERFECTION'S HEIGHTS

Philippians 2:6-9

This was, you see, the mistake of Satan. ". . . I will ascend into heaven, I will exalt my throne above the stars of God . . ." (Isa. 14:13). But God said, "Yet thou shalt be brought down to hell!" In contradistinction, it is spoken of Jesus: "Who, being in the form of God . . . but made himself of no reputation, and took upon him the form of a servant, and was made in the likeness of men: being found in fashion as man, he humbled himself, and became obedient unto death, even the death of the cross. Wherefore God also hath highly exalted him. . . .

High calling? Then walk humbly! Wesley called it, "sinking to perfection's heights." You have everything already given unto you in Christ. Therefore, wield the big stick? Crack the whip? Strike a pose? No! "With meekness . . . forbearing one another in love."

We need again to be reminded that meekness is not weakness. We conjure up a spineless specimen who is so timid he can't say "boo" to a goose! And we call that meekness. Not so! The Greek imagery is that of a soldier on a mighty stallion. That thoroughbred has the mien of majesty, poise, and virility. It is ready to strike the ground with its hoofs and bear its rider to victory. But it will not move until it has the master's command.

There is an interesting allusion to the training of horses in the Arabian desert. These horses were disciplined to the signal of the bugle. In the last test of the training process, the horses were allowed to grow intensely thirsty. Then they were brought within sight of water and released. They would venture toward those cooling, tantalizing streams. The horses which stopped and came back at the sound of the trainer's bugle would be used for service.

This is the meaning of the phrase, "followers of God, as dear children." It is the reflection of the image of Him of whom it is written, "He pleased not himself" (Rom. 15:3).

Roy Putnam

THE DISLOCATION OF HUMILITY

II Timothy 1:12

G. K. Chesterton once penned some wise words about what he called "the dislocation of humility"— "What we suffer from today is humility in the wrong place. Modesty has moved from the organ of ambition. Modesty has settled upon the organ of conviction; where it was never meant to be. A man was meant to be doubtful about himself, but undoubting about the truth; this has been exactly reversed. We are on the road to producing a race of men too mentally modest to believe in the multiplication table." Humble and self-forgetting we must always be, but diffident and apologetic about the gospel never.

But wherein does the preacher's authority lie? The preacher's authority is not that of the prophet. The Christian preacher cannot properly say `Thus says the Lord,' as did the prophets when introducing a direct message from God. He certainly dare not say `Verily, verily I say unto you,' as did the Son of God, speaking with the absolute authority of God, and as some dogmatic false prophets might, presuming to come in their own name. Nor should we become modern `babblers' and say `according to the best modern scholars,' quoting some human authority, valuable as apt quotations may be in the right place. Instead, our formula, if we use one at all, should be the well-known, oft-repeated and quite proper phrase of Dr. Billy Graham, `The Bible says.'

This is real authority. True, it is an indirect authority. It is not direct like that of the prophets, nor like that of the apostles, who issued commands and expected obedience (e.g., Paul in II Thess. 3), but it is still the authority of God. It is also true that the preacher who declares the Word with authority is under that Word and must submit to its authority himself. Although distinct from the congregation, he is one of them. Although he has the right to address them in direct `I—you' speech, he will often prefer to use the first person plural `we,' because he is conscious that the Word he preaches applies to himself as well.

John R. Stott

SLICK AND WEASEL-LIKE

Isaiah 6:1-5

God inflames the soul with a craving for absolute purity. But He, in His glorious otherness, empties us of ourselves in order that He may become all.

Humility does not rest, in final count, upon bafflement and discouragement and self-disgust at our shabby lives, a brow-beaten, dog-slinking attitude. It rest upon the disclosure of the consummate wonder of God, upon finding that only God counts, that all our own self-originated intentions are works of straw. And so in lowly humility we must stick close to the Root and count our own powers as nothing except as they are enslaved in His power.

But O how slick and weasel-like is self-pride! Our learnedness creeps into our sermons with a clever quotation which adds nothing to God's glory, but a bit to our own. Our cleverness in business competition earns as much self-flattery as does the possession of the money itself. Our desire to be known and approved by others, to have heads nod approvingly about us behind our backs, and flattering murmurs which we can occasionally overhear, confirm the discernment in Alfred Adler's elevation of the superiority motive. Our status as "weighty Friends" gives us secret pleasures which we scarcely own to ourselves, yet thrive upon. Yes, even pride in our own humility is one of the devil's own tricks.

Thomas Kelly

A LOWERED LEVEL OF EGOCENTRICITY

Psalm 25:9

The lowered level of egocentricity and the humbled self-awareness that accompany sound Christian teaching arise out of a realistic consciousness of one's actual ignorance, the limitations of one's knowledge, one's tendency to be deceived and one's egoistic interpretation of the facts (Clement of Rome to the Corinthians). It is to the humble that God teaches "his ways" (Ps. 25:9). "For the Lord, high as he is, cares for the lowly, and from afar he humbles the proud" (Ps. 138:6). "Do you see that man who thinks himself so wise? There is more hope for a fool than for him" (Prov. 26:12). Thus Scripture says, "God opposes the arrogant and gives grace to the humble" (James 4:6). *Thomas Oden*

The soul has a certain self-esteem, which is deeply hidden, and a secret contempt (*i.e.*, "pity"), for others not in its own experience. It is prone to be scandalized at their faults, and is *hard toward them*. It has a secret pride, so that it is troubled at faults committed openly, for it would fain be faultless.

It maintains a reserved bearing to others, and claims to itself the gifts of God, forgetting its own weakness; loses self-distrust, speaks rashly, and has a subtle desire to attract notice.

Although all these faults and many others are to be found deeply hidden, the soul is unconscious of them, and it even appears as if it had more humility than others, for at this stage it seems able to conceal its defects. If it falls into some visible fault it is beset with a swarm of self-reflections and when there comes any spiritual dryness it is dejected, discouraged and distressed, immediately believing that it has lost all, then endeavors to do all it can to regain the Presence of God.

It is so attached to its religious exercises that it prefers prayer to duty, and it is unyielding to those around. It is too ready to judge them, thinking it "waste of time" to enter into their interest and give them pleasure. (See Rom. 15:1-2.)

Jessie Penn-Lewis

LIKE A GRINDING MILL

Luke 18:13

So do not pay attention to the intellect, for it is like a grinding mill.

If the will desires to communicate to the intellect a portion of that fruitage of which it has entered upon, or if it labors to make the intellect remember, it will not succeed. For it often happens that the will is in unison with the intellect and that it rests while the intellect is in extreme disorder.

It is better that the will should leave the intellect alone than to go after it, and that it remain like a wise bee in the recollection and enjoyment of that gift. If no bee were to enter into the beehive, and each were employed in going after the other, no honey would be made. As a result, the soul will lose a great deal if it is not careful in this matter, especially if the intellect is keen. When the soul begins to reflect and to search for reasons, it will think at once that it is doing something if its speeches and search for ideas appear to be good.

The only reason for the soul's reflection that ought to be acknowledged clearly is that there is no reason whatever, other than God's own sheer goodness. Why should God enable us to be aware that we are so near to Him and give us the ability to pray to His Majesty for His mercies? In His presence we can ask for His gifts, and pray for the church and for those who have asked for our prayers.

Therefore, in such times of quietude, let the soul remain in its repose. Put aside learning. The time will come when learning will be useful for the Lord. It should be esteemed so that it is not abandoned for any treasure, but it should be used only to serve His Majesty. This alone is helpful.

Believe me, in the presence of infinite Wisdom, a little study of humility and one act of humility is worth more than all the knowledge of the world. For here there is no demand for reasoning, but simply for knowing what we are and that we are humbly in God's presence.

St. Teresa of Avila

AN ABSENCE OF MANIPULATION

Luke 9:48

When C.S. Lewis was a student at Oxford, he made a number of friends, some of whom became lifelong companions. Several in that close circle went on to become authors, like Lewis himself. Over the years, they loved to get together, to talk and to read to each other their works in progress. These sessions never failed to hone and shape their thinking. Among the group were Nevill Coghill and Owen Barfield, men who were cultivating the literary craft . . . but in no way as prolific or as profound as their friend. Lewis's reputation soon eclipsed them all. The ink flowed from his pen much more rapidly than theirs, and at increasingly shorter intervals, old Clive Staples was producing meaningful materials for the world to read. This could have driven a wedge between them, but he didn't let that happen.

The more popular scholar seemed to appreciate more than ever his long-standing friends. Not once did they sense that Lewis desired to control them. Barfield once admitted:

> I never recall a single remark, a single word or silence, a single look . . . which would go to suggest that he felt his opinion was entitled to more respect than that of old friends. I wonder how many famous men there have been of whom this could truthfully be said.

An absence of manipulation. No interest in pushing for his own way or putting down others, or in using his role or record of achievement as a subtle yet forceful lever.

Manipulation is the attempt to control, obligate, or take advantage of others by unfair or insidious means. It is practiced by insecure people who are attempting to look superior by making others squirm. Oh, it isn't usually done in a bold, up-front manner, but rather indirectly, obliquely. By little hints. Or well-timed comments. Or facial expressions.

Charles Swindoll

WEAK ENOUGH

II Corinthians 4:7-8

Mr. Taylor's humility was certainly a striking feature of his character. Some years ago dear Elder Cumming told me of a conversation he had had with Mr. Hudson Taylor. Remembering that, I wrote to Elder Cumming the other day and asked him if he could give me just a brief record of it, and he wrote me as follows: "At Dr. Somerville's funeral in Glasgow, Mr. Hudson Taylor and I were together and alone in the same carriage. After talking of dear old Dr. Somerville and of other subjects, I ventured to speak of the China Inland Mission, and to say that he must often have felt the wonderful honor that God had put upon him as the founder of the Mission, and that I doubted whether any one then living had had a greater honor. He turned to me and, with a voice trembling with suppressed feeling, said that he sometimes thought that God must have looked into the various countries and places to find someone weak enough to do such a work, so that none of the glory could go to the man himself, and then when He alighted upon him, God said, `This man is weak enough. He will do.'"

W.B. Sloan

A.B. Simpson did not employ the means men use to achieve leadership. He neither exalted himself nor would he allow others to exalt him. He did not exploit the public. The tricks of the advertiser he despised. He did not lay stress on organization; in fact, he determinedly opposed the introduction of much machinery. In his dedicatory address of the Madison Avenue Tabernacle he said: "I am afraid of human greatness; I am afraid of the triumphs of human praise; I am glad to have the work of God beginning in lowliness." But he believed that God had sent him on a definite mission and for a specific ministry and lived and loved and labored in the unconquerable courage and invincible strength of a true apostle.

A.E. Thompson

SUCH A DEAD DOG!

Matthew 15:27

The gentleman who had sent for David Brainerd were the correspondents in New York, New Jersey, and Pennsylvania, of the Honourable Society in Scotland for Promoting Christian Knowledge, and these instantly examined young Brainerd with a view to his fitness for this position. They were fully satisfied and discerned in the humble disciple the marks of a heroic witness for the Cross: one evidently called of God for the prosecution of this great work among the Indians. . . .

In his diary Brainerd wrote *"Thursday, Nov. 25, 1742.*—Spent much time in prayer and supplication; was examined by some gentlemen of my Christian experiences, and my acquaintance with divinity, and some other studies, in order to my improvement in that important affair of gospellizing the heathen, and was made sensible of my great ignorance and unfitness for public service. I had the most abasing thoughts of myself I think that ever I had; I thought myself the worst wretch that ever lived; it hurts me, and pained my very heart that anybody should shew me any respect. Alas! One thought how sadly they are deceived in me! How miserably would they be disappointed if they knew inside! Oh my heart! And in this depressed condition I was forced to go and preach to a considerable assembly, before some grave and learned ministers; but felt such a pressure from a sense of my vileness, ignorance, and unfitness to appear in public that I was almost overcome with it; my soul was grieved for the congregation, that they should sit there to hear such a *dead dog* as I preach. I thought myself infinitely indebted to the people, and longed that God would reward them with the rewards of His grace. . . . I spent much of the evening alone."

Jesse Page

TYRANNIZED BY HURRY

Proverbs 17:22

When you have admitted your hurried tendencies and worked at changing your attitudes toward yourself and the world, then you are ready to change your behavior. Here are some guidelines:

Improve your time management. Much hurry is caused by bad planning. For example, a few years ago I found I was always tense when I got to work. I had developed the habit of getting up rather late in the morning and not leaving enough time to complete my preparations for work. I would have to rush to the office in order to get there on time. Being "just in time" takes its toll in terms of stress. It never allows you to be leisurely, take a stroll in the garden, listen to the birds, or enjoy the slow lane on the freeway.

I have since changed my behavior pattern. Now I get up half an hour to forty-five minutes earlier. . . . I arrive at work calm and collected. Try rising a little earlier than you usually do, and see how much better you feel. If you need the extra sleep, add it on the front end—go to bed earlier.

Plan ahead. Don't be tyrannized by never having enough time and therefore always having to rush. Also, plan for time to be alone.

Learn to laugh! People hang onto the world as if their very life depended on it. They tend to take life too seriously, to believe they are indispensable and the world cannot function without them. They have trouble laughing at themselves.

Now, I am not advocating a denial of reality— far from it. There are certainly times when life's crises must be taken seriously, when it isn't time to laugh but to cry. But how often is life really *that* serious? So your tire is flat—laugh! So the milk has boiled over— laugh! So the dog has chewed up your favorite slippers—laugh!

Try reacting to irritations by laughing at them. The power of humor to keep adrenalin low is quite remarkable. It is very hard to live in an "emergency mode" while you are seeing the funny side of things.

Archibald D. Hart

WHERE THE PRESSURE LIES

II Corinthians 1:9

Rarely does a day pass when I don't hear the subject of stress discussed. The topic may be something like "burnout" or "chronic fatigue." But the real issue is stress, the pressures of daily life that place us in a weary and parched state of soul and mind.

J. Hudson Taylor, founder of the China Inland Mission, understood such pressures. He lived for years in a strange world with foreign customs. The cultural barriers of sharing the gospel were great. There was the great burden of administering a mission agency and the numerous personnel issues that had to be constantly addressed.

Hanging on the wall of my study is a quote from this godly man that has helped me personally deal with the stress that is generated from pastoring a large church and tending to all of the accompanying duties. It reads: "It doesn't matter, really, how great the pressure is. It only matters where the pressure lies. See that it never comes between you and the Lord—then the greater the pressure, the more it presses you to his breast."

Here is the answer to stress, regardless of its origin, nature, or intensity: Let the pressure drive you to the Source of all your strength, peace, and stability— the Person of Jesus Christ. The apostle Paul came to that wise conclusion after considering the many hardships he endured: "But this happened, that we might not rely on ourselves but on God" (2 Cor. 1:9).

Jesus wants to be our burden bearer. He invites us to come to him with all of our pressures and lay them before him. He asks us to submit to his lordship and realize that once we are yoked together with him, he will uphold us. Coming to Jesus in childlike dependence releases the pressure of our burdens. It lightens the load and enables us to go on. Instead of crumbling and fainting, we find new energy, energy that God himself gives.

Charles Stanley

GOD'S MEGAPHONE

Genesis 50:20

At Peace Ledge we were alone with our heavenly messengers and our questions. "When a man is to be hanged in a fortnight, it concentrates his mind wonderfully," Samuel Johnson said more than two centuries ago. Although I wasn't due for a hanging, I sometimes felt like it was what I deserved. And in that prevailing mood the mind was concentrated. It was time to search for more substantial truths about God and about self than we ever had before. We determined to do it.

Out of that came the Peace Ledge Principle:

Somewhere in those early days we equated the principle of being silent with listening. We wished to be listeners to the deep sources where certain kinds of heavenly truth are tapped only by those who have a heart to be attentive. Usually those are the hearts of the suffering or the hearts of broken-world people in search of a rebuilding effort.

We wanted to look at pain the way Joseph looked at it when he scanned the many years of slavery, imprisonment, and ill-treatment and said, "You meant evil against me; but God meant it for good" (Gen. 50:20, NKJV). Our questions were another version of that. How do you take an evil event and its consequences and squeeze good out of it? Can the worst that human beings do be forced to render something good?

Gordon MacDonald

No doubt Pain, as God's megaphone, is a terrible instrument; it may lead to final and unrepented rebellion. But it gives the only opportunity the bad man can have for amendment. It removes the veil; it plants the flag of truth within the fortress of the rebel soul.

C.S. Lewis

ATTENDING TO THE REASON FOR PAIN

I Corinthians 12:25-26

Physical pain is effective because it forces the body to cease other activities and attend to the reason for the pain. We can become the emotional incarnation of Christ's risen body. Just as the world will never learn the Good News apart from our efforts, the church of Christ will never experience a healing response to suffering unless we learn to focus on the body's pains and act as healing agents.

Dr. Paul Brand has developed this idea as a key part of his personal philosophy.

Individual cells had to give up their autonomy and learn to suffer with one another before effective multicelled organisms could be produced and survive. The same designer went on to create the human race with a new and higher purpose in mind. Not only would the cells within an individual cooperate with one another, but the individuals within the race would now move on to a new level of community responsibility, to a new kind of relationship with one another and with God.

As in the body, so in this new kind of relationship the key to success lies in the sensation of pain. All of us rejoice at the harmonious working of the human body. Yet we can but sorrow at the relationships between men. In human society we are suffering because we do not suffer enough.

So much of the sorrow in the world is due to the selfishness of one living organism that simply doesn't care when the next one suffers. In the body if one cell or group of cells grows and flourishes at the expense of the rest, we call it cancer and know that if it is allowed to spread the body is doomed. And yet, the only alternative to the cancer is absolute loyalty of every cell in the body, the head. God is calling us today to learn from the lower creation and move on to a higher level of evolution and to participate in this community which He is preparing for the salvation of the world.

Philip Yancey

WHEN THEY BLUNDER BADLY

I Corinthians 12:25-26

Last night I emphasized the absolute necessity of maintaining the fellowship of believers as a means of identification with Christ in His redemptive purpose. But the maintenance of that fellowship is a costly thing and a means of grace through suffering. Paul says, "That there should be no scism in the body; but that the members should have the same care one for another. And when one member suffers, all the members suffer with it." He also indicates the variety of gifts of different members of the body and suggests that those parts which are least comely should get more care from the rest. To us who are set for the building of the Church in India there is real challenge here. Some of our fellow workers blunder badly. It is far easier to separate ourselves from weakness than to identify ourselves with it—for its redemption. Do we disclaim all the mistakes of our co-workers and wash our hands of their blunders with pious gestures or do we suffer *with* them? Often we feel that we should like to start over again on virgin soil and escape the mistakes of earlier workers which we have inherited. These seem to cramp and bind us. O, to get free from it and start afresh somewhere else where we could build our own traditions. But the burden of Paul's word is that we are one—that the body both in time and in space is one. In space at the present moment we are one and must share our weaknesses, and in time we are one with those who have gone before and must share their weaknesses. An illustration on a large scale will make this clearer. Every day of missionary delay carries an awful penalty in the entrenchment of the enemy. The evangelization of the world before 600 A.D. could have been accomplished. But there was failure. That delay cost us Islam. Today hundreds of missionaries are working where it seems like butting one's head against a brick wall. Their suffering is acute. Why? They are one with the Church of earlier ages and share its weakness and failure. This is obvious on a grand scale like that. But we do not always see to it so clearly in our own station.

Eugene Erny

ONE VAST NEED

Philippians 4:19

A well-known Christian author and thinker once said, "Mankind is one vast need." What an apt description of the human lot. As long as our needs— emotional, spiritual, physical, material—are being met, we are relatively happy. But when one or more of our needs is unfilled, peace is a scarce commodity.

Learning to deal with such unmet needs while maintaining a positive faith is a critical step in experiencing the kind of contentment that Christ promises us for every circumstance. That learning process begins by realizing that Jesus understands our needs and has the power to meet them. In his humanity, Christ participated in the full scope of human existence, including needs. He was hungry. He was thirsty. He needed rest. He endured agony of soul before his death. And now, having suffered all of that, he feels for us. He hurts for us. He knows our needs.

"But if God knows my needs and can meet them, why hasn't he?" As a pastor, I have heard that question many times from singles who yearn to be married, from the unemployed who only want a decent job, from wives who long for their husbands to tenderly communicate love to them.

In a way, all of these are expressions of man's three basic needs—a sense of belonging, a sense of competence, and a sense of worth. These are the deepest emotional and spiritual needs of the soul; and when they are unmet, they create the most intense pain.

Yet, if we have a genuine need (as distinguished from an illegitimate desire) that is not met, we must look at several things. Have we been willfully disobedient to God in some area? Are we refusing to wait on God to meet our needs in his way and in his time? Are we wrongfully manipulating people or circumstance? Is our motivation misdirected? Is God trying to get our attention?

Charles Stanley

GROUND WELL DUG BY TROUBLES

John 15:1

The good effects of prayer abide in the soul for some time. Now it clearly apprehends that the fruit is not its own. The soul can then begin to share it with others without any loss to itself. It begins to show signs of its being a soul that is guarding the treasures of heaven, and it is desirous of communicating them to others. It desires to pray to God that it may not itself be the only soul that is rich in them.

The soul begins to benefit its neighbor as it were, without being aware of it or of doing anything consciously. Its neighbors understand the matter because the fragrance of the flowers has grown so strong as to make them eager to approach them. They see that this soul is full of virtue. They see the fruit and how delicious it is and they wish to help that soul to eat it.

If this ground is well dug by troubles, by persecutions, by infirmities, and by other detractions, they are few who ascend so high without it. If it be well broken up by a great detachment from all self-interest, it will drink in so much more water that it can hardly ever be parched again.

But if the ground which is mere waste and covered with thorns (as I was when I began) does not avoid sin, then it will be ungrateful soil that is unfit for so great a grace. It will dry up again. If the gardener becomes careless, and if our Lord out of His goodness will not send down rain upon it, then the garden is ruined. Thus it has been with me more than once so I am amazed at it all. If I had not found this to be so by experience, I really could not have believed it possible.

I write this for the comfort of souls which are weak as I am. May they never despair nor cease to trust in the power of God. Even if they should fall after our Lord has raised them to this high degree of prayer, they must not be discouraged unless they lose themselves utterly. Tears of repentance gain everything, and one drop of water attracts another.

St. Teresa of Avila

THE TRULY PATIENT MAN

Hebrews 12:4

The better thou disposest thyself to suffering, the more wisely thou doest, and the greater reward shalt thou receive. Thou shalt also more easily endure it, if both in mind and by habit thou are diligently prepared thereunto.

Do not say, "I cannot endure to suffer these things at the hands of such an one, nor ought I to endure things of this sort; for he hath done me great wrong, and reproacheth me with things which I never thought of; but of another I will willingly suffer, that is, if they are things which I shall see I ought to suffer."

Such a thought is foolish; it considereth not the virtue of patience, nor by whom it will be to be crowned; but rather, weigheth too exactly the persons, and the injuries offered to itself.

He is not truly patient, who is willing to suffer only so much as he thinks good, and from whom he pleases.

But the truly patient man minds not by whom he is exercised, whether by his superiors, by one of his equals, or by an inferior; whether by a good and holy man, or by one that is perverse and unworthy.

But indifferently from every creature, how much soever, or how often soever anything adverse befall him, he takes it all thankfully as from the hands of God, and esteems it great gain:

For with God it is impossible that any thing, how small soever, if only it be suffered for God's sake, should pass without its reward.

Be thou therefore prepared for the fight, if thou wilt win the victory.

Without a combat thou canst not attain unto the crown of patience.

If thou art unwilling to suffer, thou refuseth to be crowned. But if thou desire to be crowned, fight manfully, endure patiently.

Without labor there is no rest, nor without fighting can the victory be won.

Thomas A. Kempis

"WHY IS IT DOING THIS?"

Romans 8:17-18

When the world deals with us harshly, it makes us ask 'Why is it doing this?,' and we have got our answer, 'It is doing this to us because we are Christians.' And that makes us remember that because we are Christians we are receiving the same treatment as Christ received. And as verse 17 has said, 'If we suffer with him,' we shall be 'glorified together.' The world persecuted Him, and it is persecuting us. So persecution, far from getting us down, reminds us that we are aliens in the world; we are but 'strangers and pilgrims;' we do not belong to this world; 'as he was so are we in this world.' It already makes us see the real character of this world, and reminds us that we are now the 'children of God, and if children, then heirs,' with all the blessings that the word implies.

Trials and tribulations also force us to think of the glory which is awaiting us. In thought, we are back again to verse 18: 'For I reckon that the sufferings of this present time are not worthy to be compared with the glory which shall be revealed in us.' The trials drive us to think in these terms, and in terms of all that follows in Rom. 8: 19 to 32. They turn our attention to the promised glory. We know something of the following, 'We ourselves also, which have the firstfruits of the Spirit, even we ourselves groan within ourselves, waiting for the adoption, to wit, the redemption of our body. For we are saved by hope: but hope that is seen is not hope: for what a man seeth, why doth he yet hope for? But if we hope for that we see not, then do we with patience wait for it.' These trials and troubles and tribulations turn our minds to the glory that awaits us, and the moment they do so they become as nothing. So we are 'more than conquerors.'

Furthermore, the trials remind us, as we have been seeing, of our relationship to Him, that we are His people, that His mark is upon us. He has set His heart upon us, He has a purpose for us.

Martyn Lloyd-Jones

SAINTS OR CYNICS

Luke 10:41

Trouble does not automatically sanctify. Sometimes it does the opposite. Sometimes it breeds not saints but cynics. Sometimes it does not soften the spirit, but makes it hard and bitter. The fact is, trouble in itself is neutral. It needs something else—it needs the Spirit of God—to make it not neutral but positive and creative.

James S. Stewart

We have an Indian fern whose frond changes as it grows. As the forces of life play upon it and work within it, each little pinna divides and subdivides till, in the end, the frond is a fan of delicate lace, a feathery fan.

"What has been the effect upon him of all the trouble?" we asked a guest who had been telling us of her father, and of how he had suffered from injustice. "It has left him unable to think an unkind thought of anyone," she answered. The frond of that fern had been perfected.

If the wear and tear of life on a soul do not make for beauty, the process of the fern is reversed. The multitude of insignificant, trying things that are sure to come fret it into a ragged selfishness; and rough blows coarsen its texture. Or if it be otherwise fashioned it reacts to the touch like a jarred sea-anemone, gathering itself within itself. Then (unlike the anemone, which, if left in peace, opens again) the jarred soul gradually closes completely, and hardens, `till it acquires the power to jar others even as it was jarred. So there is loss. Fellow-lovers, who were meant to meet, pass each other coldly. They do not even recognize each other as members of one family. Each is frozen in his own ice. But the love of God shed abroad in our hearts (not filtered through various screens) can melt us and love us out of fretfulness, and out of hardness. It was said of one who lived this life, "Love gladdened him. Love quickened him. Love set him free." Love sets us free to love. And having been set free it is impossible to be bound any more.

Amy Carmichael

A RELIGIOUS ANIMAL

Isaiah 42:17

Two facts are philosophically and historically true: First, man is a religious animal and will worship something, as a superior being. Second, by worshipping he becomes assimilated to the moral character of the object which he worships.

Petronius' history furnishes evidence that temples were frequented, altars crowned, and prayers offered to the gods, in order that they might render nights of unnatural lust agreeable; that they might favor acts of poisoning; that they might cause robberies and other crimes to prosper. In view of the abominations prevailing at this period, the moral Seneca exclaimed— "How great now is the madness of men! They lisp the most abominable prayers; and if a man is found listening they are silent. What a man ought not to hear, they do not blush to relate to the gods." Again says he, "If any one considers what things they do, and to what things they subject themselves, instead of decency, he will find indecency; instead of the honorable, the unworthy; instead of the rational, the insane!" Such was heathenism and its influence, in the most enlightened ages, according to the testimony of the best men of those times.

In relation to modern idolatry, the world is full of living witnesses of its corrupting tendency. We will cite an illustration, a single case or two. The following is extracted from a public document laid before Parliament, by H. Oakley, Esq., a magistrate in lower Bengal. Speaking of the influence of idolatry in India, he says of the worship of Kali, one of the most popular idols, "the murderer, the robber and the prostitute, all aim to propitiate a being whose worship is obscenity, and who delights in the blood of man and beast; and, without imploring whose aid, no act of wickedness is committed. The worship of Kali must harden the hearts of her followers, and to them scenes of blood and crime must become familiar."

James B. Walker

HOW MAY WE WORSHIP

Psalm 29:2

In our meditations we have been seeing that the rediscovery of the worship of the living God will meet many of the spiritual needs of our day. Now, we ask ourselves in this meditation, how may we worship the Lord our God. Man's first duty is adoration, his second duty is awe; only his third is service. And in an age which has got its eye off deity and is over-concerned with humanity, it is good to remind ourselves that man's chief end is to glorify God and to enjoy Him forever.

We read in Romans, after the long catalog of sin and human failure, the basic reason for it was "there is no fear of God before their eyes." And consequently "the way of peace they have not known." And all moral failure is consequent upon this lack of vision, for where there is no vision the people cast off all restraint. The Church herself needs to learn how to tremble before the Lord her God; needs to remember that it is a fearful thing to fall into the hands of the living God. "There shall be stability in the times when the fear of God has been learned." This we are told in Isaiah 33:6, "and wisdom and knowledge shall be the stability of thy times . . . the fear of the Lord is his treasure."

Here we have a spiritual paradox: not slavish fear, because God "hath not given us the spirit of bondage again to fear," but the fear, the filial fear, which trembles before God. "There is no fear in love," we are told, "because perfect love casteth out fear." "Fear hath torment." And yet the Wesley who exults;

> Our God is reconciled,
> His pardoning voice I hear.
> He owns me as His child.
> I can no longer fear.
> With confidence I now draw nigh
> And `Father, Abba Father,' cry."

This Wesley, who says "I can no longer fear," is the same man who prays for a heart "which trembles at the approach of sin."

David Mckee

THE MISSING JEWEL

John 4:23-24

We are called to an everlasting preoccupation with God.

God is spirit and they that worship Him must worship Him in spirit and in truth. Only the Holy Spirit can enable a fallen man to worship God acceptably. As far as that's concerned, only the Holy Spirit can pray acceptably; only the Holy Spirit can do anything acceptably.

Man was made to worship God. God gave man a harp and said, "Here above all the creatures that I have made and created I have given you the largest harp . . . you can worship Me in a manner that no other creature can." And when he sinned man took that instrument and threw it down in the mud.

Why did Christ come? In order that He might make worshippers out of rebels. We were created to worship. Worship is the normal employment of moral beings. Worship is the missing jewel in modern evangelicalism.

I want to define worship, and here is where I want to be dogmatic. Worship means "to feel in the heart." A person that merely goes through the form and does not feel anything is not worshipping.

Worship also means to "express in some appropriate manner" what you feel. And what will be expressed? "A humbling but delightful sense of admiring awe and astonished wonder." It is delightful to worship God, but it is also a humbling thing.

A.W. Tozer

A UTILITARIAN GOD

Psalm 95:6

It is my belief that in the last three or four decades of Christian worship we have presented a utilitarian God to our people; a God who exists to save *them*, to bless *them*, to help *them*; a God very similar to the God Jacob had in mind when he said, "If the Lord be with *me*, and will keep *me* in the way that I should go, and will give *me* food to eat and raiment to put on so that I come to my father's house in peace, then the Lord will be my God and I will pay my tithes." This utilitarian God, a God who lives to be *used* by arrogant men and women who seek their own salvation and their own sanctification in Him instead of seeking Him for Himself, is a God who is too small. Men today ask, "Is God dead?" We can only give them a convincing answer when we ourselves have rediscovered the fear of God; when we have gone beyond the crudeness of our chummy, impertinent approaches to God; when we have learned to tremble afresh before God and His utter majesty, and yet have learned the sweetness of approaching into intimate fellowship with Him through the finished work of His Son on the cross; then we may be enabled to give a satisfactory answer to the people of our generation who have lost their way.

Dr. Tozer, in one of his splendid books, has written, "Secularism, materialism, and the intrusive presence of *things* have put out the light in our souls and turned us into a nation of zombies. We cover our deep ignorance with words, but we are ashamed to wonder. We are afraid to whisper, `mystery.'"

David Mckee

WORSHIP AND WAITING

Psalm 27:13-14

Waiting upon God. This is another aspect of Christian experience which has come under attack in the recent "Honest to God" debate. "There is no need for an ordained ministry," we are told. "Ministers would be much better to stop posing as experts in religion and go into some kind of humanitarian service. There is no need of worship as such, and withdrawal to wait upon a God who is separate from humanity is a betrayal of humanity and its needs. All work is worship and every smile is a prayer."

Dr. Temple's words are remarkably appropriate as an anticipation of this position. Writing in his *Reading in St. John's Gospel* he says, "Some people say they do not need religion. Do not need it for what? You do not need religion to make you as good as the world requires you to be. The help of the world itself is enough for that. You begin to feel the need of religion when you have a vision of Christ as the standard for your self and the world as it should be." And then he goes on to say, "Both for perplexity and for dulled conscience the answer is the same: sincere and spiritual worship. For worship is the submission of all our nature to God. It is the quickening of conscience by His holiness, the nourishment of the mind with His truth, the purifying of imaginations with His beauty, the opening of the heart to His love, the surrender of the will to His purpose, and all of this gathered up into adoration, the most selfless emotion of which our nature is capable and therefore the chief remedy for that self-centeredness which is our original sin.

Worship in the Spirit is the solution to perplexity and to the liberation from sin.

David Mckee

A DAY OF THANKSGIVING

Nehemiah 8:9-10

After five years of marriage, Sarah Hale was left a widow with five little children. She opened a millinery shop to support her family, and somehow she found time to write as well. . . . The success of her writing opened up the field of editing. In 1837, after successfully editing a smaller women's magazine, she was invited to edit *Godey's Lady's Book*. Under her leadership, subscriptions rose from 10,000 to nearly 150,000 in 1863.

Godey's was a secular magazine, but Hale did not hesitate to inject religious issues and to campaign for causes she deemed worthwhile. She was an Episcopalian and committed Christian, and she had become convinced that America, as a nation, must set aside at least one day of the year to offer thanks to God. Indeed, for thirty-six years it was her single-minded mission to establish Thanksgiving as a national holiday. She wrote to congressmen, governors, and presidents, and by 1859, the governors from thirty states had agreed to a common day for celebration, but still there was no national holiday.

In 1863, she wrote to President Lincoln pleading her cause. As the editor of the nation's most popular women's magazine, he could not ignore her. She had strongly appealed for a Thanksgiving holiday on the basis of Scripture, emphasizing particularly Nehemiah 8:10, and called on the President to do what would give honor to God. He complied. On October 3, 1863, Lincoln read the proclamation, the last paragraph of which explicitly stated the purpose of the holiday.

"I do, therefore, invite my fellow citizens in every part of the United States, and also those who are at sea and those who are sojourning in foreign lands, to set apart and observe the last Thursday of November next as a day of thanksgiving and praise to our beneficent Father who dwelleth in the heavens."

At last, she "could relax and turn her editorial attention to other issues that were on her heart, such as women medical missionaries and the spiritual role of women for their children and their children's children."

Ruth Tucker

SOMETHING FOR NOTHING

Psalm 118:1-4

One cannot but wonder at this constantly recurring phrase "getting something for nothing," as if it were the peculiar and perverse ambition of disturbers of society. Practically all we have is handed to us gratis. Can the most complacent reactionary flatter himself that he invented the art of writing or the printing press, or discovered his religious, economic, and moral convictions, or any of the devices which supply him with meat and raiment or any of the sources of such pleasure as he may derive from literature or the fine arts? In short, civilization is little else than getting something for nothing.

James Harvey Robinson

Be not afraid. I am your God, your Deliverer. From all evil, I will deliver you. Trust me. Fear not.

Never forget your "Thank You." Do you not see it is a lesson? You *must* say "Thank You" on the greyest days. You *must* do it. All cannot be light unless you do. There is grey-day practice. It is absolutely necessary.

My death upon the Cross was not only necessary to save a world; it was necessary, if only to train My disciples. It was all a part of their training: My entering Jerusalem in triumph; My washing the disciples' feet; My sorrow-time in Gethsemane; My being despised, judged, crucified, buried. Every step was necessary to their development—and so with you.

If a grey day is not one of thankfulness, the lesson has to be repeated until it is. Not to everyone is it so. But only to those who ask to serve Me well, and to do much for Me. A great work requires a great and careful training.

GOD CALLING

HONEY FROM EVERYTHING

II Samuel 22:31-36

One passage in your letter a little displeas'd me. The rest was nothing but kindness, which Robert's letters are ever brimful of. You say that ". . . this world to you seems drain'd of all its sweets!" At first I had hoped you only meant to intimate the high price of sugar! but I am afraid you meant more. O, Robert, I don't know what you call sweet. Honey and the honeycomb, roses and violets, are yet in the earth. The sun and moon yet reign in Heaven, and the lesser lights keep up their pretty twinklings. Meats and drinks, sweet signs and sweet smells, a country walk, spring and autumn, follies and repentance, quarrels and reconcilements, have all a sweetness by turns. Good humor and good nature, friends at home that love you, and friends abroad that miss you—you possess all these things, and more innumerable, and these are all sweet things. You may extract honey from everything.

Charles Lamb to Robert Lloyd

Izaak Walton's summary of David's life was that he was a man after God's heart because he abounded more in thanksgiving than any other person mentioned in Scripture. He was the thankful man of the Old Testament.

As an old man, he sang a song of thanksgiving and praise that affords a clue to the maturity of his walk with God. In it are these gems:

As for God, His way is perfect.
It is God who arms me with strength and makes
my way perfect.
The Word of the Lord is flawless.
You stoop down to make me great.

J. Oswald Sanders

YOU'VE GOT GOD

I Thessalonians 5:18

Say! You've struck a heap of trouble—
        Bust in business, lost your wife;
No one cares a cent about you,
        You don't care a cent for life;
Hard luck has of hope bereft you,
        Health is failing, wish you'd die—
Why, you've still the sunshine left you
        And the big, blue sky.

Sky so blue it makes you wonder
        If it's heaven shining through;
Earth so smiling 'way out yonder,
        Sun so bright it dazzles you;
Birds a-singing, flowers a-flinging
        All their fragrance on the breeze;
Dancing shadows, green, still meadows—
        Don't you mope, you've still got these.

These, and none can take them from you;
        These, and none can weigh their worth.
What! you're tired and broke and beaten?—
        Why, you're rich—you've got the earth!
Yes, if you're a tramp in tatters,
        While the blue sky bends above
You've got nearly all that matters—
        You've got God, and God is love.

Robert W. Service

Only he who gives thanks for little things receives
the big things. We prevent God from giving us the great
spiritual gifts he has in store for us because we do not give
thanks for daily gifts.

Detrich Bonhoeffer

THE FINGER OF GOD

John 17:1-5

'I have glorified My name.' Can you not say, looking back today along the road you have travelled, that God has indeed been doing this very thing in your life's history? Robert Browning once, voyaging in sight of Trafalgar and Cape Saint Vincent and Gibraltar, illustrious and historic name, found himself crying, 'Here and here did England help me: how can I help England?' And you today, recalling the course of your own voyage of life, and seeing certain decisive experiences standing out behind you like headlands in the sun, can say—'Here, and here, and here did God help me! Here was the divinity that shapes our ends. Here was the providence that plans and guides our way. Here was God glorifying His name in me!'

There were perhaps dark days which you could never have struggled through, if God had not been there at your right hand. There were joys so shining and so splendid that you knew at once they came to you straight out of heaven. To mention only one, there is the love of husband and wife. 'There is no surprise more magical,' wrote Charles Morgan the novelist, 'than the surprise of being loved. It is the finger of God on a man's shoulder.'

James S. Stewart

The message to me yesterday was most specific. I am to arise each morning at 6 A.M. and rejoice in the Lord. I am to praise Him with a grateful heart. I am to pour out my love for Him. I am to thank Him for everything that has gone wrong in my life. I am to do this indefinitely.

Resistance wells up inside me. I have trouble enough sleeping at nights without rising an hour earlier. But so be it. Len agreed to join me.

So this morning we sit on our patio watching the sunrise. First there was total darkness, then a deep rose above the blue. . . .

To put the focus on praise, I turned to Psalm 66:1-2: "Make a joyful noise unto God, all ye lands: Sing forth the honor of his name: make his praise glorious."

Catherine Marshall

RED-HANDED ANARCHY

Genesis 11:1-9

Anarchy is the result in civilization of Adam's sin. Sin is red-handed anarchy against God. Not one in a thousand understands *sin*; we understand only about sins on the physical line, which are external weaknesses. In the common-sense domain sin does not amount to much; sin belongs to the real domain. The sin the Bible refers to is a terrific and powerful thing, a deliberate and emphatic independence of God and His claim to me, *self-realization.* Anarchy is the very nature of sin as the Bible reveals it. Other religions deal with sins; the Bible alone deals with sin. The first thing Jesus Christ faced in men was this heredity of sin, and it is because we have ignored it in our presentation of the Gospel that the message of the Gospel has losts its sting, its blasting power; we have drivelled it into insurance tickets for heaven, and made it deal only with the wastrel element of mankind. The average preaching of Redemption deals mainly with the "scenic" cases. The message of Jesus Christ is different; He went straight to the disposition, and always said, "IF—you need not unless you like, but—IF any man will follow Me, let him give up his right to himself."

The Christian religion founds everything on the radical, positive nature of sin. Sin is self-realization, self-sufficiency, entire and complete mastership of myself—gain that, and you lose control of everything over which God intended you to have dominion. . . .

Christianity is based on another universe of facts than the universe we get at by our common sense; it is based on the universe of revelation facts which we only get at by faith born of the Spirit of God. The revelation which Christianity makes is that the essential nature of Deity is holiness, and the might of God is shown in that He became the weakest thing in His own creation. Jesus Christ claims that, on the basis of Redemption, He has put the whole of the human race back to where God designed it to be, and individuals begin to see this when they are awakened by their own agony.

Oswald Chambers

A NARROW WAY

I Peter 1:12-16

The moral quality that best points to God's incomparably good character, as one incomparable in power, is holiness, for holiness (*goddesh*) implies that every excellence fitting to the Supreme Being is found in God without blemish or limit. It also implies that all other divine moral excellences (goodness, justice, mercy, truth, and grace) are unified and made mutually harmonious in infinite degree in God (Isa. 6:1-10; 43:10-17; I Pet. 1:12-16; Rev. 4:8).

In saying such things we are struggling with frail human language to express an insight that emerges deeply from the interior life of Christian worship, a radical awareness of the difference that lies between God's goodness and our own. So deeply is this experienced that it seems impossible for fragmentary human languages to conceptualize anything at all about God's perfect goodness, because of the blemishes we feel in our moral awareness and earth-bound finitude. Indeed no propositions of Christian teaching are able to give adequate expression to God's holiness. Often we do best finally to stand in awe of God and silently celebrate God's holy presence. But because we must say something rather than nothing, and because this quality of God is so central to worship and so prevalent in Scripture—and regarded as so decisive in accounting for the character of God—it is necessary to make some attempt to express it with language.

Thomas Oden

Francis Asbury's *Journal* indicates his concern for personal sanctification in himself and others. On March 19, 1779, he wrote: "I fear I have been too slack in urging both myself and others to diligently seek the experience of this great and blessed gift. May the Lord help me from this time, to live free from outward and inward sin, always maintaining the spirit of the Gospel in meekness, purity, and love!"

Ruth Tucker

A DISCOVERED CERTAINTY

Matthew 7:21

Religion too can boast of its geniuses and experts, Paul, Pascal, St. John of the Cross, to mention only a few. But no matter how authoritatively these men speak, they cannot create the inner conviction which is the breath of a living faith. "Man," said Middleton Murry, "cannot accept certainties, he must discover them. An accepted certainty is not certainty, a discovered certainty is."

There is only one authentic approach to this problem, and that by way of obedience. In the Bible, faith and obedience are inseparable. Jesus did not look for cleverness in his disciples; He demanded obedience. "Not every one that saith unto me Lord, Lord, shall enter into the kingdom of heaven." "If any man will do His will, he shall know the doctrine." Jesus did not say "Blessed are those who persevere in searching." He said, "Blessed are the pure in heart; for they shall see God." In other words, moral obedience is the organ of spiritual knowledge. It is the key that opens the locked door to let the light from another world shine through.

It is true that religious knowledge cannot be isolated completely from other branches of knowledge. It has a rational content but it is unique by virtue of the fact that it is disclosed in the measure in which we are willing to be morally obedient. . . . Lord Byron wrote immortal verse while leading a riotously immoral life. But faith demands absolute obedience, a surrender of the entire personality.

Murdo Macdonald

It is a most strange experience to find that, even if most dreadful temptations torment a Christian, or surprise him and cause him to fall, he still cannot remain in sin, as long as the seed of God remains in him. He cannot commit sin, that is willingly, which Paul calls to "live therein."

C.O. Rosenius

SOME WHISPER FROM AFAR

I John 2:15

I have read that on the shores of the Adriatic sea the wives of fishermen, whose husbands have gone far out upon the deep, are in the habit of going down to the sea-shore at night and singing with their sweet voices the first verse of some beautiful hymn. After they have sung it they listen until they hear brought on the wind, across the sea, the second verse sung by their brave husbands as they are tossed by the gale—and both are happy. Perhaps, if we would listen, we too might hear on this storm-tossed world of ours, some sound, some whisper, borne from afar to tell us there is a Heaven which is our home; and when we sing our hymns upon the shores of the earth, perhaps we may hear their sweet echoes breaking in music upon the sands of time, and cheering the hearts of those who are pilgrims and strangers along the way. Yes, we need to look up—out, beyond this low earth, and to build higher in our thoughts and actions, even here!

You know, when a man is going up in a balloon, he takes in sand as ballast, and when he wants to mount a little higher, he throws out some of it, and then he will mount a little higher; he throws out a little more ballast, and he mounts still higher; and the more he throws out the higher he gets, and so the more we have to throw out of the things of this world the nearer we get to God.

D.L. Moody

When soldiers are on the battlefield they want only tents to live in. They do not care for palaces or mansions for their business is not comfort but warfare. They would not think of constructing fine dwellings— tents will do them well until that time when the war is over and they go home. They will leave the tent-life to enter their homes. Yes, our home too is not here. Let us be content with tent-life while we are pilgrims here. Someday this warfare shall be over for us too and we will enter the mansions prepared for us.

Selected

I WILL GIVE THEM UP

Titus 2:14

A plain, humble young Irishman heard about the blessing of a clean heart, and went alone and fell on his knees before the Lord, crying to Him for it. A man happened to overhear him and wrote about it, saying, I shall never forget his petition. "O God, I plead with Thee for this blessing!" Then, as if God was showing him what was in the way, he said, "My Father, I will give up every known sin, only I plead with Thee for power." And then, as if his individual sins were passing before him, he said again and again, "I will give them up; I will give them up."

Then without any emotion he rose from his knees, turned his face Heavenward, and simply said, "And now, I claim the blessing." For the first time he now became aware of my presence and, with a shining face, reached out his hand to clasp mine. You could feel the presence of the Spirit as he said, "I have received Him; I have received Him!"

And I believe he had, for in the next few months he led more than sixty men into the Kingdom of God. His whole life was transformed.

To be holy and useful is possible for each one of us, and it is far better than to be great and famous. To save a soul is better than to command an army, to win a battle, to rule an empire or to sit upon a throne.

Samuel Logan Brengle

Wesley believed not only in imputed righteousness, but also in imparted righteousness, i.e., in being both declared righteous by God and actually being made righteous by Him. The first he saw as a relative change in one's relationship with God, while the second he believed to be a real change within the nature of the individual. One had to do with one's objective relation to God, while the other had to do with the subjective transformation of the person. Because Wesley believed that a genuine change within the individual was a part of God's grace at work, he felt the concept of sanctification or perfection was an extension of that transforming power.

Allan Coppedge

A PECULIAR GOODNESS

II Corinthians 2:16

Goodness . . . is perhaps the hardest fruit of all time to define. It is so obvious. Of course a saint is good. But he is good in a peculiar way. The word `good' is used so freely and, even in its ethical employment, so widely, that it can mean anything and nearly nothing. A man is regarded as good in some circles if he keeps out of the hand of the police, and anyone who is `highly respectable' is judged to be good.

The goodness of the saint is a peculiar goodness. It flames with the numinous. It is a goodness which unconsciously proclaims itself. One feels it as an aura around possessor. It is *essential* goodness: goodness `in the inward parts;' it is white with whiteness `no fuller on earth can whiten.'

It is spiritually discerned. Yet its radiations are so powerful that it may be doubted whether anyone could be near it and quite unaware of it. . . . An evil man might be angered and made more hateful by it. . . . The saint is unconscious of it himself. Blissfully unaware of the impression he makes, he moves on his way *reminding people of Jesus Christ.*

W.E Sangster

We want not merely a high and full theology *acted out* in life, embodied nobly in daily doings, without anything of what the world calls "cant" or "simper." The higher the theology the higher and the manlier should be the life resulting from it. It should give to the Christian character and bearing a divine erectness and simplicity; true dignity of demeanor, without pride, or stiffness, or coldness; true strength of will, without obstinacy, or caprice, or waywardness. The higher the doctrine is, the more ought it to bring us into contact with the *mind* of God, which is "the truth," and the *will* of God which is "the law." He who concludes that, because he has reached the region of the "higher doctrines," he may soar above the law, or above creeds, or above churches, or above the petty details of common duty, would need to be on his guard against a blunted conscience, a self-made religion, and a wayward life.

Horatius Bonar

A LAST EXHORTATION

Psalm 24:4-6

If I were dying and had the privilege of delivering a last exhortation to all the Christians in the world, and that message had to be condensed into three words, I would say, "Wait on God."

Everywhere I go I find backsliders by the thousands, until my heart aches as I think of the great army of discouraged souls, of the way in which the Holy Spirit has been grieved, and of the way in which Jesus has been treated.

If these backsliders were asked the cause for their present condition, ten thousand different reasons would be given, but after all, there is but one, and that is this: they did not wait on God. If they had waited on him when the fierce assault was made that overthrew their faith, robbed them of their courage and bankrupted their love, they would have renewed their strength, and mounted over all obstacles as though on eagles' wings. They would have run through their enemies and not fainted.

Waiting on God means more than a prayer of thirty seconds on getting up in the morning and going to bed at night. It may mean one prayer that gets hold of God and comes away with the blessing, or it may mean a dozen prayers that knock and persist and will not be put off until God arises and makes bare his arm in behalf of the pleading soul.

There is drawing nigh unto God, a knocking at heaven's door, a pleading of the promises, a reasoning with Jesus, a forgetfulness of self, a turning from all earthly concerns, a holding on with determination to never let go, that puts all the wealth of wisdom and power and love at the disposal of a little man, so that he shouts and triumphs when all others tremble and fail, and becomes more than conqueror in the very face of death and hell.

Samuel Logan Brengle

A MULTITUDE OF SMALL THINGS

Galatians 5:7

With many of us the Christian life has not gone on to maturity. "Ye did run well, who did hinder you?" It has been a work well begun, but left unfinished; a battle boldly entered on, but only half fought out; a book with but the preface written, no more. Is not thus Christ dishonored? Is not his gospel thus misrepresented, his cross denied, his words slighted, his example set at nought? Are sunsets such as we have too often witnessed, the true endings of the bright dawns which we have welcomed? *Must* suns go down at noon? *Must* Ephesus leave her first love, Laodicea grow lukewarm, and Sardis cold? Are issues such as these inevitable and universal? Or shall we not protest against them as failures, perversions, crimes—altogether inexcusable?

Did a holy life consist of one or two noble deeds—some signal specimens of doing, or enduring, or suffering—we might account for the failure, and reckon it small dishonor to turn back in such a conflict. But a holy life is made up of a multitude of small things. It is the little things of the hour, and not the great things of the age, that fill up a life like that of Paul and John like that of Rutherford, or Brainerd, or Martyn. Little words, not eloquent speeches or sermons; little deeds, not miracles, nor battles, nor one great heroic act or mighty martyrdom, make up the true Christian life. . . . The avoidance of little evils, little sins, little inconsistencies, little weaknesses, little foibles, little indulgences of self of the flesh. . . . And then attention to the little duties of the day and hour, in the public transactions or private dealings, or family arrangements; to little words and looks, and tone; little benevolences, or forbearances, or tendernesses; little self-denials, and self-restraints, and self-forgetfulness; little plans of quiet kindness and thoughtful consideration for others; to punctuality, and method, and true aim in the ordering of each day—these are the active developments of a holy life, the rich and divine mosaics of which it is composed.

Horatius Bonar

MAKING THINGS RIGHT

Luke 19:8

In one of my pastorates there was a man who was often in the slough of despair. He could not seem to keep the glow in his experience. One Sunday night after meeting he confessed to me that the trouble was that he always promised God to make certain restitutions but in fact never did. We agreed then to set out the next morning together and not come back until he kept his promises. First, there was the street railway company to settle with for rides stolen when he was a boy. There was also a steam railway company upon the back end of whose trains he once or twice rode several hundred miles without a ticket. (It was interesting to observe the difficulty in these companies to decide just which officer was competent to handle such cases.) So far the offenses were gladly forgiven. Then we hunted for a long time throughout the city for an old Jew, a retired junk dealer. Back during the first World War my friend as one of a party of eight young men climbed the fence of the junk yard at night, stole a cartload of old iron, and the next morning wheeled it in and re-sold it to the Jew. They bought liquor with the money. Tears streamed down the old Jew's face as he heard our story. It did him so much good, he said, to see an honest man. He was a millionaire—through junk—and didn't want the money, but if the man wanted to clear his conscience he could give five dollars to the preacher who could give it to some widow for shoes for her children. It was done. Then there were doctor bills of several years' standing and other accounts long overdue and given up as bad debts by the creditors. And in the end, such peace and joy! Vital salvation must be based on *righteousness*.

Everett Cattell

WHAT IS IT WE LACK?

I John 4:4

Why is it that we, in the very kingdom of grace surrounded by angels and preceded by saints, nevertheless, can do so little, and, instead of mounting with wings like eagles, grovel in the dust, and do but sin and confess sin alternately? Is it that the *power* of God is not within us? Is it literally that we are *not able* to perform God's commandments? God forbid. We are able. We have that given us which makes us able. We do have a power within us to do what we are commanded to do. What is it we lack? The power? No; the will. What we lack is the simple, earnest, sincere inclination and aim to use what God has given us and what we have in us.

John Henry Newman

This was the one great aim and purpose for which Christ came into the world. "He died for all, that they who live should not henceforth live unto themselves." He gave Himself for us that He might redeem us from all iniquity, and make us a peculiar people, zealous of good works. He tells us that if we love Him, we will keep His commandments. A holy life is the only evidence that we have a living and not a dead faith, and an evidence that the world cannot deny, of the reality of religion. A holy life is just a ripening for heaven, for heaven is a place where nothing unholy can enter. Indeed, if it were possible for an unholy person to enter there, it would be no heaven to him. He would not be in a state to enjoy it. One reason that the true Christian longs to get to heaven is that he will be sinless there.

Robert Boyd

MORE THAN REMORSE

Acts 2:37-40

There is a difference between a man altering his life, and repenting. A man may have lived a bad life and suddenly stop being bad, not because he has repented, but because he is like an exhausted volcano; the fact that he has become good is no sign that he is a Christian. The bed-rock of Christianity is repentance. Repentance means that I estimate exactly what I am in God's sight, and I am sorry for it, and on the basis of Redemption I become the opposite. The only repentant man is the holy man. Any man who knows himself knows that he cannot be holy, therefore if ever he is holy, it will be because God has "shipped" something into him, and he begins to bring forth the fruits of repentance. The disposition of the Son of God can only enter my life by the road of repentance. Strictly speaking, repentance is a gift of God; no man can repent when he chooses. A man can be remorseful when he chooses, but remorse is something less than repentance. When God handles the wrong in a man it makes him turn to God and his life becomes a sacrament of experimental repentance. . .

The doctrine of substitution is twofold. Not only is Jesus Christ identified with my sin, but I am identified with Him so that His ruling disposition is in me, and the moral transaction on my part is agreement with God's verdict on sin in the Cross of Jesus Christ. Redemption means that God through Jesus Christ can take the most miserable wreck and turn him into a son of God. As long as a man has his morality well within his own grasp, Jesus Christ does not amount to anything to him, but when a man gets to his wits' end by agony and says involuntarily, "My God, what am I up against? There is something underneath I never knew was there," he begins to pay attention to what Jesus Christ says. A moral preparation is necessary before we can believe.

Oswald Chambers

A VERY SPECIAL NAME

I John 1:1

Because Jesus is God's revelation of Himself, He has a very special name: "The Word of Life" (I John 1:1).

This same title opens John's Gospel: "In the beginning was the Word, and the Word was with God, and the Word was God" (John 1:1).

Why does Jesus Christ have this name? Because Christ is to us what our words are to others. Our words reveal to others just what we think and how we feel. Christ reveals to us the mind and heart of God. He is the living means of communication between God and men. To know Jesus Christ is to know God!

John makes no mistake in his identification of Jesus Christ. Jesus is the Son of the Father—the Son of God (I John 1:3). John warns us several times, in his letter, not to listen to the false teachers who tell lies about Jesus Christ. "Who is a liar but he that denieth that Jesus is the Christ?" (2:22). "Every spirit that confesseth that Jesus Christ is come in the flesh is of God; and every spirit that confesseth not that Jesus Christ is come in the flesh is not of God" (4:2-3). If a man is wrong about Jesus Christ, he is wrong about God because Jesus Christ is the final and complete revelation of God to men.

Warren Wiersbe

When Jesus is present, all is good and nothing seems difficult; but when Jesus is absent, all is hard.

When Jesus speaks not inwardly to us, all other comfort is worth nothing; but if Jesus speak but one word we feel great comfort. Did not Mary rise immediately from the place where she wept, when Martha said to her: "The Master is come, and calleth for thee" (John 11:28)? Happy hour, when Jesus calls from tears to spiritual joy!

How dry and hard are you without Jesus!

Thomas A. Kempis

THE NARROWEST MAN

Matthew 7:14-15

It was not the Bible or Christian doctrine, according to E. Stanley Jones, that made Christianity unique among the world's religions, but rather it was Christ, and thus he believed that Christ alone should be exalted. On one occasion when he was complimented by a Hindu for being a "broad-minded Christian," he responded: "My brother, I am the narrowest man you have come across. I am broad on almost anything else, but on the one supreme necessity for human nature I am absolutely narrowed by the facts to one—Jesus." Jones went on to explain, "It is precisely because we believe in the absoluteness of Jesus that we can afford to take the more generous view of the non-Christian systems and situations."

Ruth Tucker

We are apt to discard the virtues of those who do not know Jesus Christ and call them pagan virtues. Paul says—If there is any virtue anywhere in the world, think about it because the natural virtues are remnants of God's handiwork and will lead to the one central Source, Jesus Christ. We have to form the habit of keeping our mental life on the line of the great and beautiful things Paul mentions. It is not a prescribed ground. It is we who make limitations and then blame God for them. Many of us behave like ostriches, we put our heads in the sand and forget altogether about the world outside—"I have had this and that experience and I am not going to think of anything else." After a while we have aches and pains in the greater part of ourselves which is outside our heads, and then we find that God sanctifies every bit of us, spirit, soul and body. God grant we may get out into the larger horizons of God's Book.

Oswald Chambers

OBJECTIVE AND MYSTICAL REALITY

Ephesians 2:22

The salvation I speak of is not merely a subjective, psychological thing—a self-realization in the order of nature. It is an objective and mystical reality— the finding of ourselves in Christ, in the Spirit, or, if you prefer, in the supernatural order. This includes and sublimates and perfects the natural self-realization which it to some extent presupposes, and usually effects, and always transcends. Therefore this discovery of ourselves is always a losing of ourselves—a death and a resurrection. "Your life is hidden with Christ in God." The discovery of ourselves in God, and of God in ourselves, by a charity that also finds all other men in God with ourselves is, therefore, not the discovery of ourselves but of Christ. First of all, it is the realization that "I live now, not I but Christ liveth in me," and secondly it is the penetration of that tremendous mystery which St. Paul sketched out boldly—and darkly—in his great Epistles: the mystery of the recapitulation, the summing up of all in Christ. It is to see the world in Christ, its beginning and its end. To see all things coming forth from God in the Logos Who becomes incarnate and descends into the lowest depths of His own creation and gathers all to Himself in order to restore it finally to the Father at the end of time. To find "ourselves" then is to find not only our poor, limited, perplexed souls, but to find the power of God that raised Christ from the dead and "built us together in Him unto a habitation of God in the Spirit" (Ephesians 2:22).

Thomas Merton

THE REAL AND ESSENTIAL WORD

John 1:14

Visions are in the inferior powers of the soul, and cannot produce true union—therefore, the soul must not dwell or rely upon them, or be retarded by them; they are but favors and gifts—'tis the Giver alone must be our object and aim.

It is of such that St. Paul speaks, when he says, that "Satan transforms himself into an angel of light," II Cor. 11:14; which is generally the case with such as are fond of visions, and lay a stress on them; because they are apt to convey a vanity to the soul, or at least hinder it from humbly attending to God only.

Ecstacies arise from a sensible relish, and may be termed a kind of spiritual sensuality, wherein the soul letting itself go too far, by reason of the sweetness it finds in them, falls imperceptibly into decay. The crafty enemy presents such sort of interior elevations and raptures, for baits to entrap the soul; to render it sensual, to fill it with vanity and self-love, to fix its esteem and attention on the gifts of God, and to hinder it from following Jesus Christ in the way of renunciation, and of death to all things.

And as to distinct interior words, they too are subject to illusion: the enemy can form and counterfeit them. Or if they come from a good angel (for God himself never speaks thus), we may mistake and misapprehend them; for they are spoken in a divine manner, but we construe them in a human and carnal manner.

But the immediate word of God has neither tone nor articulation. It is mute, silent, and unutterable; for it is Jesus Christ himself, the real and essential Word—who in the center of the soul, that is disposed for receiving him, never one moment ceases from his living, fruitful, and divine operation.

Madame Guyon

TO HAVE A STANDARD

John 15:5

The essential thing for holiness of life is to have a standard, and then to live without deviation by that standard. The Lord Jesus Christ has set the standard for us.

"I am the vine, ye are the branches; he that abideth in me, and I in him, the same bringeth forth much fruit; for without me ye can do nothing"—John 15:5.

There is a threefold thing that He shows us here; oneness in Christ, likeness to Christ, the fullness of Christ.

Ruth Paxton

The moment I consider Christ and myself as two, I am gone.

Martin Luther

May the powerful grain of faith remove the mountains of remaining unbelief, that you may see things as God sees them. . . . Then you will cry out with St. Paul, `O the depth!' . . . Then you will take Christ to be your life; you will become His members by eating His flesh and drinking His blood: you will consider His flesh as your flesh, His bone as your bone, His Spirit as your spirit, His righteousness as your righteousness, His cross as your cross, and His crown (whether of thorns or glory) as your crown; you will reckon yourselves to be dead indeed unto sin but alive unto God through this dear Redeemer. O my friends, let us believe and we shall see, taste and handle the Word of Life.

John Fletcher of Madeley

THE MEN WHO KNEW HIM BEST

Acts 4:13

It is freely allowed that no man is a hero to his valet. The world may speak of him in superlative terms, but the servant who sees him at all odd hours—at night when he is overtired; in the morning before he is properly awake; when business overpresses; when disappointment comes; when he is off-guard and under no temptation to pose—this man does not normally think of his master as a hero. He knows the other side.

It is easily possible to know too much about some people. I remember from my college days that the head gardener never came to the college chapel when a student was planned to preach. He said, half in jest and half in earnest, 'I know 'em. I'm like the man who works at a jam factory; he has no taste for jam.'

Who was it first claimed that Jesus was sinless and used of him the awesome name of God? The disciples! The men who shared every kind of experience with Him that mortals could share; who had seen Him at all hours of day and night; who had seen Him tired, hungry, disappointed, scorned, abused, and hunted to death; who had ridden with Him on a wave of popularity and hidden with Him from inquisitive miracle-mongers; who had met Him when He came down from a sleepless night of prayer on the hillside, and known Him physically overworked and emotionally over-wrought . . . these were the men—eleven of them, who, with amazing unanimity, declared Him, at the last, to be the sinless One. . . . No thinking man can doubt the quality of Christ's character . . . if he gives attentive heed to the unanimous testimony of the men who knew Him best.

W.E. Sangster

NOT A WORD AGAINST HIM

John 18:38

Once at a meeting in Hyde Park, London, an atheist lecturer ventured to attack the Founder of Christianity. He held up the central Figure of the Gospels to ridicule and what he thought was devastatingly clever caricature. But his audience, secular and unbelieving as many of them were, would not have it. Out from the crowd stepped a working man, strode up to the speaker and dared him to go on, and then turning to the crowd exclaimed—'Men, let's give three cheers for Jesus Christ!' And they gave them with a will. Crude? Yes, no doubt—yet magnificently right! For that gesture meant, you can vilify Christendom if you like, tear the Church to tatters, but—not a word against Christ! We find no fault in Him. . . .

Carlyle once walked with Emerson on a Scottish moor, and suddenly he stopped and gripped his companion's arm. 'Christ died on the tree,' he exclaimed, 'that built Dunscore kirk yonder—that brought you and me together.' Yes, and if anything is to bring men and nations together still, and storm and scatter the darkness of the world, it is that same luminous message that will do it: 'the power of God unto salvation . . . .'

It was told that when Savonarola was being marched to his death, the watching crowd saw that the martyr was repeating something over and again to himself, and those who were nearest heard what the words were. 'They may kill me if they choose—but they will never, never tear the living Christ from my heart!' This is the victory.

James S. Stewart

WE CAN MAKE SURE OF HIM

II Corinthians 1:22

When Christ has made sure of us, we can make sure of Him. A seal bears witness to a completed transaction. When the seal is placed, the business is settled. Christ is Lord! No more booming out of hollow words from the drumbeat of empty lives. Our faith is lifted out of the realm of vagueness and unreality. The seal brings a new definition to life. Fellowship with the living God is vitalized. A new intimacy with the Lord Jesus is realized. Communion with the Holy Spirit becomes exhilaratingly real! Listen to the testimony of Robert Murray McCheyne as he writes to Andrew Bonar, saying "Andrew, I seem to know Jesus Christ better than any of my earthly relatives." The Holy Spirit is not the sealer. He is the seal, taking this gospel of ours out of history, out of eternities, out of doctrine and ratifying it experientially in our souls.

Roy Putnam

I am begging you not to miss the voice of heaven, not to think the revelation any less valid or authentic, when it comes, as so often it does come, through human relationships. `You're Christ to me,' cried the dying soldier in the Crimea to Florence Nightingale as she went round the ward at night carrying her lamp, `you're Christ to me'—then he fell back and died. And Augustine had the same experience about Monica. It was said about a veteran Scots missionary returned from Livingstonia that there was something about Dr. Donald Fraser's smile which on a grey day would light up a rainswept Glasgow or Edinburgh street—and those of us who knew Donald Fraser would agree with that from the heart. In every congregation there are people who would testify that they have found in human love and sympathy and understanding the authentic touch of the divine, and the assurance that `underneath are the everlasting arms.' `I have seen thy face, as though I had seen the face of God.'

James S. Stewart

December 20

WONDERFULLY ILLUMINATING
CONTRADICTIONS

Matthew 5:3-6

I cannot see that Jesus ever advocated a reform of any kind, or supported any human cause, however enlightened. His teaching ranged between the sublimest mysticism and the bluntest realism, leaving out the middle-ground, the lush pastures and liberalism and goodwill, where editorialists and Media pundits graze, and a stifling sirocco wind of rhetoric endlessly blows. He gave us, not a plan of action, nor even a code of ethics, certainly not a programme of reforms, but those wonderfully illuminating contradictions of his—the first to be the last, the poorest the richest, the weakest the strongest, the most obscure the most celebrated. He silenced the stridency of the ego, freed the elbows and unharnessed the shoulders from their urge to push and shove, abated the will's rage and the flesh's obduracy. The meek, he told us, would inherit the earth, and he showed us how to be meek, humility being the very condition of virtue. . . .

Men say: Get rich and be happy. Riches bring everything desirable—travel, speed, the delights of love and every human bliss. How beautiful are the bodies of the rich as they run, laughing, into the sea! Or as they sit at the wheel of a fast car, or look at one another's perfection across a white table-cloth beside the blue Mediterranean, Gatsby-like in their whiteness and fragrance and freshness! Who in his senses could suppose that the opposite state—poverty—is to be preferred? Poverty, as Bernard Shaw vehemently insisted, is dirty, squalid, unmanicured and ungroomed; not just unblessed, but a fall from grace, a sinful condition imposed by a cruel and unjust social system. Yet Jesus dared to say that the poor were blessed, and what is more, through the centuries the choicest spirits have not just agreed with him, but often, in order to participate in this blessedness, embraced poverty themselves in its extremist form. As blissful at being naked on the naked earth as others are at being tucked up in newly laundered linen sheets; as joyous in their lack of possessions as others are in their yachts, their convertibles, their swimming-pools.

Malcolm Muggeridge

JOY TO THE MALL

Luke 2:1-2

And it came to pass in those days, that there went out a decree from the U.S. Treasury, that all of America should go shopping. (And this decree was first made when leading economic indicators dipped to their lowest point.) And all went out to shop, each to his own mall.

And a Christian also went up from his suburban home to the city with its many malls because he wanted to prove he was from the household of prosperity. And with him was his wife, who was great with economic worry. And so it was, that while they were there, they found many expensive presents, pudgy-faced dolls, trucks that turn into robots, and a various assortment of video games.

And there were in the same county children keeping watch over their stockings by night. And, lo, Santa Claus came upon them; and they were sore afraid (expecting to see the special effects they had seen in the movies), and Santa said to them, "Fear not . . . for unto you will be given this day, in your suburban home, great feasts of turkey, dressing, and cake—and many presents, wrapped in bright paper, lying beneath an artificial tree adorned with tinsel, colored balls, and lights."

And suddenly there was with Santa Claus a multitude of relatives and friends, praising one another and saying, "Glory to you for getting me this gift; it's just what I wanted."

And it came to pass, as the friends and relatives were gone away into their own home, the parents said to one another, "I sure am glad that's over. What a mess! I'm too tired to clean it up now. Let's go to bed and pick it up tomorrow." And when they had said this, they remembered the statement that had been told to them by the storekeepers: "Christmas comes only once a year." And they that heard it wondered at those things that were sold to them by the storekeepers, but the children treasured all their things in their hearts, hoarding their toys from each other.

Chris Dolson

THEY RECEIVED HIM NOT

John 1:11-13

Some in our day seem satisfied to sit back and belabor the Jews for not receiving Jesus. But Jesus taught very plainly that we should take the plank from our own eyes in order to see clearly to remove the speck from our brother's eye (Matthew 7:5).

We have 2,000 years of Christian teaching and preaching that the Jews did not have. We have both an Old and a New Testament. We have the indwelling presence of the Holy Spirit.

In short, not for one minute ought we to assail the Jews who rejected Jesus and thereby comfort our own carnal hearts. The same situation is all around us today. Millions of men and women with an understanding of the revelation of God in Jesus Christ are not willing to commit themselves to Him whom the very angels and stars and rivers—His creation— received.

People hesitate and delay because they know God is asking the abdication of their own selfish little kingdom and interest. They will not consent to the thorough inward housecleaning that is involved in full commitment to Christ.

Our Lord will not inhabit any place that is not clean. Some would rather have the dirt than to have the presence of the Son of God. They prefer to stay in the darkness than to come to the Light of the World.

They have every kind of spiritual opportunity, but they will not receive Jesus. They do not want their spiritual houses to be clean. This is the great tragedy of mankind. They have rejected Jesus from their hearts because they must have their own way.

The true meaning of Christianity is a mystery until we have been converted and brought in by the miracle-working, transforming power of the new birth. Until Jesus Christ is sincerely received, there can be no knowledge of salvation, no understanding of the things of God.

"He came . . . and his own received him not." That is the great tragedy of mankind!

Alliance Witness

THE MOST STUPENDOUS EVENT

Luke 2:8-10

An idea becomes close to you only when you are aware of it in your soul, when in reading about it, it seems to you that it has already occurred to you, that you know it and are simply recalling it. That's how it was when I read the Gospels. In the Gospels I discovered a new world: I had not supposed that there was such a depth of thought in them. Yet it all seemed so familiar; it seemed that I had known it all long ago, that I had only forgotten it.

Tolstoy

The coming of Jesus into the world is the most stupendous event in human history.

As it is, belonging to a civilization which began with the birth of Jesus some two thousand years ago, and reaching the conclusion—to me inescapable—that whatever is truly admirable in the achievements of the succeeding centuries, in art and literature, in music and architecture, in the quest for knowledge and in the pursuit of justice and brotherliness in human relations, derives from that same event, I cannot but see it as towering sublimely above all others. I have to add, too, that over and above this, the revelation Jesus provided, in his teaching, and in the drama of his life, death and Resurrection, of the true purpose and destination of our earthly existence, seems to me, even by comparison with other such revelations, to be of unique value and everlasting validity. The fact that I happen to have come into the world myself at a time when the revelation's impetus in history gives every sign of being almost spent, and when Western Man is increasingly inclined to reject and despise the inheritance it has brought him, only serves to make me the more appreciative of it.

The laughter of the saints has drowned the trumpets of the great; the nakedness of the saints mocked the splendor of captains and kings; the foolishness of the saints confuted the wit and wisdom of the learned.

Malcolm Muggeridge

CROWDED OUT

Luke 2:7

"No room!" The Lord was crowded out! And I suggest that this incident at the birth of our Savior is symbolic of the tragedy of our relationship to Him today. He has been excluded from the central place. He has been hustled into the outer courts. No room has been offered Him in the inn. He has been crowded out!

And I further suggest that the only place in which He can make His home today is the inn of the soul, the secret rooms of the personal life. We sometimes sing, in one of the most tender and gracious of our hymns, "O make our hearts Thy dwelling place," and that is just what the Lord is willing and waiting to do. "O make our hearts Thine inn!" But when He moves toward us, He finds the inn already thronged. There is no room for Him, and He is relegated to the cold and grudging shelter on the outside of our lives. He is crowded out!

Now what do we offer the Lord in the place of a room in the inn? We build Him stately *material temples.* We expend boundless treasure in their erection. Art joins hands with architecture, and the structure becomes a poem. Lilywork crowns the majestic pillar. Subdued light, and exquisite line, and tender color add their riches to the finished pile. And the soul cries out: "Here is a house for Thee, O Man of Nazareth, Lord of Glory! Here is the home I have built for Thee." And if the soul would only listen, there comes back the pained response, "Where is the place of My rest?" saith the Lord. "The most High dwelleth not in temples made with hands;" "I dwell in the high and holy place, with him that is of a contrite and humble spirit." The Lord of glory seeks the warm inn of the soul, and we offer Him a manger of stone.

J.H. Jowett

THE FIRST CHRISTMAS WREATH

Isaiah 53:3-4

A sure sign of approaching Christmas season is the appearance of festive wreaths that trim countless doors. These gaily decorated reminders prepare us once more to commemorate the wondrous birth of Christ our Savior.

Christmas, after all, should be a time of warmth and celebration. A blazing fireplace, the smell of pine, a brightly lighted tree with gifts spilling out in every direction, the sense of families drawing closer, the shining smiles of eager youngsters—these and a myriad of other personal touches and traditions make this a most special time of the year.

But ironically, this joyous season becomes a time of stress and dread for many. Endless traffic and irritating crowds. Financial tensions. Anxiety in the choice and cost of gifts for others. Fractured families who shuttle children back and forth and spend more time awkwardly carving up a schedule than they do the turkey. Rolaids and ruined toys. Traffic deaths and body counts. Loneliness, alienation, depression, fatigue.

Such is the bittersweet nature of Christmas. And yet these very feelings of lostness and despair are what Christmas is really all about. Because Jesus Christ has come to identify with fallen humanity, the celebration of Christmas flows out of divine consolation. He shared our pain . . . He gives us hope.

Christ was "a man of sorrows, and familiar with suffering" (Isaiah 53:3). As a young man He experienced the death of Joseph, His human stepfather. As the eldest son He knew backbreaking labor and the weight of responsibility to provide for His household. His ministry and mission were misunderstood by His loved ones. He faced the humiliating accusation of illegitimacy all His life. And He accepted His betrayal by a friend. He patiently bore the hostility and taunts of His enemies and the injustice of being wrongly accused. He humbly submitted to arrest, torture, and the cruelest of deaths.

Christmas—A Celebration of Life.

"Surely He took up our infirmities and carried our sorrows" (Isaiah 53:4). "We do not have a high priest who is unable to sympathize with our weaknesses, but we have one who has been tempted in every way, just as we are—yet was without sin" (Hebrews 4:15). He understands. He lived as we live. He died and rose again that we might really live. "I tell you the truth, whoever hears My word and believes Him who sent Me has eternal life and will not be condemned; he has crossed over from death to life" (John 5:24).

Christmas, then, is a celebration of life for God's people, a time of triumphant rejoicing and praise. We can wholeheartedly do so because our Savior has come. His suffering has brought freedom and hope to us all. "Christ died for sins once and for all, the righteous for the unrighteous, to bring you to God" (I Peter 3:18). Have you embraced the hope that Christ offers?

Why can we celebrate each year with the Christmas wreath? Because Christ wore the first one— a crown of thorns.

Jimmy Williams

A SKELETON FROM THE PAST

Hebrews 11:31

It is quite probable that someone reading my words this moment is fighting an inner battle with a ghost from the past. The skeleton in one of yesterday's closets is beginning to rattle louder and louder. Putting adhesive tape around the closet and moving the bureau in front of the door does little to muffle the clattering bones. You wonder, possibly, "Who knows?" You think, probably, "I've had it . . . can't win . . . party's over."

The anchor that tumbled off your boat is dragging and snagging on the bottom. Guilt and anxiety have come aboard, pointing out the great dark hulks of shipwrecks below. They busy themselves drilling worry-holes in your hull and you are beginning to sink. Down in the hold, you can hear them chant an old lie as they work: "The bird with the broken pinion never soared as high again. . . ."

Allow me to present a case in opposition to these destructive and inaccurate accusers. It may be true that you've done or experienced things which would embarrass you if they became public knowledge. You may have committed a terrible and tragic sin that was never traced back to you. You may have a criminal record or a moral charge or a domestic conflict that, to this moment, is private information. You may wrestle with a past that has been fractured and wounded by a mental or emotional breakdown. . . .

But wait a minute. Before you surrender your case as hopeless, consider the liberating evidence offered in the Bible. Take an honest look at men and women whom God used *in spite* of their past! *Abraham*, founder of Israel and tagged "the friend of God," was once a worshipper of idols. *Joseph* had a prison record but later became prime minister of Egypt. *Moses* was a murderer, but later became the one who delivered his nation from the slavery of Pharaoh. *Jephthah* was an illegitimate child who ran around with a tough bunch of hoods before he was chosen by God to become His personal representative. *Rahab* was a harlot in the streets of Jericho but is numbered among the saints in the Hebrews 11 Hall of Faith.

Charles Swindoll

THIS — SIDEDNESS

II Corinthians 4:18

Men nowadays take time far more seriously than eternity.

German theology of a century ago emphasized a useful distinction between This-sidedness and Other-sidedness, or Here and Yonder. The church used to be chiefly concerned with Yonder; it was oriented toward the world beyond, and was little concerned with this world and its sorrows and hungers. Because the sincere workingman, who suffered under economic privations, called out for bread, for whole-wheat-flour bread, the church of that day replied, "You're worldly-minded, you're crass, you're materialistic, you're oriented toward the Here. You ought to seek the heavenly, the eternal, the Yonder." But the workingman wasn't materialistic, he was hungry; and Marxian socialism promised him just the temporal bread he needed, whereas the church has rebuked him for not hungering for the eternal Bread.

All this is now changed. We are in an era of This-sidedness, with a passionate anxiety about economics and political organization. And the church itself has largely gone "this-sided," and large areas of the Society of Friends seem to be predominantly concerned with this world, with time, and with the temporal order. And the test of the worthwhileness of any experience of Eternity has become: "Does it change things in time? If so, let us keep it, if not, let us discard it."

I submit that this is a lamentable reversal of the true order of dependence. Time is no judge of Eternity. It is the Eternal who is the judge and tester of time.

The possibility of the experience of Divine Presence, as a repeatedly realized and present fact, and its transforming and transfiguring effect upon all life— this is the central message of Friends. Once discover this glorious secret, this new dimension of life, and we no longer live merely in time but we live also in the Eternal.

Thomas Kelly

"I HAVE NOT GOT THE TIME"

II Corinthians 6:2

Think of the privilege, my friends, of saving a soul. If we are going to work for good, we must be up and about it. Men say, "I have not the time." Take it. Ten minutes every day for Christ will give you good wages. There is many a man who is working for you. Take them by the hand. Some of you with silver locks, I think I hear you saying, "I wish I was young, how I would rush into the battle." Well, if you cannot be a fighter, you can pray and lead on the others. There are two kinds of old people in the world. One grows chilled and sour, and there are others who light up every meeting with their genial presence and cheer on the workers. Draw near, old age, and cheer on the others, and take them by the hand and encourage them. There was a building on fire. The flames leaped around the staircase, and from a three-story window a little child was seen who cried for help. The only way to reach it was by a ladder. One was obtained and a fireman ascended, but when he had almost reached the child, the flames broke from the window and leaped around him. He faltered and seemed afraid to go further. Suddenly some one in the crowd shouted, "Give him a cheer," and cheer after cheer went up. The fireman was nerved with new energy, and rescued the child. Just so with our young men. Whenever you see them wavering, cheer them on. If you cannot work yourself, give them cheers to nerve them on in their glorious work. May the blessing of God fall upon this afternoon, and let every man and woman be up and doing.

D.L. Moody

We must act like men who have the enemy at their gates, and at the same time like men who are working for Eternity.

Mazzini

Every minute was an opportunity.

John Macpherson

IT TAKES TIME

Philippians 3:10

It takes time to get to know ourselves; it takes time and eternity to get to know our Infinite Lord Jesus Christ. Today is the day to put our hand to the plow, and irrevocably set our heart on His goal for us—that we "may know him, and the power of his resurrection, and the fellowship of his sufferings, being made conformable unto his death" (Phil. 3:10).

"So often in the battle," says Austin-Sparks, "we go to the Lord, and pray, and plead, and appeal for victory, for ascendancy, for mastery over the forces of evil and death, and our thought is that in some way the Lord is going to come in with a mighty exercise of power and put us into a place of victory and spiritual ascendancy as in an act. We must have this mentality corrected. What the Lord does is to enlarge us to possess. He puts us through some exercise, through some experience, takes us by some way which means our spiritual expansion, and exercise of spirituality so we occupy the larger place spontaneously. `I will not drive them out from before thee in one year; lest the land become desolate, and the beast of the field multiply against thee. By little and little I will drive them out before thee, unto thou be increased' (Ex. 23:29-30)."

One day in the House of Commons, British Prime Minister Disraeli made a brilliant speech on the spur of the moment. That night a friend said to him, `I must tell you how much I enjoyed your extemporaneous talk. It's been on my mind all day.' `Madam,' confessed Disraeli, `that extemporaneous talk has been on my mind for twenty years!'

Miles J. Stanford

JUMBLED PRIORITIES

John 11: 9

When we stop to evaluate, we realize that our time dilemma goes deeper than shortage of time; it is basically the problem of priorities. Hard work does not hurt us. We all know what it is to go full speed for long hours, totally involved in an important task. The resulting weariness is matched by a sense of achievement and joy. Not hard work, but doubt and misgiving produce anxiety as we review a month or year and become oppressed by the pile of unfinished tasks. We sense uneasily that we may have failed to do the important. The winds of other people's demands have driven us onto a reef of frustration. We confess, quite apart from our sins, "We have left undone those things which we ought to have done; and we have done those things which we ought not to have done."

Several years ago an experienced cotton-mill manager said to me, "Your greatest danger is letting the urgent things crowd out the important." He didn't realize how hard his maxim hit. It often returns to haunt and rebuke me by raising the critical problem of priorities.

We live in constant tension between the urgent and the important. The problem is that the important task rarely must be done today, or even this week. Extra hours of prayer and Bible study, a visit with that non-Christian friend, careful study of an important book: these projects can wait. But the urgent tasks call for instant action—endless demands pressure every hour and day.

Charles E. Hummel

A TYRANT AND A FRIEND

Revelation 1:8

"Father Time" is looked on as both a tyrant and a friend. Time will write wrinkles in our faces, scribble crow's feet about our eyes, turn our hair white (if it doesn't take it away altogether), rob us of our vision and vigor. But time can also be a corrector of errors, a confirmer of truth, a healer of sorrows, our best tutor. Andrew Marvell describes the remorseless rush of time in unforgettable lines:

> But at my back I always hear
> Time's winged chariot hurrying near.

But Jesus has no beginning nor ending. He is eternal. Even our calendars pay homage to His superiority over time.

There is another intriguing and inspiring dimension to this title. The alphabet represents absolute wholeness, completeness. It is an inexhaustible resource for all to tap. The same 26 letters used by Shakespeare to write immortal lines have been used by lovers to express their feelings, by judges to pass sentences, by Presidents to issue proclamations, by a parent to guide a child. Jesus Christ as our Alpha and Omega is our resource and inspiration for the whole realm of life and communication.

As our Alpha and Omega, He is also the Lord of our beginnings and endings. He is there at the thresholds of our lives—birth, growing up, when the young person goes off to college, at the marriage altar, at the start of a career, when the first child comes, new undertakings, and all our important beginnings.

He is there in our endings—when we leave home, at the completion of a task, the end of a stay, leaving a place and friends behind, loss of a loved one, retirement, death.

We take comfort and courage from this title with its assurance that our times are in the hands of the eternal, our life becomes complete in Him and He is the Lord of our beginnings and endings.

Henry Gariepy

ACKNOWLEDGMENTS

We gratefully acknowledge permission granted by the following publishers to use excerpts from their copyrighted books.

Abingdon Press
> *Salute Thy Soul*, Clarence Macartney
> *Science, Technology and the Christian*, C.A. Coulson
> *The River of Life*, James S. Stewart
> *The Way*, E. Stanley Jones

Baker Book House
> *Each New Day*, Corrie Ten Boom
> *Listening to the Giants*, Warren Wiersbe
> *Wayward Genius*, Bentley Taylor

Back to the Bible
> *Go Ye Means You*, Norman Lewis

Ballantine Books
> *The March of Folly*, Barbara Tuchman

Banner of Truth
> *Romans*, Martyn Lloyd Jones
> *The Sermon on the Mount*, Martyn Lloyd Jones
> *Spiritual Depression*, Martyn Lloyd Jones

Beacon Hill Press
> *The Spirit of Holiness*, Everett Cattell

Bethany House Publishers
> *The Bible and I*, E.M. Blaiklock

Bristol Books
> *The Love Exchange*, Margaret Therkelsen

Christian Alliance Publishing House
> *The Life of A.B. Simpson*, A.E. Thompson

Christian Literature Crusade
> *Abide In Christ*, Andrew Murray
> *Calvary Road*, Roy Hession

Humility, Andrew Murray
Made In Pans, Amy Carmichael
Marching Orders for the End Battle, Corrie Ten Boom
The Key to Missionary Service, Andrew Murray

Christian Publications
The Incredible Christian, A.W. Tozer
The Tozer Pulpit, A.W. Tozer

Cokesbury Press
The Missionary Imperative, Elmer T. Clark

Collins Fontana Press
Jesus Rediscovered, Malcolm Muggeridge

Coppedge, Allan
John Wesley in Theological Debate

Creation House
The Coming Revolution in World Missions, K.P. Yohannan

Crossway Books
How Should We Then Live? Francis Scheaffer
Open Windows, Philip Yancey
Who Speaks for God?, Charles Colson

Daybreak Books
Sacred Stories, Ruth Tucker

Dell Books
No Man is an Island, Thomas Merton

Discovery House Publishers
Run Today's Race, Oswald Chambers

Doubleday (Image Books)
Orthodoxy, G.K. Chesterton

Edward England Books
He is Able, W.E. Sangster

Evangelical Missions Quarterly
> *Requirements for Making a Really Great Missionary,*
> Janice Dixon

Fleming H. Revell Co.
> *Daily Readings from W.E. Sangster,*
> *Letters by Modern Mystic,* Frank Laubach
> *Seven Reasons Why a Scientist Believes in God,*
> A. Cressy Morrison

Fontana, Collins Publishers
> *Fernseed and Elephants,* C.S. Lewis

Gospel Light Publications
> *Who Says?* Fritz Ridenour

Grosset and Dunlap
> *Abide in Christ,* Andrew Murray

Harcourt Brace Company
> *Letters of C.S. Lewis,* W.H. Lewis

Harold Shaw Publishers
> *Finding Your Place after Divorce,* Carole Streeter
> *Five Evangelical Leaders,* Christopher Catherwood

Harper Collins Publishers
> *A Testament of Devotion,* Thomas Kelly
> *Celebration of Discipline,* Richard Foster
> *Christ and the Meaning of Life,* Helmut Thielicke
> *The Incendiary Fellowship,* D. Elton Trueblood
> *The Validity of Christian Mission,* D. Elton Trueblood
> *Where is God When it Hurts?* Philip Yancey

Harper and Row
> *A Severe Mercy,* Sheldon Vanauken
> *Discovering An Evangelical Heritage,* Donald W. Dayton
> *The Man Who Lives,* Malcolm Muggeridge

Higley Press
> *God's Wisdom in the Plan of Salvation,* James B. Walker

Hodder and Stoughton
> *Smoke on the Mountain,* Joy Davidman

Inter Varsity Press
> *Death in the City,* Francis Scheaffer
> *Genesis in Time and Space,* Francis Scheaffer
> *Henry Martyn,* Constance Padwick
> *Jesus Christ, Lord of the Universe, Hope of the World,*
> David Howard-editor

Kennedy, James
> *The Vital Importance of the Bible*

Kinnear, Angus
> *The Normal Christian Life,* Watchman Nee
> *Sit, Walk, Stand,* Watchman Nee

Little Brown Co.
> *The Last Lion,* William Manchester

The Macmillan Company
> *The Abolition of Man,* C.S. Lewis

Marshall, Morgan and Scott
> *Oswald Chambers, His Life and Work,* Dinsdale T. Young

Moody Press
> *Daily With the King,* W. Glyn Evans
> *Enjoying Intimacy with God,* J. Oswald Sanders
> *Heaven and How to Get There,* D.L. Moody
> *Reason for Our Hope,* Vernon Grounds
> *Science Speaks,* Peter W. Stoner
> *Spiritual Maturity,* J. Oswald Sanders
> *The Story of Sadhu Sundar Singh,* Cyril J. Davey

Multnomah Press
> *Seasons of Life,* Charles Swindoll

Penguin Books
> *The Silver Chair,* C.S. Lewis

Overseas Missionary Fellowship
> *Mountain Rain,* Eileen Crossman
> *The Life of J. Hudson Taylor,* Mrs. Howard Taylor
> *Hudson TaylorCThe Open Century,* A. Broomhall

Random House
> *The March of Folly*, Barbara Tuchman

Readers Digest Association
> *The Family Treasury of Great Biographies*

Regal Books
> *C.S. Lewis, Mere Christian*, Kathryn Ann Lindskoog
> *Spreading the Fire*, C. Peter Wagner

The Salvation Army
> *Portrait of a Prophet*, Clarence Hall

Servant Publications
> *Against the Night*, Charles Colson
> *Total Surrender*, Mother Theresa

Simon and Schuster Inc.
> *The Closing of the American Mind*, Allan Bloom
> *Man's Search for Meaning*, Victor Frankl
> *The Story of Philosophy*, Will Durant

Skogland, Elizabeth
> *More Than Coping*

The Society for Promoting Christian Knowledge
> *Toward Jerusalem*, Amy Carmichael

John R. Stott
> *Christ the Controversalist*

Thomas Nelson
> *D. James Kennedy, The Man and His Work*,
> Herbert Lee Williams
> *Rebuilding Your Broken World*, Gordon MacDonald

Tyndale House Publishers
> *The Kingdom of Love*, Hannah Hurnard

Victor Books
> *Be Real*, Warren Wiersbe
> *Be Mature*, Warren Wiersbe
> *Harvest of Humanity*, John T. Seamands
> *One Hundred Portraits of Christ*, Henry Gariepy

Viking Press
> *Memoirs of a Modernist's Daughter*, Eleanor Munro

Warner Press
> *David's Song*, Maurice Berquist

Weybright and Talley Publishers
> *Shaw, An Autobiography*, Stanley Weintraub

William E. Eerdmans Publishers
> *The Preacher's Portrait*, John R. Stott
> *The Quest for Serenity*, G.H. Morling

Word Books
> *A Reasonable Faith*, Anthony Campolo
> *Say Yes to Your Potential*, Skip Ross, Carole Carlson
> *The Body*, Charles Colson
> *The Challenge*, Billy Graham
> *The Hidden Link Between Adrenalin and Stress*,
> Archibald Hart
> *The Splendor of Easter*, Floyd Thatcher

World Wide Publications
> *A Shepherd Looks at the Twenty-Third Psalm*,
> Philip Keller

Zondervan Publishers
> *A Touch of His Peace*, Charles Stanley
> *Daws*, Betty Skinner
> *God's Best Secrets*, Andrew Murray
> *Kingdoms in Conflict*, Charles Colson
> *Knowing the Face of God*, Tim Stafford
> *Purple Violet Squish*, David Wilkerson
> *Touch the World Through Prayer*, Wesley Duewel

OTHER BOOKS BY ED ERNY

This One Thing, the biography of missionary leader and statesman, Eugene Erny. A member of the famed Asbury College Missionary team, he held evangelistic meetings throughout Asia in 1929-30. In China he met, courted, and won the hand of a young missionary, Esther Helsby. Together they served in China and India and as OMS mission president for nearly 20 years. $7.00

Under Sentence of Death, the epic story of a young pastor, Henry Steel, who upon learning that he is dying of Hodgkin's Disease, determines to give himself unreservedly to reaching the nations for Jesus Christ. $3.95

The Quest, a small booklet, explaining in simple language what one needs to do to be a Christian. More than 100,000 copies in print, *The Quest* has been translated into a number of foreign languages. $.50

The Key Goose, and other lessons God taught me, with Mildred Rice. Rich spiritual lessons seasoned with humor, gleaned from a lifetime of missionary service in China, Japan and Taiwan. $4.50

Princess in the Kingdom with Evelyn Lallemand Bellande. Born into a wealthy, aristocratic Haitian family, a young lady finds her dreams broken by a failed marriage and the dark diagnosis of cancer. In her despair she discovers life and a mission to her own people. $4.00

Thrice Through the Valley with Valetta Steel, widow of Henry Steel *(Under Sentence of Death).* She tells of the series of tragedies that bereft her of her entire family, testing her faith to the limits of human endurance but also leading to unprecedented joy and fruitfulness. $3.95

Another Valley, Another Victory, Another Love (which contains the original book, *Thrice Through the Valley*), with Valetta Steel Crumley, describes her courageous journey facing three tragedies. From her tears, new dreams grew. In spite of a criminal attack and rape while in overseas ministry, she believes the LOVE of Jesus overcomes the darkness. Recently married to Al Crumley, M.D., they continue their lives of ministry. $5.99 (40% discount for ten or more copies for churches and Christian workers. Copies are also available in Chinese, Russian, and Japanese.)

Nobie, with Nobie Pope Sivley, describes a life begun in shame and remorse. Nobie finds beautiful fulfillment at mid-life and travels from West Texas to the remote waterways of Colombia, South America, to offer relief from pain and the message of Salvation during violent times. $5.00

He Goes Before Them by Meredith and Christine Helsby, missionaries, who find themselves as Japanese prisoners of war in China during World War II. A moving story of God's miracle provision and quiet courage in the darkest days of this century. $5.00

Lord, This is Not What I Had in Mind, a series of humorous and embarrassing episodes in the life of a missionary family. $3.00

My Grave Was No. 12, short stories of outstanding nationals on OMS fields in Asia, South America, and the Caribbean. $4.00

Legacies of Faith, Volume I, daily devotional readings drawn from great Christian writers through the centuries from St. Augustine to C. S. Lewis. $8.00

The Story Behind Streams in the Desert with Lettie Cowman from her 1924 diary, the final year of the life of her husband, Charles. A window into the crucible of physical pain and emotional and spiritual turmoil from which emerged the classic devotional, *Streams in the Desert*, destined to bless millions of sufferers. $7.00

Yippie in My Soul, with Margaret Bonnette. An adventuresome young woman, determined to live life to the hilt, Margaret was once engaged to three men at the same time! Later, with her beloved husband's death sentence, she finds her dreams shattered and her life empty. Her search for God eventuates in a life-changing encounter and a date with destiny as God's healer in the remote mountains of Haiti. $5.00

What Now Lord? with Margaret Brabon. The story of Harold and Margaret Brabon who helped pioneer the work of The Oriental Missionary Society in Colombia, South America, during the dangerous years of "La Violencia." This is a true romance in which a beautiful, idealistic college coed engaged to a ministerial student improbably falls in love with a brilliant young chemist working for Henry Ford. $6.00

OMS BOOK ROOM

Order from OMS Bookroom, Box A, Greenwood, IN 46142.
For single books, include $1.50 postage. USA prices listed.

Phone: 317-0881-6751, or e-mail
Pwinfrey@omsinternational.org

OMS INTERNATIONAL

OMS International, (formerly the Oriental Missionary Society), was founded in 1901 by two Chicago telegraphers, Charles E. Cowman and E. A. Kilbourne. Its ministry includes 1) aggressive evangelism 2) establishing fully indigenous churches 3) training national believers for leadership, and 4) joining them in partnership to reach the world.

OMS now ministers in 18 nations: Japan, Korea, Taiwan, Hong Kong, Philippines, Indonesia, India, Spain, Colombia, Ecuador, Brazil, Haiti, Hungary, Russia, Mexico, the Republic of Ireland, Mozambique, and East Asia. Today, over 450 missionaries work in partnership with over 6,900 national co-workers. A total of 4,116 organized churches tallies membership exceeding one million. In 1998 over 63,000 decisions were made to follow Christ.

The mission operates 26 seminaries training institutions with over 5,000 students preparing for ministry. Secondary, primary, and vocational schools are conducted, along with camps and cottage-industry training.

Through door-to-door visitation, 218 evangelism teams, including 614 team members, plant new churches.

As a member of CoMission II, OMS also currently sponsors missionaries in the former Soviet Union, Mozambique, Hungary and East Asia.

Radio station 4VEH and Good Shepherd Radio target audiences in Haiti and Ecuador, respectively. Christian broadcasts are also effective in Colombia, Japan, and Korea. Medical teams treated over 40,000 last year. Ministries of compassion--in cooperation with national churches--provide care for orphans, widows, and delinquents.

Men For Missions International (MFMI), the laymen's voice of OMS, involves thousands of men and women from all walks of life in the cause of world missions.

A quarterly publication, OMS Outreach, is sent to donors of $15 or more per year to the work of OMS.

OMS International, Inc.

World Headquarters: P.O. Box A, Greenwood, IN 46142-6599

Australia: P.O. Box 897, Ringwood, VIC 3134

United Kingdom: 1 Sandileigh Avenue, Didsbury, Manchester M20 3LN

Canada: 2289 Fairview Street, Unit 105, Burlington, ON L7R 2E3

New Zealand: P.O. Box 962, Hamilton

South Africa: P.O. Box 640, Roodepoort TVL 1725

NOTES

NOTES

NOTES

NOTES

NOTES